S0-FQY-765

Francestown
Fifty Years of Growth and Change
1970-2020

Kevin Pobst

Copyright © 2022, Kevin Pobst
All rights reserved.

ISBN 9798353990949

To

Mindy
Candor, Patience, Kindness

CONTENTS

Preface	i
Chapter 1, Growth and Change, 1970 - 1985	1
Chapter 2, The Tipping Point, 1986 - 1990	33
Chapter 3, An Era of Good Feeling, 1990s	47
Chapter 4, A Bumpy Night: Town Governance 2003 - 2020	73
Chapter 5, Projects that Defined the Town, 2000 - 2020	109
Chapter 6, Key Organizations	131
Chapter 7, Joyful Living	177
Chapter 8, Key Citizens	197
Afterward	223
Appendices	227

    Births, Population, Building Permits by Year

    Political Party Presidential Voting, Registration

    BOS, Moderator, 1970-2020

    Budget by Year

    Budgets by Department by Decade

    Value of Town Property by Decade

    Conservation Fund and Land Acquisition

    Years of Governance Service to the Town

Index	235

"Time flies over us but leaves its shadow behind."
Nathanial Hawthorne

PREFACE

In 2008, local students interviewed sixteen residents of Francestown who had either grown up here or moved to town before 1970 or shortly thereafter. Videos of the interviews are available at the George Holmes Bixby Memorial Library. The interviewees were asked to talk about the changes they had observed in Francestown and the community over the years. Initially, most respondents emphasized continuity more than dramatic change. They said things like "not too much [changed]," or "[it] changed quite nicely," or "not much ... the town does a nice job of keeping things in character," or "same mountain, same lakes, skiing, golf, a store, the same houses on Main Street." One town veteran said that the town was "still friendly, still loving."

A listing of changes emerged from the discussion. The commentators identified things there are "more of" -- taxes, cars, houses, committees, town services, and commuters – and "less of" – barns and farms, places to hunt, open fields, stately trees lining Main Street. A consensus described the town as "a bedroom community for bigger towns." The interviewees were of two minds about the new reality that "things we used to do for ourselves are now done by the town." Some saw it as a blessing, others as a loss of self-reliance. Jack Curren concluded his interview on a light note. Waving vigorously while sitting in his yard, he complained that "The black flies are still bad."

The history of Francestown from 1970 to 2020 was summarized well by these sixteen witnesses. During the years after 1970, the year-round population tripled as did the number of homes. Debate over development became an issue for the first time against a background movement for "conservation" and "environmentalism." Ironically, the people who accounted for the population growth, new housing, and demand for improved public services were often the same people who led the movement to "preserve the rural character" of their adopted town. Town government grew as new residents sought public services they were used to in the larger towns, suburbs, and cities from which they migrated.

In the simplest terms, the story of Francestown over the last fifty years, particularly in the 1970s-90s, is a story of growth and the response to that growth. Change is not easy whether it comes personally or communally. The town has actively managed change, but not without rough patches. When asked to describe someone or something we love, the temptation is to be nostalgic. It's been said, "nice people" avoid talking about unappealing characteristics or inconvenient details in "polite company." The sixteen town veterans probably were influenced by this inclination to gloss over those things that have been lost or changes of which they disapproved. Even so, the oldsters' generally sunny views probably validate Francestown's success at managing change to the satisfaction of the majority.

The index to this book, which only lists individual and family names, has nearly 700 entries. That is a far cry from the anonymity I intended when I started this project. When interviewing residents about their experiences in town over the years and their interpretation of events between 1970 and 2020, I assured them that I did not intend to include many names in telling this story. I wanted to avoid leaving anyone out who deserved recognition or characterizing someone in a fashion they or their loved ones found objectionable. I had no intention of ruffling feathers. This is, after all, a town history by an amateur historian with great affection for Francestown. However, as I wrote I overruled my initial intention. I listened to people, read documents, and reflected. I was impressed by how personal the story is to most of those who were involved in town affairs. Great impersonal forces may push history one way or another, like economic trends or national movements. However, often an individual's leadership makes a tremendous impact. Individuals make differences and key individuals make key differences. This has certainly been true in Francestown.

Writing history is storytelling, and the story of the town is more than a collection of events, leaders, organizations, and statistics. Each time I interviewed a resident I asked them to tell me what they thought had been the town's "theme" in the time they've lived here. For most interviewees this was a difficult question to answer, but the themes described below were suggested by many interviewees.

Growth and development. A prevalent factor in shaping Francestown's story over the last fifty years has been how the town responded to growth and development. From the late 1970s until the early 2000s, waves of new residents challenged traditional ways of doing things. New residents often had different expectations regarding the services the town provided and how it ought to be governed. Development, whether subdividing lots for new homes, or building resorts for skiing and golf, has been viewed by some with favor and by others with concern or disdain.

Maintaining the "rural character of the community." Growth challenged the rural character of the town. A concern over the last fifty years has been how to maintain "the rural character of the community." Those concerns coincided with the national movement to conserve land, wildlife, and resources. In Francestown that led to a campaign to preserve undeveloped land,

and a corresponding pushback against government regulation of landowners' rights.

Town government. Some disputes about growth and development boiled down to competing views of what was the appropriate scope of the town's provision of services, as well as its regulatory authority. The challenges presented by a growing and changing population led to disputes that were resolved through the awkward but revered apparatus of traditional New England democracy: the Town Meeting.

"Natives" & Newcomers. Demographics have played a role in how the town managed change. Three groups of residents – "natives," "summer settlers" (people whose families were summer visitors but transitioned to full-time residence), and "move-ins" from distant towns, cities, and suburbs – have sometimes differed in how they wanted "the rural character of the community" defined. Generational differences played a role as well. Established native leaders in the 1970s aged-out in the 1980s-90s and ensuing generations, both native and move-in, did not always see eye to eye.

Using labels such as "natives," "summer settlers," and "move-ins" runs the risk of over-generalizing. A couple of wise long-time residents warned me to take care with such labels. One grew up summering in Francestown and the other moved in thirty years ago and has intentionally befriended residents of all stripes. They observed that one of Francestown's social strengths is bringing together people with different backgrounds and interests by focusing on what we have in common: "Groups with competing agendas have done an amazing job of finding middle ground." They assert that Francestown is less "siloed" than other towns. The long-time summer resident said, "Francestown has been a place where you could transcend the differences between year-round and summer; the town tried hard to make it work for everyone for a long time through recreation – baseball, tennis, the beach, dances – as well as varied entertainment at the Meeting House." In his view, Francestown has ensured multiple uses of conserved land befitting the multiplicity of residents' interests: "The town has tried to walk a line to keep Francestown special for everyone by respecting everyone's reason for thinking it's special."

Caroline Lord, the town's librarian in the 1940s-50s, celebrated that aspect in her book, _The Diary of a Village Library_ when she describes the Labor Day event. "September 1, 1952: Today is a big day in this town. The history of this annual celebration began with the Village Improvement Society's raising money for the Red Cross during World War I by means of a carnival on Labor Day.... [over the years] the day became a real Old Home Day. The entire town participates in the event, which has been the means of bringing together both summer and winter people until the difference between the two is less and less observed. Committees are composed of local year-rounders and non-residents of all ages. Everyone works like fury, cooking, soliciting, building, collecting, vowing never to do it again, and having such fun that the next year is the same, only more so. Some kinds of 'tired' are glorious, and Labor Day tired is that kind."

In the story that follows, I've tried to heed these celebrations of brotherhood, but have acknowledged times when the politics in town governance have appeared to be influenced by differences between "natives," "summer-settlers," and "move-ins."

Chapters 1, 2, 3, and 4 divide the story of town governance into chronological periods: 1970-1985, 1986-1991, 1992-2002, 2003-2020. Chapter 5 describes two big projects illustrating how the scope of the town's governance changed from the 1970s to the 2000s. But there was more to life in this town than governance. Chapter 6 will bring into this story key private or quasi-governmental organizations that the townspeople cultivated: the Volunteer Fire Department, the Community Church, the Improvement and Historical Society, the Old Meeting House, Inc., as well as profiles of several other organizations. Chapter 7 recognizes that the period of 1990s into the 2000s was a time of community spiritedness in Francestown, of abundant activity and fun. It celebrates the joy of "being Francestown." Chapter 8 is a collection of short profiles that provide recognition to key people in the last fifty years of the town's history. The Afterword provides a summary of the sources for the information presented in this book.

There is not a single definitive version of the town's story. What follows is one telling.

Kevin Pobst
2022

[***Interviewees**: Fran Arnold, Mit Boyle, BJ Carbee, Scott Carbee, Dick Cilley, Stewart Clark, Frank Jones, Junior Foote, Bart Hardwick, Joe Ludwig, Ethel MacStubbs, Dariel Peterson, Pat Place, Marcy Tripp, Connie Varnum, Carolyn Woodbury. **Interviewers and film makers:** Hilary Weisman Graham, Diana Place, Nancy Gagnon, Katie Ennis, Adam Baer, Joel Barwood, Kendal Bush; Kelsa Danforth, Cailin Ennis, Matt Foote, Jimmy Gombas, Colby Goodrich, Austin Hoffman, Stephanie Leandri, Marybeth MacKay, Emily Peters, Jack St. Jean, Elizabeth Taft, Jakob Rupp.]

CHAPTER 1

GROWTH AND CHANGE

1970- 1985

Francestown in 1970 was a tiny, rural New England town with a secure base of small farmers, tradesmen, and small businesspeople, who enjoyed a quiet community life. "Summer People" came to relax, doubling the population during that season with a sizable and influential cohort of seasonal residents. An important feature of the town was its Main Street, lined with classic 18th and 19th century New England homes framed by a canopy of majestic hardwoods. The town was much the same as it had been in 1960, 1950, and 1940. Few of the natives expected or wanted change.

EARLY TOWN GOVERNMENT AND RESOURCES

Town governance was bare bones. The annual budget was just shy of $53,000. The town clerk and tax collector worked out of their homes. The Board of Selectmen met weekly in an office on the second floor of the Town Hall on the Common. They handled all the town's administration. Property assessments were determined annually through their personal inspections. A count of livestock was still included in their assessments of real property values. There were frequent conversations with property owners about the accuracy of assessments. The town collected a "head tax" and a "poll tax." Both were meager. The Selectmen were also charged with finding jurors for the county courts, which they did by drawing names from a box. Records of Select Board meetings were kept in long hand by the most junior Selectman. Several years would pass before the town owned a typewriter or employed a woman -- of course, it would be a woman – who would assist the three men -- of course, they were men – in keeping the town's records.

Facilities and resources for first responders were also rudimentary. The police chief was also the fire chief. He had held both positions for well over a decade. As police chief, he operated out of his home and used his own vehicle to patrol and respond to calls. He had scant connection to a larger network of policing; his car was equipped with a radio for the first time in 1968. The Francestown Volunteer Fire Department (FVFD) operated out of a small station built on the spot of a prior school building on the Town Common. FVFD used lovingly maintained, but elderly equipment. This department, even in 1970, served not only to provide public safety, but also as social and fraternal organization. These functions have remained integral to its identity through the past 50 years.

Governing boards and commissions met occasionally and drew little attention to their work. A Conservation Commission was founded in the mid-1960s. It celebrated the first "Earth Day" with the rest of the nation in 1970 and focused on reducing litter and on small beautification projects. Though the town had a Planning Board (PB) and a very basic Zoning Ordinance, it did not yet have a long-term land use plan. The Highway Department, arguably the most crucial institution in a town of long unpaved roads that became a boggy morass each spring, owned only two vehicles. Snow plowing in the long winters was contracted with several residents who owned trucks and blades. Grading and graveling of the roads were taken care of by the elected road agent mostly using his own, or rented, equipment. The 1970s saw one bridge after another reach a crisis and face expensive, but usually temporary, repair. Household garbage was taken to the "dump," where open-air burning of garbage was still legal.

KEY STRUCTURES

The key architectural structures from 1970 are recognizable in 2020. The aging Town Hall – mostly used for occasional dances, school physical education, and homespun events – was cold in the winter and in need of regular, costly repairs. On Main Street a three-room school built in 1940 served fifty students. Francestown had recently been consolidated into a regional school district comprised of the small schools in nine regional towns – the Contoocook Valley Regional School District (ConVal). Students from Francestown who continued past the eighth grade had previously traveled at their own expense to the high schools in Peterborough or Antrim; the town paid their tuition. With the advent of consolidation, students were bused to Antrim for Junior High School and to a newly built ConVal High School in Peterborough. There were two churches. A small Unitarian congregation met in the Meeting House building in the summer. This building was without heat and in serious need of repair. A larger non-denominational congregation met in a church structure on Main Street, built in the 1880s. This group had ties to the historic Congregational-Presbyterian tradition. The church had been re-incorporated in 1959 and the families who founded the church still comprised its core membership. The minister who served in 1970 was young, energetic, and popular, but the church was on the threshold of decades of frequent ministerial turn-over. The library was in a handsome 145-year-old brick house on Main Street, its current location. The building was dedicated to George Holmes Bixby Jr., a Civil War hero and well-regarded 19th century obstetrician. His daughter donated the residence to the town in 1923 to be used as a library and historical museum.

EARLY BUSINESSES AND ORGANIZATIONS

There was only one store, Vadney's, a classic New England general store. It was the second oldest continually operating store in the United States. Its longtime competitor, Colburn's, burned down in 1964. Grandmother's House, a restaurant serving comfort food befitting its name, was on the road to the ski hill. The Crotched Mountain ski area, founded in the mid-1960s, was the dominant business in town in 1970. It catered to day-trippers from the region, providing important seasonal employment for residents. By 1970 most of the townspeople were tradesmen, commercial agriculture was declining.

Several social and service organizations characteristic of rural towns across the country were part of the fabric of Francestown: a Grange, the 4-H club, Masons, the Order of the Eastern Star, a Women's Guild, and the Improvement and Historical Society. The last functioned as the town's recreation department and put on an "Old Home Days" style celebration on Labor Day weekend every year.

There was a Currier and Ives aspect to Francestown in the 1970s. However, a more blunt and grudgingly realistic profile of the town circa 1970 was presented in a 1997 issue of *The Francestown News*. It captures challenges faced during the next fifty years: "In the 1960s, after more than 100 years of steady decline, Francestown was 'rediscovered.' Families began moving into what was a relatively poor, run-down, town with a neglected infrastructure. Francestown's bare-boned services were designed for a small number of people with a philosophy of limited government and a custom of community service…Francestown was ill prepared to absorb the impact of new growth." The burgeoning population of the mid-1970s through the 1990s placed a conundrum on the town. The new residents expected town government to respond to their demand for more public services.

1972 BICENTENNIAL

The quaintness of the town is illustrated by events surrounding the 1972 Bicentennial celebration. The Bicentennial was celebrated over the three days of Labor Day weekend after years of planning by a committee chaired by John Schott, the author of *Frances' Town*. According to the Town Report for 1972, "the town…had a lot of fun." Though the town allocated funds for the celebration, none of those monies were needed; the event was self-supporting. Commemorative silver and bronze medals were struck for the Bicentennial and offered for sale as well as commemorative early American glass flasks, town maps, and town history books. Friday night opening ceremonies took place in a packed Town Hall. Arthur Lord "with his dry Yankee wit" was the master of ceremonies. The night included an historical pageant with a large cast. On Saturday, over 700 people participated in the Open House Tour of Main Street. Many former residents of the town took this opportunity for a "homecoming." A reception was hosted on the Common for home comers and their friends and families on Saturday afternoon. Several historical exhibits were available on Main Street, and the annual Grange Fair was held on Saturday. That evening, a formal Bicentennial Ball, with many attendees dressed in 18th century style clothing, spilled out of Town Hall into a great tent on the Common.

A community-wide religious service orchestrated by the leaders of the two town churches took place Sunday morning, followed by a box lunch picnic and band concert at the ski area. In the evening Monadnock Music, conducted by Francestown resident James Bolle, presented a concert featuring classical music including a piece by Francestown's Edward Burlingame Hill. On Saturday evening, as John Schott describes in his characteristically grandiose style, a party for the town at the ski lodge on Crotched Mountain was a "frolicsome bedlam." Labor Day events on Monday drew the largest crowd to town in anyone's memory to watch "the grandest parade in the town's history." The Molly Stark cannon, borrowed from the town of New Boston, out of which a sizable chunk of Francestown was carved in 1772, was fired with an impressive report. The Fire Department held its annual Firemen's Supper on Monday evening followed by a square dance, which included some demonstrations of styles of dance from earlier times.

This celebration was preceded by interpersonal dynamics that characterize Francestown. A mild dispute occurred regarding the use of Town Hall for the Bicentennial Ball. Could the town that loved a good cocktail party serve alcohol *in* Town Hall? Alcoholic beverages were banned from Town Hall events. When the organizing committee proposed an exception for the big ball, the Select Board stood fast on the traditional rules. With only a few months to go before the celebration, the event chair, John Schott, resigned in protest for a couple of days. He re-engaged and negotiated a compromise. A set of punch bowls was placed outside the building in the tent, one pure and the other sullied. Directions for the supervision and placement of the bowls was part of the deal that was struck. This was, and is, Francestown.

SHIFTING DEMOGRAPHICS

Over the following decade, the town was on an increasingly steep trajectory to modernize due to the influence of a steady stream of new people moving from cities and suburbs as well as summer residents who were now settling here full-time. This profile of newcomers is drawn from census data, surveys, and interviews. The population in town grew by almost 5% per year in the 1970s. From 1975-1979 two hundred and twenty-one new residents moved into town. Though the town was tilting younger the percentage of residents over retirement age still exceeded the state average, and the median age, 40, was also above the state average. The population growth trend continued into the mid-1980s with over 30 new residents per year. Most of the increase in population between 1970-1985 came through migration rather than births; the birth rate did not increase until 1985. In 1970, 85% of town residents had lived in the same house five years earlier; that number dropped to 57% by 1990. At no time in Francestown since the 1820s-30s has the population grown so fast. In 1970 the percentage of people in Francestown who had moved to town within the last five years was 15%; it was around 40% in 1980. Sixty percent of town residents in 1980 had been born outside New Hampshire.

The percentage of town residents whose employment was classified by the U. S. Census Bureau as professional, managerial, technical, or sales grew substantially from 1970 to 1980. In 1970, 30% of residents had not graduated from high school while 32% had completed college. By 1980 the non-high school graduate cohort dropped to 13% and the college graduates rose to 38%, and by 2010 the figures were 4.5% and 44%. Francestown residents living below the poverty line in 1970 (13%) was double the NH average. That measure dropped to 9% in 1980 and 3.5% by 1990, which was well below the state average. Median family income was lower than the state average in 1970, but through the 1980s it rose and by 1990 it exceeded the state average by 15%. The move-ins tended to be college-educated and had robust incomes. Francestown was a refuge for young, college-educated professionals from the Merrimack River Valley and Massachusetts.

The new residents wanted the town to spend more on roads, recreation, waste disposal, and other public services. From 1970-1980 the town's population grew by 55%, but town expenditures rose by 375%, school costs by 549%, and property taxes collected by 516%. The increases in revenue and spending in this decade were made possible due to the increasing value of property, including the ski area, golf course, and adjacent development. Over 200 new subdivided lots and many new houses were added to the tax roll. The valuation of land in town rose from $5m in 1970 to $29m in 1980. The number of housing units, stand-alone homes as well as condominiums, grew by more than 100 between 1970 and 1980. A bigger jump came in the second half of the 1980s. In those years around 200 dwelling units were built. These figures do not count the number of families who moved into pre-1970 houses and spent thousands of dollars improving the market value of those homes. By 1990 50% of all housing units had been built since 1970. Vacation dwellings were a substantial percentage of the housing stock in 1970, but new "camps" played little role in the town's post-1970 growth. By 1995 there were 69 camps in town but only 16 had been built after 1970.

The "new" Francestown was of two minds about growth and development. Many of the move-ins wanted a more modern way of doing municipal business and better public services. They were willing to pay taxes and authorize municipal spending to make that possible. Ironically, they did not want the town to change. Even as they passed Warrant Articles at town meetings that set the stage for fundamental change in the way the town was governed, they embraced the mantra of "preserving the rural character of the community."

This desire for both change and preservation led to the town's struggles in the following decades.

REGIONAL GROWTH

Residents who were concerned about growth and development were not alone in the Monadnock region. Concern was present in every town. Peterborough, the big town to the south, pioneered land use regulation in the region. It experienced a commercial and residential building boom between 1963 and 1973. Three hundred new homes and nearly 200 apartments were built in Peterborough during this period. National Cash Register, New Hampshire Ball Bearing, and Brookstone expanded. Growth slowed during the "energy crisis" of 1973-74. Even after the slow-down, the town's commercial expansion continued. Eastern Mountain Sports moved its headquarters to Peterborough. The new Plaza on Route 101, including a new A & P grocery store, opened in 1973. An article in the *Peterborough Transcript* in 1972 titled "Is This Inevitable: Must Plan for 'Double Population?'" reported residents' concerns about growth. Later in the year, another *Transcript* article presented the planning challenges facing small towns and called for towns to adopt Master Plans. A group was formed in Peterborough in 1972 to place a freeze on big residential developments.

That same year, in the Milford Cabinet, editor W. B. Botch decried that the call for managing growth by preserving "open space" was being tagged as a "subtle form of snobbery." He observed that when a town preserves open land, it is accused of "forcing land values up... driving lower income people out of the buyers' market." "You're on the side of the Angels by saving the environment, but at the same time you're keeping out the poor folk." Thus the "greatest enemy" of those who campaign to preserve open space is "not the real estate developer, the highway builder, or the growth of industry, it is this 'suspicion of elitism.'" He countered by asserting that "it is the ordinary family" not the elite or the rich who "are going to need state parks, town forests and recreation space as more and more private land is taken out of circulation." "Before writing off the ecologists and the environmentalists as a selfish elite, we hope people will pause and ask themselves: what will this place be like 20 or 30 years from now if we don't take steps to preserve open space today?"

Other small towns in the region experienced a growth spurt like Francestown's. town meetings around the region in 1973 faced Warrant Articles attempting to address zoning, planning, and subdivision issues in Peterborough, Antrim, Bennington, Temple, Mason, and Greenfield.

Peterborough's Town Meeting limited subdivisions to two lots. Dublin's Town Meeting passed a one-year building permit freeze. By 1974, Peterborough's Town Meeting approved the creation of what was the region's first municipal Master Plan. There was opposition to managing development. At Greenfield's Town Meeting a petition Warrant Article to repeal zoning and subdivision ordinances and to disband "snob zoning" was debated. The petition article fell short, but it drew a 65% turnout to Town Meeting. The petitioners' complaint was simply stated as "too much control." The Transcript labeled the campaign in Greenfield an "anti-planning movement."

In 1974, the *Peterborough Transcript* reported on a campaign of the Society for the Preservation of New Hampshire Forests (known as The Forest Society or SPNHF). This organization was promoting a new open land preservation mechanism that was gaining a following. Called a "conservation deed," SPNHF recommended that such "conservation easements" (in the parlance soon to be adopted) be monitored by local banks. The headline for the article was "Landowner's Tax Break." That is probably not the angle on the story that SPNHF preferred. Their vision was land protection not tax shelters. The Forest Society also sponsored "Guiding Growth" workshops. One was held at ConVal High School. SPNHF encouraged anyone to attend, but especially local government officials and town lawyers.

Such was the regional context that Francestown residents would have read about in their local newspapers or heard about in conversations with friends in neighboring towns. Covering Planning Board discussions in Francestown, the *Peterborough Transcript* reported the concern felt by some residents: "Is Francestown about to be Overcome by Condominiums and People?"

THE FIRST DEVELOPERS

Another aspect of the tussle over "development" that unfolded in the late-1970s was the role of "developers." Town leader and historian John Schott's attitude toward "developers" represented one view, based on a bogeyman stereotype. He noted that between 1965 and 1970 the Zoning Ordinance was amended and expanded. This was, in his view, "a hopeful effort to affect some community control over the use of land before Frances' Town was raped by self-seeking developers and others anxious to cash in on what could someday become just another bedroom community serving Manchester or Boston, or a honky-tonk recreational area perverted by gas stations, rooming houses, trailer camps, and road-side hot dog stands." A grim vision of the future and a clear condemnation of developers. Ultimately, the Planning Board records of the 1970s tell a story that corrects this caricature of developers. Dozens of long-time native residents of Francestown sought, and received, subdivisions of their land into buildable lots which they put on the market. To a significant extent, the town was filled with developers.

Most of the development in town was proposed by locals who were active members of the community. William MacAdam (Francestown Mountain Land Associates) had been the moderator in town since 1953, and Ted Bixby (Francestown Development Associates) had deep roots in a long-standing family in town. They led efforts to build houses and condominiums adjacent to the ski area on Crotched Mountain. There were some "move-in" developers, but often they engaged in the life of the community. Land/Vest, the new owner of the ski area in 1970, designated Tim Gannett to run the operation. Eventually he owned the ski area independently, moved his family to town, and was active in local society. Robert Cloutier, an active speculator in subdivided tracts, served on town committees. After Cloutier bought the Foote Farm subdivision, he came to the Select Board seeking advice about how to respond to the suggestion that since he was a developer he should resign as chair of the Planning Board. The Select Board assured him that unless there was a written complaint about a specific conflict of interest, Cloutier was properly seated.

There were out-of-town speculators. The LaRoche brothers bought a tract from Land/Vest to construct 33 small colonial-style homes on the mountain. This project never matured but it may have represented Schott's vision, though there was no plan for a hot dog stand. Richard Tremblay bought Tavern Farm and began developing it as a golf resort. The town was constantly in conflict with him over his casual approach to regulations. The most contentious Planning Board and ZBA meetings at the turn of the decade were about the golf course development.

Much of the interaction with developers was directly with the Planning Board and ZBA, but separate, informal appeals came to the Select Board because, in many cases, developers and board members were friends and neighbors. The Select Board walked with Bixby where he planned to build condos. On another occasion, Selectmen examined five condominium units which were models of sixty-one planned for by Francestown Mountain Land Associates, prior to a decision about them by the Planning Board. At one point, they listened to Bill MacAdam vent his frustration. He demanded a special Town Meeting to amend the Zoning Ordinance so that he could proceed with his condo plans. No such meeting was held. Gannett complained about not being permitted to build on lots where the access road wasn't deemed good enough for subdivision standards. He alleged discrimination against subdividing lots on Crotched Mountain. Lawsuits were filed to fight the town over subdivision denials and rejections of applications for variances and special exceptions. In some cases, the town settled, and in others it prevailed. The Zoning Ordinance evolved through a steady flow of amendments until it was completely re-written with professional consultation and approved at Town Meeting 1985.

LINES ARE DRAWN

By the end of the decade of the 1970s, the dominant theme that reverberated through the next forty years was established in the discourse of the town: development versus preservation. This debate started as a generalized concern about how, and how much, to manage growth. Over time, advocacy for conservation of open spaces for both environmentalist and aesthetic reasons --"preserving the rural character of the community" -- became a dominant theme. The growth control and management camp were a mix of town natives, summer folk who became year-rounders, and the swell of new residents seeking "Brigadoon."

Development was appealing to residents who worked in the trades or who wanted to derive income from selling their land. Yankee tradition inclines away from regulatory governance. Often both natives and newcomers who shared discomfort with what growth and development might mean for the town, also were uncomfortable with town policies that limited individual control over private property or entrepreneurial initiative. Early on, the possible implications of growth and development were not clear to many residents; they hovered between the two poles. That may explain why the make-up of some committees in town – such as the Planning Board, Zoning Board, Conservation Commission – were pendulums swinging back and forth between openness and restrictiveness.

"Modernization" was a companion theme influencing the town's story. This was especially the case in the 1980s. That actual term was seldom uttered, but it was implied in the reasoning articulated by influential leaders who worked to improve governance. By no means did the impulse toward traditionalism wane for many residents. Hence the back-and-forth arguments through these decades. In 2020, "traditionalism" still had a strong pull on many residents. Alan Thulander, who served in town leadership through four decades, was a "bridge figure" spanning the divide between the "if it was good enough in 1965, its good enough for 2000" attitude and the "let's run the town like the business it is" mentality. He appears to have been drawn to each way of thinking at different times on different issues. To that extent Thulander probably represented the town's center.

Three formal groups played important roles in the struggle over development, the Select Board (SB), the Budget and Advisory Committee (BAC), and the Planning Board (PB). The Select Board's challenge was whether the government of the town was prepared to efficiently provide the level of public services new residents expected. The new and somewhat surprising actor in this drama was the Budget and Advisory Committee. Planning Board meetings were the public arena where much of the angst and frustration were displayed.

TOWN LEADERS IN THE 70S

In the 1970s the town's leaders were gentlemen and gentlewomen of America's "Greatest Generation" (born between 1908 and 1926) or the first half of the "Silent Generation" (born in the late 1920s and the 1930s). They experienced the economically depressed years of the 1930s and many served in WWII or the Korean conflict. In 1970 the oldest members of this cohort reached their early sixties, the youngest were just moving into their forties.

Stereotypically, these generations were conservative, parsimonious, and committed to a do-it-yourself practicality.

The keel of Francestown's ship of state was its long-serving native, traditionalist leadership. Herman "Bing" Miller was midway through his 45-year career as town clerk and tax collector. The Trustees of the Trust Funds and the Zoning Board of Adjustment – all men – were from families who had been town leaders for many years and would continue to serve the town into the 1980s. Women served as library trustees and on the Conservation Commission. Priscilla "Sibby" Kunhardt chaired both groups for most of two decades stretching from the 1950s into the 1970s. She was joined on the library board by Connie Dodge who for much of the 1970s was Town Historian. Dorothy Miller, Bing's spouse, was on the Cemetery Commission; she would become a long-serving deputy town clerk and tax collector. Norman Stewart was the long-tenured chief of both the police and the volunteer fire department. Stewart was "Mr. Francestown." His influence stretched beyond his public safety hats. He was the dog catcher, clock winder, and summer home watchman. If a dispute needed mediation, Norman Stewart took care of it. Though he stepped down from official police and fire leadership by the mid-1970s, his influence continued for several years.

The Board of Selectmen in 1970 were Franklin Mace, Donald Hoyt, and Walter Dodge, conservative men who worked with their hands and embraced Yankee individualism. Hoyt was also the Civil Defense Director and Mace was Overseer of Public Welfare (formerly, and more bluntly, Overseer of the Poor). The Select Board preferred to spend as little money as possible and to provide bare bones public services. They swallowed the bitter pill of borrowing money more willingly than they raised taxes. The largest expense for the town in 1970 was debt service.

A Few Contentious Issues

Some of the issues the Select Board wrestled with in the early 1970s exemplified this traditionalism. A Bible Hill landowner hosted a "Woodstock-style" outdoor music festival – young people, motorcycles, and rock and roll. After consulting the town's attorney, the Select Board sent a "cease and desist" letter and no similar events were allowed in the future. The tax collector had traditionally been paid one-half of one percent of the total of what he or she collected. This practice originated in colonial times. Town Meeting changed this to a flat stipend of $500, but the currently serving officer objected to her pay being changed during her term of office. Her rights were restored until the next election.

One classic battle between Yankee leaders in town was settled only by a petitioned vote at Town Meeting. In 1974, the Select Board authorized car window permit stickers for use of the dump and the beach. Several officers of town government demanded stickers, but refused to pay for them, including

Town Clerk Bing Miller, who argued that the $1.00 sticker constituted illegal taxation unless it was authorized by a Town Meeting. The Select Board dug in arguing that the stickers were not a tax. At Town Meeting 1975 a petition Warrant Article rescinded the sticker order, barred such a policy going forward, and provided refunds for all who sought them.

Other issues facing the Select Board in the early 1970s were chronic, but manageable. The need to repair the Bixby-Creamery Pond dam popped up in each successive decade. In 1973 the Select Board directed the road agent to repair the Cressy Hill Road bridge and to open the road; it had been closed since 1969. Town Hall was closed at times due to the expense of heating, particularly during the National Energy Crisis of 1973-1974. It took three years for the Select Board to decide what to do with the long wooden benches in Town Hall; these had been student seating when the Hall was the Francestown Academy. The board wanted to replace them with folding chairs, which they did (the incredibly heavy blue steel chairs that are still in the first-floor closet in 2020). The difficult decision was how to dispose of the benches. Eventually they were auctioned off to town residents.

One change in Select Board operation laid a foundation for the board to modernize its work in the coming years. In 1973, the board hired its first clerical assistant and paid her $2 per hour. This led to another hurdle: should the town own a typewriter, and should it be new or used? In 1974 they bought a new typewriter. A couple of other clerical assistants followed before Betty Behrsing was hired. Soon after, Betty was elected as the town's first selectwoman. A member of the Select Board from 1979 to 1987, she then again served for several years as the board's administrative assistant.

PROPERTY ASSESSMENTS, TAX MAPS, AND CURRENT USE

Perhaps the most important function of the Select Board in the 1970s was property assessment. It required an abundance of time and attracted a lot of attention. Each year, most visitors to Select Board meetings were there to challenge their assessments. The board began trying to improve its accuracy and process. Their meeting minutes from the 1970s are dominated by swarms of taxpayers descending on the board meetings seeking a review of their tax assessment. In Peterborough, the Town Meeting had authorized their Select Board to hire a professional assessment firm to revalue property. It took over a decade for successive Francestown Select Boards to succeed in convincing Town Meeting to permit professional, paid, reassessment. Left to their own devices as amateur assessors, they took a step forward by contracting to have tax maps made by a firm in Maine. The town had never had a set of tax maps. The board hoped that maps would increase transparency and efficiency. No sooner were the maps made available for public inspection than a litany of complaints began. The maps were rife with errors, misrepresentations of property lines and miscalculations of acreage. They eventually hired a local surveyor to make corrections.

The advent of "Current Use" complicated the assessors' work. New Hampshire Governor Walter Peterson (1969-73) led a campaign, "Yes on 7," for a constitutional amendment that would allow land to be taxed based upon its "current use value," and not its "highest and best use value," which the state constitution required. Current Use tax assessment reduction was an attempt to address a situation that had arisen in NH in the 1960s. New Hampshire's population was growing, and land values were rising rapidly. Higher property taxes were forcing farmers and woodlot owners to sell their lands. Traditional industries of agriculture and forestry were threatened. In 1968, a constitutional amendment was approved by two-thirds of voters. In 1973, the NH legislature followed through by enacting a Current Use taxation law, aimed at ensuring reduced taxation of undeveloped farm and forest lands.

In Francestown, there was a rush to enroll property in the Current Use (CU) program. The town has 18,700 acres of land, excluding bodies of water. In 1974, the first year of the Current Use program, 954 acres were enrolled. By 1979, acreage in the program increased to 8,765 acres. Acreage peaked at 13,423 in in 1999. That constituted 440 properties, encompassing 72% of land in town. Statewide, nearly 3 million acres owned by about 27,000 landowners were enrolled in the CU program by 2020, representing about 60% of the state's taxable private land. The program has played a significant role in preservation of undeveloped open spaces for wildlife conservation and recreation.

In 1976, the town was facing many challenges: increasingly complex assessment, non-compliance with the Zoning Ordinance and Planning Board permitting, rambunctious meetings, an ever-growing highway department budget even as dissatisfaction with the roads grew, a need for weighty decisions to be made about waste disposal, and a population explosion and building boom. The Select Board of 1975 had taken some small steps to corral these issues, but pressure was escalating. A key concern was the deterioration of the town's infrastructure. The town's buildings and bridges were aging and requiring more maintenance, particularly the library and Town Hall. The fire house and highway department facilities were inadequate. The Horse Sheds were on the verge of collapse. The care of the roads ate up nearly 80% of the budget.

SELECTBOARD LEADERSHIP IN THE 70S

In 1971, Alan Thulander, young, relatively new to town and not a New Hampshire native, was elected to the Select Board. This represented the first step in a transition from boards bound by tradition to the more activist boards of the late 1970s-early 1980s. He was the leading edge of a new wave of town leaders. With the election of John Schott (1975-78), Jack Arnold (1976-79, 1981-1984), and Bob Abbott (1977-1983) the Select Board changed, if not so much generationally, then in its degree of insularity and professional background. Schott, though he came to town in the early 1960s, and Arnold who had summered in town before settling here in the late 1960s, had lived and worked extensively in the wider world outside New Hampshire, and Abbott, though a Francestown lifer, was young and commuted daily to work near Boston. Schott held a nostalgic vision of Francestown but recognized that steps needed to be taken to increase the efficiency of public services and to support growth management.

Jack Arnold's election to the board tipped the scale away from traditionalism toward activism. Arnold won a race against four-term incumbent Frank Mace. Rarely were incumbents challenged nor did they lose an election. As a successful lawyer and businessman, Arnold offered a more business-like approach to governance. One long-time observer of Francestown governance said that Arnold was impatient with "seat of the pants decision-making" and introduced to the Select Board "a more codified process and structure." The board's meeting minutes testify to an abrupt change of tone. Arnold instituted required attendance of department heads – Highway, Police, Fire, Waste Disposal – at all Select Board meetings. They were expected to report and to participate in discussions about issues in their areas of responsibility.

In 1976 and 1977 some minor issues were resolved in a way indicating change in the town's governance culture. Town Meeting decided that dogs could no longer run free. Their owners must be with them, or they must be restrained. Smoking was banned at town meetings. The town joined the New Hampshire Municipal Association so they could buy affordable group medical insurance for town employees, including for the full-time highway employees and their families.

The proposed Tenneco pipeline was not a minor issue. The way the town responded was another indication of a changing culture. In 1977, Tenneco, Inc. announced plans to build a natural gas pipeline from New Brunswick, Canada to Pennsylvania. The pipeline would have bisected Francestown, entering near the Weare-New Boston northeast corner and exiting near the Greenfield-Lyndeborough southwest corner. Bill Hansen, the publisher of an antiques magazine and catalog, who was becoming actively involved on town committees, organized an ad hoc committee to push back. The Citizens Organized to Protect the Environment (COPE) mounted a vigorous campaign against the pipeline. Though committee members were from towns throughout the region, members from Francestown were at the heart of the mobilization. A special Town Meeting was called in May 1977 and after that the Select Board joined the campaign of opposition. The Select Board filed as an official intervenor when the case was scheduled to be heard by the Federal Power Commission. The committee rallied politicians from all levels and numerous jurisdictions. The campaign's success came in two steps. First, Tenneco agreed to re-route the pipeline to an existing easement for Public Service NH power lines further south, and in 1978 Tenneco dropped its plans.

RISE OF THE BUDGET AND ADVISORY COMMITTEE

The most significant action of the Select Board in the period from 1977-1985 was to seek authorization for a Master Plan committee. That committee set to work in 1979 and by 1980 had prepared a plan. The Master Plan was a direct result of the rise of a new force in town governance, the Budget and Advisory Committee.

The Select Board could see that they were falling behind in addressing the mounting issues. They reached out for assistance in strategizing how to meet the challenges by seeking the advice of a dormant town board, the Advisory Committee. This group was renamed the Budget and Advisory Committee (BAC) in 1978. From 1977 to 1982 the BAC was a broadly influential power in town governance. After that burst of influence, the BAC narrowed its scope of advice. From the mid-1980s to 2000 the BAC confined itself to assisting the Select Board in building a budget. Periodically after 2000, Select Board's brought the BAC into a wider scope of decision-making once again.

The BAC nudged the Select Board to address growth, development, and governance efficiency issues and to quit kicking cans down the road. They advised the Select Board and Planning Board to create a Master Plan. The aggressiveness of their recommendations was surprising, and ironic, given their recent experience. The BAC of 1977-1979 included two former Selectmen, Walter Dodge and Frank Mace, who were not known as advocates for increasing the scope of town government. They had not been activists as Selectmen. Perhaps the freedom they felt as advisors insulated from actual decision-making, enabled them to rise to the moment faced by the town. Their published statements convey considerable chutzpah: "Our advice is asked for. It can be either accepted or rejected, but our point of view will be known.... We are a 'watchdog,' to try and develop a system that will assure that the town gets full value for all it spends." In the 1979 Town Report the BAC's assertiveness continued: "BAC recommends the budget to Town Meeting as submitted, not as a 'rubber stamp'... but because for the first time ever, the budget is a distillation of many jawboning sessions held between the Selectmen, ... department heads, and the Budget and Advisory Committee."

By passing Article 26 at Town Meeting in 1978 residents and the Select Board affirmed their confidence in the value of the BAC by re-commissioning and re-naming the committee. The article provided a new charge of responsibility. The Budget and Advisory Committee was given a broad mandate to advise and assist the Select Board about "any matter affecting the town." The BAC was to actively participate with the Select Board in the preparation and final compilation of the annual town budget, and to publicly post, prior to Town Meeting, the committee's recommendations on each item in the budget and on articles proposing capital expenditures.

In the next few years, the BAC was asked to advise the Select Board on an array of issues. They recommended relocation of town offices to the former fire station with handicapped accessibility, hiring a town manager, appointing a permanent Board of Assessors, providing offices for the town clerk and tax collector, hiring assistance for processing Current Use applications, updating tax maps, setting line-item maximum increases in the budget, and bidding of all purchases over a $1000. The BAC also weighed in on immunity insurance for town officials, increased compensation for town employees and officials, control of fuel costs for police, fire, highway, and refuse transfer, charging developers for necessary infrastructure upgrades, and seeking payment for material that would off-set the expense of recycling. They called upon the town to build a new facility for the Fire Department and observed that the town's pattern of setting aside 5% of the budget per year for Capital Reserves was insufficient. Placing 10% in reserve funds would be more prudent. Many of these recommendations were not acted on, but the BAC's aggressiveness represented a strong impulse to modernize governance in Francestown.

The BAC was focused especially on seeing the Select Board "take control of the Highway Department" by appointing the road agent. At that time road agents were elected. It was clear to the BAC that if the roads continued to consume most of the town's budget that many other needs facing the town would not be met. The BAC was most aggressive in insisting that the road budget was out of control and far above what it should be at "cost per mile." For three years running they recommended cuts in the budget proposed by road agents. The BAC compared the road budgets of seven adjacent towns in the period between 1974 and 1979. The comparison led them to determine that Francestown's highway budget was 25% greater than it should be. A study of area towns allowed them to conclude that the town should purchase its own highway equipment. The Committee's 1980 report included acknowledgement of Kris Stewart's leadership during his one year (1980) as the elected road agent: "We would like to commend him on the fine report he submitted to this committee in which he detailed the work done last year... Most of the roads in town have been greatly improved and a head start of sorts has been affected thanks to Kris' diligence as road agent."

Many town bridges needed attention. The BAC recommended that when bridge repair or replacement projects were budgeted that each project should include "retention of competent engineering design services." Prior to this, the road agent served as the "engineer." Phil Ireland, a licensed engineer, was brought into numerous projects over the next decade. Ireland also served on the Planning Board and was the town Moderator from 1985-1993.

Throughout the 1980s, the Budget Committee retained its skepticism about the financial efficiency of the Highway Department and the quality of its services to the town. However, in the late 1980s the BAC handed over the baton of overseeing town roads to the Planning Board and its new Capital Improvement Plan (CIP) process. The CIP, by the early 1990s, included a subcommittee that generated the first formal Road Improvement Plan.

PLANNING BOARD AND EARLY ZONING

The third leg of the stool balancing the future of Francestown in the late 1970s and early 1980s was the Planning Board (PB). Their meetings served as the playing field where the contestants skirmished over the town's management of its growth and development. One veteran of Planning Board meetings in this period referred to them as "The Tuesday Night Fights." The town adopted a Zoning Ordinance (ZO) in 1951. The Planning Board was founded in 1963 as a state requirement for the town to receive certain types of funding. Until 1979 members were appointed by the Select Board. From the mid-1960s through 2020 the ZO was changed at many town meetings. Subdivision regulations were added in 1964 and amended regularly through the following decades. The history of the Planning Board is a story of increasing regulation with the stated goal "to preserve the character of the town." The following table illustrates how zoning changed in the 1970s with respect to the basic home-building lot. The last permit for a new home on a one-acre lot was issued to Peter and Kay Flood in 1973. The home was named The Last Acre.

Zoning Ordinance for the New Home Construction			
Year	Lot Size	Frontage	Setbacks
1965	1 acre	200'	75' from the center of road
			25' from neighbor's property line
1972	2 acres	250'	
1977			50' from neighbor's property line
1979	3 acres	300'	100' from the center of the road
		100' lake	75' from high water line of ponds/river

At the beginning of the decade of the 1970s, the PB's tool kit was growing, but it still lacked a full array of gadgets. The Town Report for 1970 does not include an entry from the PB, as it was not yet considered on the front line. Only five permits for new houses were issued that year. The state added to the board's responsibilities when it passed the Scenic Road law in 1971. In 1972 Town Meeting designated 21 town roads as "scenic." This meant that cutting trees along such roads required a public hearing.

Twenty permits for new houses were applied for in 1971 and 1972 resulting in a ripple of concern. That ripple became a wave from 1975-1980. The workload of the previously sleepy PB increased from a few meetings a year to twice-a-month or more. A greater concern than individual building permits was subdivision, particularly for multi-unit dwellings. Land/Vest, the owners of the ski area in the early 1970s, launched a condominium project that preoccupied the board. Controversy arose when the PB approved large condominium and housing developments. Planning Board meetings were occasionally rambunctious. To opponents, these projects represented "growing speculation in Francestown land by outsiders.... [including a] disturbing number of property transfers and subdivisions now taking place in town.... [this] raises concerns about how development should go." Phrases such as "controlled growth," "worrisome rise in taxes," "destroy the more attractive features of our town," and "vigilance" peppered the debate. In 1974 a petition signed by 243 residents asked the PB to make even more changes to the ZO and subdivision regulations. The signees called for "more adequate control of the subdivision and development of land in Francestown." Town Meeting approved new ZO amendments regarding hotels, inns, and condominium projects. One of the most infamous Planning Board meetings took place in December of 1977. Seventy residents attended and the conversation became rowdy. During the meeting, two PB members resigned to protest the attendees' incivility. Selectman Jack Arnold talked with both men during the following week; one agreed to rejoin the board.

RISE OF THE CONSERVATION COMMISSION

In 1977, with the addition of Herb Benedict and Bill Hansen to the board, and the subtraction of members more positively disposed to development, the board began serious discussion about the advantages of a comprehensive land use plan, a Master Plan. "Explosive growth" leading to "suburbanization" was feared. The Conservation Commission (ConCom) began to take an interest in growth and development issues when Brenda Parker became chair. Parker and ConCom activist David Jonas sought to increase the scope of the Commission's focus. Parker conveyed to the Select Board "the ConCom's interest in Zoning and the Planning Board." This was a first. The ConCom was moving beyond its traditional portfolio of recycling, roadside clean up, environmental education, and beautification, and beginning to engage with the issues of growth, development, and land use.

Though each Town Meeting added detail to the Zoning Ordinance, and building permits were required for new construction or substantial remodeling, compliance was not a given. Enforcement was necessary. Town Meeting 1973 had created the position of Building Inspector. The Select Board wearied of facing down residents who saw no need for a building permit or misrepresented their project. A notice was placed in local newspapers informing everyone that fines could be administered if a project was not properly permitted. There was some skepticism about whether the board would follow through. Harry Varnum, chair of the ZBA, openly criticized the Select Board for their casualness in issuing building permits. In early 1974 several violations were reported by the new Building Inspector and the Select Board supported him. The board checked with the town's attorney and then challenged a dozen landowners who were not conforming to the Zoning Ordinance; this included the names of some property owners serving on town committees. The Select Board's backbone stiffened in 1976 and 1977, when the board refused to permit construction by Land/Vest on a road that "had not been brought up to standards."

MASTER PLAN DEVELOPMENT

Town meetings 1978 and 1979 were momentous, and lengthy. Voters faced 34 Warrant Articles in 1978 and 40 in 1979. Town Meeting 1978 approved the writing of a Master Plan/Land Use Plan. The Select Board appointed a Master Plan Committee. It included Herb Benedict, Bill Hansen, and Bob Caskie from the Planning Board, Bob Abbott from the Select Board, David Jonas from the Conservation Commission, Alan Thulander from the ZBA, and three at-large members, Donald Marsden, Janet Munson, and Connie Varnum. Hansen was the chairman. Town Meeting authorized the committee to seek technical assistance from the Southwestern New Hampshire Regional Planning Commission. Before the end of 1978 the committee surveyed citizens to solicit their input on the state of the town and their wishes for the future. Responses came from 85% of full-time residents (453) and 41% of part-time residents (148). Town Meeting 1978 changed the Planning Board from appointed to elected. A majority on the newly elected PB was more tolerant of development than were the members of the Master Plan Committee. Conflict was guaranteed since a proposed Master Plan would be submitted to the Planning Board for approval. This contrast between the two committees represented the division in town.

Town Meeting 1979 approved two petition Warrant Articles that called for limits on building permits and subdivision approvals. Increasingly restrictive zoning amendments were on the ballot and were approved in both 1978 and 1979. Some of the amendments addressed non-conforming structures, accessory dwellings, and mobile homes.

Work on the Master Plan continued through 1979. As it did, the interaction between a new developer and the Planning Board led some residents to question whether the board would genuinely follow through on a Master Plan if it called for more aggressive management of development. The developer in question was Richard Tremblay. In 1978 Tremblay began construction of a golf course-resort on the site of the former Crotched Mountain Country Club (closed in the 1930s), most recently known as Tavern Farm and owned by Don Prince. Phase One of the "Hall of Fame Golf Club" was to open an 18-hole course, a swimming pool, and a hotel and restaurant in the old Gibson Tavern building. Phase two was yet unclear, but it appeared that it would involve the construction of a large hotel or time-share condominiums to create a year-round resort. The ski areas were less than ten minutes from the golf course.

The "Hall of Fame" course opened in June of 1979. Tremblay immediately approached the Planning Board about expansion. Tremblay had demonstrated a casual attitude toward compliance with ordinances and permitting. Several times the town issued "cease and desist" orders to Tremblay for unpermitted activity.

The Master Plan draft was completed by the end of 1979, but the Planning Board did not prioritize approving it. Public hearings for the draft plan were scheduled for 1981. The board did not officially embrace the Master Plan until 1982. The attitude of some board members at public meetings and the slow approach to final acceptance of the plan led some town residents to suspect that the board might resist implementing the plan. These suspicions were exacerbated by an accommodating approach the Planning Board appeared to be taking with respect to Tremblay's moves to expand his resort.

In the spring of 1980, a large ad hoc committee was organized as a "watchdog" for the Planning Board. The committee's purpose, expressed in a document sent to its membership, opposed the "pro-development stance" of the Planning Board. The leaders of this committee were Jack Arnold, Herb Benedict, Bill Hansen, Ron Baptiste, and Phil Browne. Thirty-three members were organized into five "study groups" or subcommittees designated as Political Action, Economic, Environmental, Legal, and Media. A campaign was set in motion. Committee members were dispatched to attend Planning Board meetings to encourage acceptance and implementation of the Master Plan. Eventually, the PB endorsed the Master Plan in January 1982 with only modest editing.

The findings and recommendations of the three Master Plans – 1980, 1995, and 2015 – are described in Chapter 3. In comparison with the subsequent plans the 1980 Master Plan was brief, but the conceptual foundation it established is easily recognizable in the two plans that followed. Decisions made by select boards, planning boards, conservation commissions, and other town committees in the late 1980s and early 1990s reflected this foundation. The following paragraph provides the gist of the 1980 plan.

The Master Plan of 1980 was primarily a statement of principles rather than a list of detailed recommended policy steps. The plan's statement of purpose --"The purpose of a Comprehensive Plan of Development is to serve as a flexible framework to guide the orderly growth of a community over a period of years" -- was followed by the plan's most fundamental conclusion: "It is the expressed desire of Francestown residents to keep their town very much as it is today; a small, rural New England community, devoid of commercialism; a permanent community dominated by its citizens; an attractive, well-ordered town that retains its simplicity in spite of the complexity of modern life." In the community survey conducted by the Master Plan committee, 65% of respondents preferred that the town remain "as it is now." Seventy-two percent (72%) said that "rural lifestyle" was "very important" in their decision to live in Francestown. "The large majority of Francestown's residents wish to avoid growth for growth's sake, or growth simply for commercial profit. They will continue to resist ventures that usurp control of the town's destiny.... And they appreciate their fellow-citizens' healthy awareness of the community's architectural, natural, and social attributes. Francestown's residents have never sought purely personal gain at the expense of the town's classic beauty, its unique fitness as a place to live and raise children, or its sense of community."

The plan provided "statements of general policy" which included

- "The Town will seek in every legal, moral, and responsible way to retain its present character, which is one of simple rural beauty, reinforced by a history of architectural responsibility."
- "The Town will encourage and support a high quality of life for all its residents, but it will not support services or facilities inconsistent with the expressed desire of its citizens."
- "The Town's resources for the fifteen years of this plan might permit a growth rate of up to three percent per annum in the total population."
- "The Town will resist speculative ventures that threaten to change its character, but it will encourage 'cottage industries,' and other means of economic betterment that help it retain that unique character."

That last bullet was undoubtedly aimed at the plans for the golf course and the possibility that the two facilities – ski and golf -- might merge and become a major residential resort.

The Master Plan proved to be a pressure release valve, albeit temporarily. The work of the Planning Board from 1982 through 1985 became more routine. Population growth in 1981-1984 abated some -- about 100 new residents and 55 permits for new dwellings. The golf resort's plans for expansion were delayed, and then the course was sold, though soon the new owner escalated residents' concerns. That episode will be explored in Chapter 2. The Zoning Board was exhausted. Harry Varnum retired from the board after more than fifteen years. His steady hand was replaced by that of another: Alan Thulander. During Thulander's time as chair, the ZBA continued a hectic pace with an average of a dozen hearings each year. Beginning in 1983, the Planning Board began a complete overhaul of the Zoning Ordinance to match the expectations of the Master Plan and to increase coherence after years of incrementally adding amendments. The new Zoning Ordinance passed overwhelmingly by Town Meeting 1985.

Highway Department Struggles

The major preoccupation of the Select Board and the Budget and Advisory Committee (BAC) in the late 1970s and early 1980s was the care and cost of roads. They struggled to control the budget and to influence the operational decisions of the elected road agent. At the 1982 Town Meeting, citizens surrendered the practice of electing the road agent; the road agent was to be appointed. Town meetings through the 1980s approved, however slowly, acquisition of a fleet of town-owned trucks and apparatus. The first equipment purchased was army surplus or well-used, but it was a start. The Select Board, to break deeply entrenched patterns, hired an outsider as road agent in 1983, Tony Roberts. He served three years before leadership of the department was returned to the Foote family. Clayton "Junior" Foote, nephew of Robert Foote (road agent in the 1970s), was appointed road agent in 1987. Junior led the department until 2006.

The town owes a great deal to the Foote and Paige families, who have cared for the roads for decades. They worked hard often using low quality equipment to keep the roads passable, roads that had not been built for the weight and volume of the traffic they were expected to carry with the increasing population. Most of the town's bridges were just culverts. They constantly needed to be cleared of debris and winter ice. The highway crew may not have represented the image that new residents to town recognized as the outward appearance of professionalism, but their knowledge, skills, and pride in their work was strong.

It is easy to see why the BAC and Select Boards were concerned about the cost of town roads. In 1970, the combined cost of the road budget and warrant articles for roads and bridges was $33,400, by 1980 it grew to $138,000, and reached $332,000 in 1990, ten times the 1970 figure. Expenditures per capita were $165 in 1980 and around $300 in 1990. Roads consumed 64% of the town's budget in 1980 but only 53% in 1990, though that was due mostly to the expansion of spending on Waste Disposal, Recreation, and other departments. Expenditures per mile were $273 in 1970, $1,247 in 1980 and nearly $5,000 in 1990. It wasn't just about the bottom line of the budget. The select boards and budget committees wanted control. They viewed the Highway Department as too independent. For example, at Town Meeting 1981, the BAC supported the purchase of a single sander but opposed Warrant Articles to purchased five other pieces of equipment and any allocation for sealing blacktop roads. However, once the road agent was an appointee the BAC routinely supported such requests. Even as they praised Kris Stewart's exemplary year as road agent in 1980, they opposed his recommendations for the purchase of equipment and funds for preventive maintenance. It was about control, and, to some extent, "culture." The Highway Department had a reputation for hard work and conscientiousness, but also for coloring outside the lines.

The battle between the Budget and Advisory Committee and the Highway Department from the point of view of a road agent was succinctly captured by John Paige, the last elected road agent, in the 1982 Town Report: "Considering the outrageous price of rebuilding a piece of road, I find the lack of responsibility of the town to have a yearly sealing program totally ridiculous, and senseless. It's like paying a dentist a large sum of money to have your teeth fixed, then not taking care of them. It costs more, in many ways, more patch for potholes and shoulder breakage, and a lot more unneeded abuse to cars and trucks, etc." Paige continued with specific examples – mud, culverts, brush cutting, tree removal -- where "funds were not allowed" for the department to do necessary preventive work. Paige's final shot was "Maybe careful consideration of the people appointed to the budget committee would help, people who use town roads on a daily basis may be better qualified to judge the needs of this department." Once the road agent was an appointee the Select Board responded with praise. They noted that town roads were improving, and that the road agent was doing a good job. The Budget Committee now supported re-graveling of deteriorated roads, a re-paving cycle to stay ahead of deterioration of paved roads, a "concerted attack against the takeover of the roads by brush," and preventive maintenance on town-owned equipment.

Even with the progress made in the mid-1980s the highway department's working conditions and equipment situation were still substandard. An oft repeated joke was that the highway crew spent more time under their equipment than in it. The main highway "barn" built in 1957 was a poor place to do maintenance. There were some improvements in the 1980s -- a salt barn, a fuel containment structure, a parts room, and an office; though, the "office" was a 6' x 10' steel container. A sand pile sufficient for one winter was maintained on the site. With more equipment the inadequate work and storage space became even more problematic; working conditions were unsafe at times. Most equipment had to be left outside even in the winter, which led to cold start-ups for plowing. Professionalization of the department still had a long way to go. But, by the late 1980s, the department was on a trajectory of improvement to which town leaders were committed.

Fire Department

The Fire Department's two dozen members brought little controversy into the governance of the town. A contributing factor to that may well have been stable leadership whose thinking was well-aligned with those who made decisions about budgeting and planning. Many of the participants on town governance committees were members, or leaders, of the fire service. An overall summary of the history of the Fire Department is in Chapter 6.

Fire equipment was changing, particularly in size, cost, and complexity. Newer fire truck models were significantly larger. The firehouse, built in 1962, and the department's vehicles were well-maintained, but they were aging. From 1970 to 1980 the number of calls the department received increased substantially, particularly in medical emergencies. With the town's population growth, calls for rescue service were increasing. Because of these factors, the small firehouse on the Common was insufficient; it would not be able to house newer model vehicles nor was there room for any additional apparatus, like a rescue truck. A study committee reported to Town Meeting 1980 that a new firehouse, on a new site, was needed. At a special Town Meeting voters approved the purchase of a plot of land on the south turnpike adjacent to the highway department barn and a Warrant Article to borrow most of the funds needed for the new facility. Construction proceeded smoothly and by 1982 the department moved to its new 5,000 square foot, three bay garage with an office, maintenance area, rest rooms, meeting room, and kitchen. A training tower was added in the 1990s. In 1984, the town purchased a new tanker-pumper and the following year the new station's parking lot was paved.

The old firehouse was renovated and re-named the "Town Hall Annex." John Schott's assessment of that structure was ungenerous: "an eyesore on the Common," though "serviceable." As called for by the BAC, it became the offices of the Select Board, Town Clerk, Tax Collector, Police Chief, Planning Board, ZBA, Conservation Commission, and it provided a public rest room. There was a 40-person meeting room upstairs. However, precious little parking was available.

POLICE DEPARTMENT

From 1973-1976 the Francestown Police Department had four different chiefs. The period began with long-time Chief Norman Stewart in charge. By mid-1976 the Select Board settled on the leadership of young Peter Flood, son of the former police chief in Antrim. Flood lived in town and was married to the daughter of the town's fire chief, Clifton Foote. He developed a comfortable and trusting relationship with town residents and leaders. Flood served as chief for 25 years.

Statistics reveal a substantial growth in reported police activity. Some of this was undoubtedly due to Chief Stewart's preference for settling issues of conflict through conversation and mediation. His annual activity reports show only a modest number of arrests. But, by 1980 the expansion of skiing, golf, and the overall population was reflected in Chief Flood's succinct annual report: "more crime, more traffic, more work for the police." By the time Flood became chief, there was a dedicated phone installed in his home so that the public could more easily reach him. Town Meeting 1974 purchased the first town-owned police vehicle, though officers often still used their personal vehicles. Motor vehicle violations were the primary policing concern for the town in the 1970s. In 1970, Chief Stewart recorded 58 motor vehicle stops. By 1978, Chief Flood and his officers stopped about 750 vehicles. A chronic concern of Main Street residents was speeding, particularly in the winter as skiers dashed to and from Crotched Mountain. In 1974, state police made a special patrol on a Saturday during ski season and counted 727 cars between 3:30 pm and 6:00 pm. They stopped 98 for speeding.

By 1980, for the first time all the officers employed by the department were state certified. In 1983 there were seven part-time officers, an animal control officer, two vehicles, and a radar device. Policing the ski area increased the town's need for officer hours. A police department office was opened in the Town Hall Annex. Don Abbott began serving as the Animal Control Officer in 1983 and continued to serve through 2020.

Recycling Comes to Francestown

In 1970 the town's "dump" was a landfill where unsorted refuse was piled and burned periodically. It was not fenced and had no paid supervision. The dump was a danger for surface water and aquifer contamination and lacked available material for covering the burned refuse. Occasionally the fire would burn too aggressively, and the Fire Department had to respond. There was no systematic recycling. The Select Board was aware that changes needed to be made to waste disposal practices. As early as 1968 the Select Boards of Francestown, Hancock, and Greenfield held joint meetings to discuss the implications of new state legislation regulating disposal of trash. A state edict banned open burning after 1975, though at that time the compliance date was extended to 1977.

Everything changed by 1980 as the environmental movement and the concept of "recycling" found its way to Francestown. Connie Bicknell's personal zeal was responsible for the rapid evolution of recycling in town. Her passion was supported by ConCom stalwarts Sibby Kunhardt and Pat Place. In 1972 the town began recycling newspapers, and the effort quickly expanded to include glass, cans, and all sorts of paper. In one year, eight tons of glass, two tons of metals, and three tons of paper were transported to vendors in Massachusetts and Connecticut. The materials were carried in private vehicles and transport was paid for through private donations. Bicknell did most of the haulage. Sheds were added to the dump for recyclables. The National Guard had a program for hauling away discarded appliances and junk cars. Members of the ConCom attended a statewide meeting where they displayed photos of Francestown's recycling program, which generated interest from across New Hampshire. The town was recognized as a model for its voluntary recycling program.

The Select Board investigated options for managing trash and recycling. A Waste Disposal Committee recommended that the town enter into a cooperative agreement with Bennington and Antrim to share a landfill. To implement this recommendation the town would need a compactor or several roll-off containers, fixed hours of operation, and supervision. Recycling was formalized, both to keep re-useable material out of landfills, and to reduce the cost of trash hauling. An agreement with Bennington and Antrim was approved in 1976 and renewed for ten years in the early 1980s. The newly christened transfer station collected trash in roll-off containers that were transported to

Bennington. In 1978 the town hired the first recycling supervisor to assist the transfer station's supervisor. In 1985 a compactor on a concrete pad replaced the roll-offs.

Implementing a formal recycling program was not without hiccups. At one point, Bicknell, in frustration, informed the Select Board that she would no longer oversee recycling unless she received more support. She called upon the Select Board to create a Recycling Committee, which they did in 1975. The new committee held fund-raising events including a town talent show which played to a standing-room-only crowd due the performance of its all-male chorus line including Junior Foote, Dick Leavitt, Alan Thulander, Phil Ireland, Bob Bewley, Leighton Bicknell, Lou Gallop, and Bob Toppan. Donations paid for the new recycling sheds at the dump. Robert "Dud" Parker became the leader of the Waste Disposal and Recycling Commission (WDRC) in 1976 and led the department through the 1980s. His dedication to efficient waste disposal brought stability to the program. Parker regularly exhorted residents to do a better job separating their recyclables.

In 1978 the town's landfill was covered with soil, and permanently retired. The Budget and Advisory Committee called upon the WDRC to cover the cost of recycling with the sale of recyclables. The national market for recyclables was unprepared for the volume generated in the 1970s. There was a glut of recyclables and revenue declined. Parker reported that "The principal disappointment in the operation of the Waste Disposal and Resource Recovery operation...is the volatile market for recyclable materials."

RECREATION COMMISSION

Town meetings and town officials in the 1970s-1980s showed much more enthusiasm for developing waste disposal facilities than they did for creating a recreation program and facilities. Town residents engaged in recreation – tennis, baseball, swimming, dance – but the dominant philosophy was that recreation ought to be paid for privately. It was not considered a fundamental municipal service.

The Francestown Improvement and Historical Society (FIHS) was the town's de facto "recreation department." In 1972, facing high demand for tennis court time, the town negotiated with FIHS to lease some of their land to install a second public tennis court. FIHS built the original court, provided the swim float and safety equipment at the town beach on Scobie Pond (aka Haunted Lake), organized skating on the Creamery-Bixby Pond or in the Colburn lot, funded the baseball program, and supported ad hoc recreation initiatives like hockey, and dancing at Town Hall. Summer tennis lessons were privately organized by a group of mothers. In addition to using the town courts, lessons were offered on courts owned by the Taylors, Hills, and at the Inn on Crotched Mountain. Also, privately organized cross-country skiing was hosted by Prince's Tavern Farm, and several young horse riders from Francestown joined the Frog Rock Pony Club in New Boston.

A Recreation Commission (RecCom) was formed at the suggestion of the BAC following a kerfuffle over maintenance for the swim raft and supervision of teenagers at the beach. The new commission was appointed with Carol Prest as chair. The new RecCom sponsored Contra dancing and dance lessons, swim lessons at the town beach, and parties for children on Halloween and before the Christmas holiday. Town Meeting 1978 provided the first funding for recreation programs from tax revenue, including paid lifeguards for the beach. By 1985 the town budgeted $5,600. The RecCom program in the 1980s expanded to include Cub Scouts, 4-H, Little League, men's softball, an "Adventure Program," tennis lessons, a "Summerfest" on Crotched Mountain, theatre camp through Andy's Summer Playhouse, aerobics and exercise classes, volleyball, a golf clinic, and round-robin tennis tournaments. Ninety children took swim lessons in 1985. An immediate concern of the Recreation Commission was the leased town beach on Scobie Pond. The RecCom favored a new location for the town beach on land that the town would own. The commission sought a location with more parking, a natural beach, and adjacent space for picnicking. A proposal was made to buy land off Journey's End Road with frontage on the pond. The purchase was not approved. A decade later, the RecCom proposed to buy another lot on Scobie, but again without support from Town Meeting. The RecCom also attended to the existing baseball field. The town's field was rehabilitated in 1980 and dedicated to long-time Little League booster, John "Jack" Underhill. At the ceremony, the FIHS President read a long list of the ways that Underhill supported baseball and town beautification.

Residents' continued ambivalence about publicly funded recreation showed in the community survey conducted for the 1980 Master Plan. Only 30% wanted recreational facilities "increased." By 1995 the town had moved past the expectation that programs would be self-supporting through user fees and budgeted $40,000. As of 2020, other than forests, the town has never purchased any land for recreational purposes.

CONVAL SCHOOL DISTRICT TAKES OVER

The number of students in Francestown's elementary school grew substantially from 1970 to 1985. So did the town's tax burden for support of the ConVal School District. The last year of Francestown's independent school district was 1967-1968. The district shared a Superintendent with Wilton. The budget was $59,000. On July 1, 1968, the new Contoocook Valley School District assumed full operating responsibility for the school in Francestown. The new "cooperative" organization had nine member towns. A thirteen-member school board governed the district. Each year the budget was submitted to the voters in a district-wide meeting that was structured as a Town Meeting.

The ConVal Articles of Agreement provided for a Selectmen's Advisory Committee (SAC) that would give direct input to the district's board and Superintendent. Frequently criticized by various towns' leaders, particularly those from Francestown, the SAC seldom mustered the weighty voice that its designers imagined. A 1973 Transcript article's title "Confrontation Looms Over Who Runs the Schools" captures towns' leaders crankiness with ConVal. In 1972 the Select Board chose to remit a couple of monthly payments to the district "under protest." A letter from the ConVal Superintendent scolded one of the selectmen for giving the district's bookkeeper a "bad time." Selectman Alan Thulander, never a fan of the ConVal schools, complained that the district's budget was "not lean enough." And, since it was the 1970s, there was an "open forum" in Peterborough where parents and administrators exchanged views on "drugs, permissiveness, too much free time, and poor communication with parents." In 1974 Antrim's Town Meeting entertained a Warrant Article for the town to withdraw from the school district; it failed. The new school district had a junior high school, so Francestown's 7th and 8th graders were bused along with the high school students. A new high school facility, completed in 1970, was described by John Schott as "elaborately-appointed." Schott, eulogizing the town's independence, called this "another chapter in the dispersion of the town's population and disintegration of the town as a self-sufficient, independent community.... its older children, like their parents in search of jobs, ... left town."

Joining ConVal doubled the cost of schooling for taxpayers. By 1972 schools were 76% of a resident's property tax bill. School district budgets rose even more rapidly than the town's budget with an increase of 184% in the 1970s. The district's assessment from each town was calculated based on two factors: the number of students attending from each town, the "average daily membership" (ADM) and the "equalized assessed valuation" (EAV) of a town's property. Francestown's share of the district's costs rose from 6% in 1970 to 7.5% in 1979. In 1980, per pupil spending by the ConVal district was substantially higher than all other school districts in the region from Milford to Keene.

Enrollment at Francestown Elementary School (FES) grew modestly during the 1970s. In 1967, 78 students, grades 1-8, attended the Red School. There were three teachers and three classrooms. Sixty-seven students in grades 1-6 attended the school in 1979. Families moving into town pushed the school's enrollment steadily higher. Though 5th and 6th grade students were attending middle school in Antrim by 1994, the Red School enrolled 115 children that year. The district brought in portable classrooms to house the overflow from the three classrooms. Parent volunteers, in classrooms, on the playground, and before and after school, were a necessary feature of how the Red School coped with steady growth. In 1979 a group of parent volunteers built a new playground for the school children; another parent-initiated playground project took place in the 1990s. A push for a new, more modern, and more spacious school building began in the late 1980s, but not until 1997 would ConVal open the FES building on the south turnpike that serves the town's children in 2020.

In 1970, with no public-school kindergarten at the time, a group of parents in Francestown, Bennington, and Greenfield started the Tri-Town Kindergarten located in the Community Church's basement. A push for ConVal to offer kindergarten was persistent but not until 1992 did ConVal establish kindergartens. A parent cooperative, Francestown Community Preschool (FCP), was founded in the 1970s. In the 1980s, the community preschool was housed in the lower level of the post office building; it provided licensed preschool for up to 20 children. Town Meeting 1980 rejected a Warrant Article that would have provided FCP with town support.

LOCAL ECONOMY AND SMALL BUSINESS

John Schott well summarized the economy of Francestown in the 1970s, "Newcomers brought no jobs with them, and few came to work here in self-employed occupations; rather, for the major part, they came to rest and relax. Nor did they require services beyond those already provided within the town ... carpenters, electricians, plumbers, and general handymen, satisfied their minimal needs. No local industry was therefore encouraged by these newcomers, nor did they bring industries with them. Indeed, those who were not retirees tended to earn their living elsewhere, the more seasonal newcomers in Boston, and the year-rounders in Peterborough, Nashua, or near-by towns."

The ski area and, beginning in 1978, the golf course, were multi-million-dollar enterprises employing double-digit numbers of employees. Most of their workers were seasonal. Skilled tradesmen dominated the economy of the town in the 1970s-1980s and still did in 2020. The backbone of excavation and construction have been Miller Plumbing and Heating, and Francestown Sand & Gravel. The Miller brothers -- Rick and Steve -- continued their father Richard's business and were the men in town who would address any problem from major excavation to a clogged toilet, with quiet thoughtfulness, deft skill, and conscientious dependability. Kris Stewart started the business that evolved into Francestown Sand & Gravel. His leadership service to the town will be described in later chapters. George Whipple Construction and the Robson Corporation also played important roles in major town projects. Home building, remodeling, and repair employed many tradesmen. Builders included Don Hoyt, Peter Bixby, William McNeill, Thomas Bournival, Rob Ames, Robert Rokes, Blair Hardwick, Eric Grenier, Paul Knight, Larry Kullgren, Jay Creighton, Jeff Tarr, James Gibbons, Charles Wasserloos, Rino Sanchioni, Scott Smith, Gordon Sherman, Steven Brown, and Paul St. Cyr. Painting, plumbing, and electric were provided by Richard Leavitt, Jennifer Noonan,

Harry Maybee, Bruce Dennis, Robert Schroeppel, Arthur Buzzell, Bruce Harrington, Thomas Clark, and Gavin Gordon.

As in any town in America, small businesses were born and passed away during these five decades. For many native residents Vadney's general store in the historic "Long Store" building served as their grocery store. The Vadney family owned the store until the mid-1980s. They were succeeded as store operators by Kip and Kim Dalley and in the 1990s by Ben and Song Moeller. Following the Vadneys, the building owner was Henry Tiffany who operated a ski shop in the southern most section of the structure for a few years. The town disapproved of this use of the building and sued to stop it. The resulting court ruling, in favor of the town, led to severe restriction on the use of the south end of the building for many years.

When the new Rt. 101 Plaza in Peterborough opened in the early 1970s, the new A&P drew a lot of town customers. Many new residents who worked out of town bought their weekly groceries in Milford, Goffstown, or Peterborough and used Vadney's mostly for urgent needs. Boutique antique businesses were a growth industry in Francestown in the 1980s-90s. Several residents had home-based shops. Francestown was a destination for antique collectors due to the density of dealers including Barbara and Derald Radtke, Elsie Mikula, Ann and David Stewart, Ashley Prest, Bonnie Lizotte, and Alan Thulander. Peddling real estate has provided income to more than a dozen Francestown-based realtors. Country Brokers, owned in succession by Mary Lindstrom, Sarah Pyle, and Judi Miller has been a major home-grown realty from the 1990s through 2020. Other realtors in town worked for firms in Peterborough or other larger towns in the region. A potpourri of small businesses included Camirand's Car Care, Jerry Kerouac's and Kelly Socia's liveries, Andrew Grant's tree service, Mark Couturier's chimney cleaning, and David Rowean's and Bev Abbott's Yankee Pools. More than fifty entrepreneurs operated out of their homes through the decades.

In the late 1960s a horseback riding camp opened on 240 acres off Dennison Pond Road as Kingsbury Hill drawing campers and staff from around the world. The extensive facilities supported training in show jumping and dressage. A dozen people were employed at Kingsbury Hill during the summer camp season. Another equestrian facility was developed in the 1980s off New Boston Road near the town line. Harmony Hill boarded horses and provided training and instruction. Specialized small businesses in town have included Luis Gallop's Booted Sheepherder, Nancy Angell's Portrait Studio, Yankee Pools, Henry Camirand's Car Care, Andrew Grant's Tree Service, and Scott Carbee's Field Restoration. Many have produced maple syrup including the Cilleys, Hardwicks, and Harringtons. Various farming operations are described in Chapter 3.

Anyone who moved to town after 1993 would be surprised that at one time there was a very good restaurant in town. Anna Yoss owned and prepared comfort food meals at *Grandmother's House* on Mountain Road from 1967 to 1985. Immigrating from Germany before World War Two, Ms. Yoss owned restaurants in New Jersey before she and her husband moved to Dublin, New Hampshire to run the Dublin Inn. She then purchased the restaurant in Francestown known as *Granny Ketch*. The ski area was new, and that traffic made the location promising. Yoss built up the restaurant's reputation. In 1985 Robert Jean LeJacq took over *Grandmother's House,* re-naming it *Maitre Jacq*. Trained as a chef in his native France, LeJacq immigrated to the U.S. and worked in restaurants in New York City, Manchester, and Milford – Hampshire Hills -- before launching *Maitre Jacq* as a white tablecloth French bistro. LeJacq was a strong supporter of conservation, an avid hunter, and loved rambling the hills of Francestown. He moved his family to Francestown. In November 1992, LeJacq was shot and killed in a hunting accident near the restaurant. He was sixty. His children briefly attempted to keep the restaurant going but it closed in 1993. From that time forward, only the series of restaurants in the old Gibson Tavern on the north turnpike, part of the golf course business, provided meals in Francestown.

WATER COMPANY

The Francestown Water and Electric Company was founded in the 1920s as a private utility. A well was bored on the north side of the Village and water pipes were installed to carry potable water to customers in the Village area of the town. John Schott characterized the situation of the Water Company and its customers in 1970, "Plagued by perforated pipes, inoperative meters, a lowering of the water table, accusations of administrative laxity, and dwindling financial reserves, by the middle 1960s the company had been written off by many of its stockholders, bred ulcerous despair among its users, and was considered by Concord officials as a rather bad joke about which the less they heard the better. Finally, in 1971, a 'user revolt' led to the voting in of new local management, presided over by Harold Varnum, in hopes that at least something might be salvaged from the existing system and steps taken to resuscitate this failing private venture into a needed public service."

The Water Company re-incorporated itself as a not-for-profit cooperative in 1977 with the goal of renovating its infrastructure. Most of the project's cost was covered by a grant from the Farmers' Home Administration. The company members voted to float a bond that was paid off through monthly user fees. Town Meeting agreed to an easement through town-owned property. In 1978 the "new" Water Company upgraded 9,000 feet of pipes and installed a 30,000-gallon water storage tank. A six-inch main replaced a one-inch iron pipe that had been in place since 1877. As a result of new piping and improved storage, the company met all relevant water quality standards and delivered water to fifty-five residences in the Main Street village area.

A project completion celebration was held in October 1979. Margery Foster, president of the Water Company, cracked a bottle of wine on the new storage tank and then made a short speech of appreciation for all those who made the improved main line and new connections possible including this wry observation, "Now we all will be able to take showers at once, even on the second floor."

END OF THE FIRST WAVE

By 1985, Francestown had navigated the first wave of in-migration. A Master Plan was in place to guide town governance, at least in principle. The problematic areas of town administration -- roads, waste disposal, and property assessment – were on a more efficient footing. Regulation of residential and commercial development was in place; growth management had been embraced. Town leadership was a mixture of older natives and younger newcomers, and the mixture appeared to be compatible. There were still occasional rambunctious Planning Board or Zoning Board hearings, but these were more about situational details than the overall trajectory of the town.

Unbeknownst to the citizens, looking back it is clear that Francestown was poised for a "tipping point" experience beginning in 1986 and extending through 1990. By 1990 the town would be set on a path that continued up to 2020. No single event would characterize this "tipping point" but the changes would prove to be substantial.

CHAPTER 2

THE TIPPING POINT
1986-1990

During this period, new initiatives by the Conservation Commission (ConCom) and Planning Board (PB) led to fundamental change in Francestown's governance. At an opportune moment in the town's evolution leaders emerged who proved to be key agents of change. Scot Heath, chair of the Conservation Commission, and Abigail Arnold, chair of the Planning Board, strongly influenced the next thirty years of the town's history. They led a newly acquisitive Conservation Commission and an assertive and modernizing Planning Board. A third development was also consequential: the demise of the ski and golf resorts. The failure of the two largest businesses in Francestown cleared away the dream, for some, or the nightmare, for others, of Francestown becoming a resort community, the Vail of southern New Hampshire. Francestown's core identity remained: a picturesque, rural, hill country town. For many of its residents that was just fine.

CONSERVATION COMMISSION RISING

The Conservation Commission's scope of responsibility broadened in the late 1970s when the ConCom chair, Brenda Parker, told the Select Board that it wanted to be involved in reviewing Zoning Ordinance amendments and growth management initiatives. With Johanna Staub as chair in the 1980s, ConCom members attended statewide conferences and legislative hearings on growth and its consequences. The ConCom urged the Select Board to convene a public meeting about Scenic Road tree-cutting which led to the appointment of a Special Roads Committee to investigate the highway department's road maintenance practices. The ConCom also organized a Wetland Evaluation Team to consider how best to protect local wetlands. The next step in expanding its portfolio was dramatic: acquisition of conservation lands.

Into this context many believe that the right man arrived in the right place at the right time. Scot Heath moved to Francestown in 1984 as a recent college graduate having just begun a career in real estate appraisal. Heath grew up in Merrimack next to a large farm and forest owned by his family. His consciousness of the desirability of land preservation was shaped by watching how that acreage was whittled away by development. In Heath's view, the loss of this open space led to a permanent change in the way of life of the citizens of Merrimack. It did not take him long to join a coalition of Francestown residents who sought to conserve undeveloped forest land. His own vision was preserving undeveloped land for protection of wildlife and water resources, but also for recreational uses. In 2020, a long-time leader in town observed, "It's hard to picture what Francestown would look like today if Scot Heath had not moved here when he did."

CONSERVATION LAND ACQUISITION

There have been two periods of substantial additions to the acreage of protected land in Francestown, 1987-1990 and 2003-2010. Heath directly led the first campaign and worked behind the scenes to encourage and support the second. As chair of the Conservation Commission from 1986 to 1991 he negotiated land donations, purchases, and easements that created the Crotched Mountain Town Forest and brought together the team that founded the Francestown Land Trust (FLT). In 1987 the town owned 28 acres of conserved land; by 1991 conservation land owned by the town or held in conservation easements exceeded 1,000 acres. There are 18,700 acres in town, not including lakes and the river. By 2020, the total of conserved land owned by Francestown and FLT, or protected by easements held by the town, FLT, or other land trusts, exceeded 6,000 acres. Much of this protected acreage is along the Piscataquog River and its headwater streams or in backcountry tracts with steep slopes and wetlands accessible only from Class VI or abandoned roads. In 1986-1990 the ConCom included: Ellen Arnold, Connie Varnum, Mary Lindstrom, Frank Hanchett, Taisto Holm, Randy Wheeler, David Goodrich, Sirkka Holm, Kenneth Marks, Suzanne Birchard, Patricia DeAngelis, Barbara Kraus, Marvin Armstrong, and Sara Allen.

At the 1987 Town Meeting, Warrant Articles were approved to create a Conservation Fund (ConFund) and to appropriate $10,000 for the fund. This pattern of support by townspeople continued each time the ConCom proposed such a Warrant Article for the next 18 years. Between 1987 and 1990, $45,000 was added to the fund. Between 1991 and 2010, town meetings approved $380,000 for the ConFund. In addition to that, Town Meeting 2005 approved a $1,000,000 bond for land acquisition. Due to Heath's advocacy and the support of the Planning Board, Francestown became the first town in the state of New Hampshire to have a land conservation fund included in its Capital Improvement Plan budget.

As ConCom chair, Heath conducted a letter-writing campaign. More than one hundred letters went out to landowners of large holdings considered to have "conservation value." The letters informed the owners about how they could protect their land from development. The map of targeted properties was very ambitious. Crotched Mountain, Bullard Hill, and Shattuck Pond were considered "high value" targets. Though most of the "asks" did not bear fruit initially, several of them did; others came to fruition years later. When asked about Heath's efforts, his colleagues from that era talk of "persistence" and "focus," as well as "coaxing" and "cajoling." Said one colleague, "There was no one he would not approach; he spent countless hours cultivating relationships that in many cases eventually led owners to make a decision to conserve their land."

The project that set off the dominoes of land preservation was an expanse of farmland, abutting the original Lord Town Forest, owned by Fred and Lillian Harrigan. The Harrigans purchased the Lord Farm on lower Bible Hill and wanted to protect it in perpetuity. Complex negotiations ensued leading to the farm's protection. For the Conservation Commission to purchase sizable tracts of land, money beyond what was in the ConFund had to be raised. Grants, from state and private organizations, played a key role over the next three decades. Winning grants was competitive. A grant application was more likely to be successful if there was evidence town residents were supporting land conservation by putting conservation easements on their land. To facilitate this, Heath organized Francestown Land Conservation, Inc., later renamed the Francestown Land Trust. Eventually the new land trust might purchase land or easements, but in its origins, it was a tool to leverage grant funds.

Shortly after this first project was completed, former NH Governor John King called Heath. King owned hundreds of acres in Francestown and wanted it protected. The project moved forward with grants from the state's Land Conservation Investment Program (LCIP) and the Forest Society. Conservation easements on lands owned by Ellen Hill, and Harry and Connie Varnum made the grant applications more competitive. This synergy resulted in 388 acres of land on the slopes of Crotched Mountain becoming a town forest. Later, donations and purchases from the Merrills and Schultzes brought the size of this forest to 630 acres. By 2020 it grew to 948 acres. During this period, Francestown was successful in winning a substantial amount of grants.

In the late 1980s, towns to the east -- Weare and New Boston -- were experiencing a push for subdivision of land for home building. Many residents expected this tide to rise into Francestown. Heath brought to the Planning Board a new growth management tool. Town Meeting 1991 amended the Zoning Ordinance to designate "overlay districts." The overlay district system allowed the Planning Board to regulate development of land in vulnerable areas such as "steep slopes," "shorelands," or "wetlands." Thousands of acres fall within these overlay districts.

How Much is Too Much?

Between 1991-1999 the trajectory of the ConCom's land preservation campaign plateaued. This was due to several factors including a downturn in the national and state economy which led the state to end the LCIP grant program. Another key factor in the pause was that Scot Heath moved out of Francestown. He moved back to town in time to play a supporting role in the second wave of aggressive protection of open space that kicked-off in the early

2000s when another passionate leader, Betsy Hardwick, emerged. That story is in Chapter 5.

Another factor in the direction of the Conservation Commission in the 1990s was opposition to its appetite for land. Opponents argued that the town forests provided sufficient recreational opportunities and observed that they were not well used. The Master Plan of 1995 admitted that most residents "either do not know there are town-owned forests or do not know where they are located." The ConCom's original impetus had been to conserve land for recreation, wildlife habitat, and water resource preservation. Some advocates for open space preservation were motivated primarily to control development and maintain the aesthetics of rural life. They called for "the protection of…more *visible* tracts" (emphasis added) along the town's major roads to make permanent a rural "look." Opponents of ConCom land purchases were able to argue that this aesthetic motivation did not justify spending thousands of taxpayer dollars. An example of some town leaders' skepticism about additional open space preservation came in 1992. The ConCom proposed accepting a donation of land on Pleasant Pond as an additional town forest. Alan Thulander, having rejoined the Select Board, questioned whether town residents and the ConCom were on the same page regarding the scope of land protection. Thulander cited conversations with residents who thought the town was taking too much land off the tax roll. In response, the ConCom conducted a survey of town residents that showed broad public support for commission activities past and present. The land acquisition project fell off the ConCom's agenda for the remainder of the 1990s. Through the 1990s, the ConCom partnered with the Planning Board (PB) in land use policymaking and management. ConCom members participated in site inspections for development proposals, served on the Road Improvement sub-committee, and worked with the PB in developing land use regulations and the Master Plan of 1995. The ConCom supported the Waste Disposal Commission's hazardous waste collection days.

Though there was a pause in land acquisition, a commitment to land protection in Francestown was established between 1987-1990. A "tipping point" was reached. Taking land out of the development market would begin again in the 2000s, and the scope would be much greater. Steady, incremental preservation of open space became a pattern in town through 2020.

THE PLANNING BOARD'S CHALLENGES IN THE LATE 80S

The period of 1986-1990 was tumultuous for both the Planning Board (PB) and its partner the Zoning Board of Adjustment (ZBA). Three factors were at play: an unparalleled demand for subdivision and home construction; multi-million-dollar speculative resort development projects came forward; and the idea that modern municipal governance ought to be based on long-range planning was consummated.

SUBDIVISION

The PB and ZBA faced subdivision and dwelling unit construction unlike anything the town had experienced since the 1830s. Growth in the mid-to-late 1980s exceeded the building boom of the late 1970s. Between 1981 and 1989, 165 lots were created out of 73 subdivisions. Building permits were issued for 155 dwelling units. For the first time in over a century, births significantly exceeded deaths in town. Births don't lead to houses, but they did lead to seats in a school building that was already too small. The population of the town rose by about 250 residents in the four years from 1986 through 1989. The statistics cited represent dwellings actually built on individual lots. In addition to the reality of new dwellings, there was apprehension about speculative proposals for building at the ski area and golf course. The building boom threatened to exacerbate preexisting town infrastructure problems, particularly road issues. The wave of subdivision also led to a sense of "I better get mine before this is over!" among some residents holding undeveloped land.

As in the previous decade, there was a spectrum of disagreement among members of both the PB and ZBA that reflected divisions within the town. At one end of the spectrum were those eager to see large commercial development and abundant housing construction. The opposite pole harbored those who wanted to "pull up the drawbridge," allowing no development at all. Most residents fell in between. The idea of "controlled growth" appealed to many. Some of the residents had a personal business interest -- they owned land that could be subdivided. While some saw development offering "promise" to the town – jobs, business, expanded recreation, a larger tax base – others feared how increased housing density or commercialization might change the culture of the town. Richard Tremblay's development plans for his Hall of Fame golf resort and Tim Gannett's proposals for more condominiums near the ski area led to occasionally raucous Planning Board and ZBA meetings in the late 1970s and early 1980s. That phenomenon returned when similar commercial growth proposals were advanced in 1985-1987. The development plans of ski resort owners kindled concerns of over-commercialization of the northside of town. The ski area was the major business in town. The huge tract of land along Mountain Road that had been the Winslow family's Hob and Nob Farm was broken up and sold in the late 1950s. A substantial amount of the property was purchased by an investor group that opened the Crotched Mountain ski area in 1964 under the stewardship of Bill MacAdam. It was the first major business founded in town since the soapstone quarry and mill closed in the early 1900s.

CROTCHED MOUNTAIN EXPANSION

A second ski area was carved out on the Bennington side of Crotched Mountain by 1970. The two areas merged in the 1980s and Ski Crotched became a truly major enterprise averaging over 100,000 skier visits per year. Crotched was a major day-trip destination for skiers from northern

Massachusetts and southern New Hampshire. Crotched Mountain doubled its snowmaking capabilities by adding state-of-the-art equipment for both areas: "twice the snow in half the time." Night skiing was offered at half the price of day skiing. The area advertised that it was "uncrowded," with "crisp air, starry skies, ... and crackling fires with live entertainment in our lounge," all at "New Hampshire's largest night skiing area!" The combined ski complex had twenty-six trails and seven lifts.

The ski business in Francestown faced daunting challenges. Annual snowfall was erratic and declined over the years. Even though Crotched pioneered artificial snowmaking in New England, at times it was not able to maintain sufficient base. Profits from ski areas are generally modest leaving ski business owners and investors vulnerable to the seductive siren song of the greater profits to be gained in resort development: condos, timeshares, hotels, restaurants, and year-round recreation. The initial development of condos on the east side of the mountain was moderately successful, but a subsequent residential project was foiled by the economic downturn of the late 1970s and early 1980s. In the mid-1980s, further significant investment was made in expensive snowmaking equipment and Gannett revealed plans for a $5 million condominium development. Increased debt, the real estate slump, workmanship complaints from condo owners, and chronically snow-deficient weather led to a cloud of impending foreclosure during the 1988-1989 season. Ski Crotched Inc. and Trailside Development Inc. filed for bankruptcy in October 1989. Combined, the two companies had $13.9 million in debt and liabilities compared to only $7.5 million in assets.

A substantial number of residents of Francestown lost employment, mostly seasonal jobs, when "the Mountain" closed. Workers had groomed the slopes, moved the compressors that made snow, parked cars, run and repaired the lifts, served food in the cafeteria, rented skis and boots, served on the ski patrol, and taught lessons in the ski school. Perhaps a more serious impact was the loss of its social function; it brought together workers and customers across lines of class and status in town. Some ancillary businesses that counted on ski area traffic closed as well. Property tax rates were increased to compensate for the loss of revenue from the ski area. The value of the condos on the mountain fell. The new incarnation of the golf course, Tory Pines resort, undoubtedly became a shakier proposition when the ski area closed. No ski area operated on Crotched Mountain again until 2003; Francestown's area, the eastside, never opened again.

Golf in Francestown

The site of the present Crotched Mountain Golf Course has a long history of commercial use. The Georgian-style mansion, known as the Gibson Tavern after its first owner, was built in 1800 to accommodate travelers on the newly opened Second New Hampshire Turnpike. After the tavern closed, the site was used for farming until 1927, when it was purchased for use as the Mount Crotched Country Club. Well known in the area, the club, with its nine-hole course designed by famed golf course architect Donald Ross, operated through the 1930s, until the Great Depression and other economic challenges on the cusp of World War II led to its closing. The property then reverted to agricultural use for a second time. At the beginning of the 1970s it was owned by Donough Prince and operated as a dairy called Tavern Farm. In the mid-1970s, about ten years after the opening of the ski area, the property was purchased by Richard Tremblay for development as a golf course and resort with the sobriquet of "Hall of Fame." Tremblay's expectations for the success of the resort did not materialize and he sold the business to a new owner in 1985.

The new owner was Fred T. Fish. He sought to redevelop the "Hall of Fame" into "Tory Pines." Some who met Fish say he had an air of "Harold T. Hill" about him. His vision was ambitious and expansive. Fish, and his sidekick attorney, Thomas Welch, came to the Select Board, Planning Board, and Zoning Board with a series of development proposals that were long on "phases" but short on details. An initial obstacle was that the town had made an agreement in 1982 with the prior owner for a five-year moratorium on construction on the golf course property. That threatened to push consideration of Fish's plans back to 1987 at the earliest. The drama began.

TORY PINES RESORT PROPOSALS

An early brochure for the *future* "Tory Pines Resort" included these pitches, couched in the past tense: "Under the watchful eyes and personal hands-on involvement of owner Fred T. Fish, the golf course has been expanded and upgraded to become one of the top-rated 18-hole championship courses in New England;" "Gibson's Tavern has undergone a half-million-dollar renovation and is now home to the Tory Pines Pro Shop, Harry's American Bar, and the Snooty Fox Restaurant…;" "Championship Golf of America has added a recreational complex *to the overall plan* for Tory Pines, with facilities for swimming, tennis, and other sports."

"Championship Golf of America" was a grandiosely named organization created by Fish solely to manage this lone golf course. In February 1986, the *Manchester Union Leader* featured a gushing review of Sunday brunch at the Snooty Fox. Phase One of Fish's development project called for an expansion of the restaurant and existing hotel beginning as soon as possible. Fish and his attorney came to all three boards simultaneously, looking for someone willing to negotiate. Initially, there was unity among the boards; the moratorium was not negotiable. Alan Thulander (ZBA), Ellen Arnold (PB), and Betty Behrsing (BOS) held firm. But there were fissures between the boards and within the Planning Board. Fish's proposal rekindled the broader ongoing dispute over development. Attorney Welch assessed the situation accurately in June 1986 when he told the Planning Board "if...the fears are fear of change, development, and increased activity, then perhaps we are stuck before we start."

In response to Fish's campaign, the Planning Board began consideration of a proposal for an "interim growth management ordinance." This was not only a reaction to Tory Pines' plans. It was a general response to the soaring demand for subdivisions, building permits, and the ski area's condo plans. The Master Plan of 1980 had called for a population growth target of 3% per year, and the current growth was well over 5%. The proposed "interim growth management ordinance" called for a limit of 15 building permits per year, and no more than one subdivision of three lots per year for any tract. The most controversial part of the ordinance was that permits would be issued by lottery, not on a first-come-first-served basis.

HITTING THE BRAKES

In 1986 the Planning Board had four members who favored a "slow down" in growth. They were skeptical about commercial development proposals coming to the PB for site plan review. Four of the members of the board favored the proposed ordinance, including the chair, Ellen Arnold. The other three members thought a limit on growth went too far. A special Town Meeting was scheduled for December 1986, with the proposed ordinance as its sole agenda item. Several realtors vigorously opposed the ordinance. Planning Board member Bill Hansen asserted that the demand for subdivision was so great that the board was meeting 4-5 times a month and 41 permits had been issued in the last 12 months. Chairman Ellen Arnold contended that permit issuance in the last three years was 50% higher than in the total of the previous 12 years. At the special Town Meeting secret ballot votes were held on the two proposed growth management ordinances. Turnout for the meeting was 71%. Both the residential growth ordinance and the commercial growth ordinance were rejected by 55% of voters. Arnold told the *Peterborough Transcript* that the Select Board had worked against the ordinance. The town clerk, Bing Miller, openly opposed the proposed ordinance and was quoted as saying "I hope the Planning Board got the message." Arnold summed up this episode: "It was a very ugly race with a lot of misinformation and personal attacks.... they don't understand what's going to happen when spring arrives, but they will." At the next Planning Board meeting the agenda featured four pending subdivisions for thirteen building lots.

TORY PINES EXPANSION

In 1987 two development skeptics left the Planning Board leaving Hansen and Arnold as a minority on a board more open to growth. The pro-growth majority replaced Ellen Arnold as chair with Charles Eggert Sr. By the end of

1987 the "FTF Trust," Fred T. Fish's ownership entity, was granted final approval for the restaurant expansion. His "Phase Two," a 120-unit hotel, was given conditional approval. A maintenance facility was built, and construction began on an extensive sewage lagoon system to process solid waste into fertilizing irrigation for the golf course. An additional 200 acres of adjacent undeveloped land was purchased by Fish for his planned sports complex. The next phase for which Fish sought approval was for hundreds of vacation units. Residents were curious about subsequent phases that had been announced – such as the conference center, the sports complex, and the lake for trophy fishing. But Fish provided few written descriptions of his plans.

The Zoning Board pushed back. The ZBA, led by Alan Thulander, had been stolidly stable for five years with the same membership – Paul Lawrence, Bobby Abbott, Herb Benedict, and Clifton Foote. These men were steady stewards of the Zoning Ordinance. The ZBA insisted that Fish pay for a "total impact study" for the hotel project. Fish sued. Due to the suit, Alan Thulander resigned for reasons related to his employment. The new chair, Paul Lawrence, spelled out in detail to Fish's attorney the ZBA's dissatisfaction with Fish's non-compliance with ZBA requests including the key point of conflict with the hotel plan: "confirmation" that Fish understands that the hotel units cannot become "residences." Later in the year, for reasons related to his position as a judge, Paul Lawrence resigned from the board as well. The two new members replacing Thulander and Lawrence on the ZBA were more amenable to Fish's plans. Other turn-over on the board from 1987 to 1988 resulted in a completely different ZBA in 1988 than was seated in 1986. This unprecedented turnover helped move along Fish's project.

From the first announcement of the Tory Pines hotel project, skeptics had been suspicious that the new facility – sixteen buildings with "apartment-style" units – would not be a hotel, but rather a set of time-share condominiums constituting year-round residences. Bill Hansen suggested that Fish planned to build 120 new residences under the cloak of a hotel. At an April 1987 joint meeting of the PB and ZBA, several members echoed Hansen's concern. Charles Eggert, the new PB chair, dismissed the difference between "hotel rooms" and "condos" as "mere word-smithing." Hansen called for all plans for the project to be reviewed by an independent expert. The board majority defeated his motion, provoking former Selectman Jack Arnold to challenge the board for "total neglect of your duties. It's unlikely this town will have another project that will have as dramatic impact on Francestown as will this one.... I'm appalled at the board's decision to refuse to get the best possible advice on this project. What are you afraid of?"

The plot thickened. In late January 1988, with a contested Planning Board election looming, Planning Board Chair Charles Eggert, ZBA Chair Dick Mikula, and Select Board Chair Betty Behrsing met with Fred Fish in an unannounced and non-public meeting. Referred to as a "secret meeting" by detractors, the confab became a *cause celebre* in the election campaign. Former ZBA Chair Paul Lawrence summed up the view of those for whom the meeting was suspicious by observing that "people deserve to know all the facts of the meeting… The appearance of impropriety is great." The parties to the meeting refused to provide any account of what was discussed. This provoked a lawsuit against the town by a set of Tory Pines' abutters who contended that Tory Pines' plans violated the 1980 Master Plan's core assertion that the town should remain a "small, rural community void of commercialism." Nothing came of the suit, but it intensified the drama. During this ruckus, the PB majority voted to ease the conditions of their site plan approval, allowing Fish to begin building the hotel before the sewage system was completed.

With this set-up, the Town Election of 1988 was a doozy. The Peterborough *Transcript* closely followed the race. Three seats were open, no incumbents were running. Three candidates vied for two three-year seats on the PB, and two other candidates contested a single, one-year seat. Two of the five candidates were realtors. If they were elected realtors would fill four of the seven PB seats. Neither realtor was elected in 1988, though both won seats in 1989.

Pro-Growth and Anti-Growth Candidates

The theme of the election, for all the candidates, was to end the "pro-growth," "anti-growth" divide. The candidates' campaign statements were very similar, beginning with denial that there was really such a polarized division among the residents of the town. The candidates' public position was that "everyone is well-meaning" and "we have more in common than that which divides us." Scratch the surface of most public officials, amateurs or professionals, and you find a politician. All candidates endorsed capital improvement planning. No candidate was avowedly "pro" or "anti" development. Dean Mottard had only been a town resident for about 18 months. He positioned himself as a "swing vote," an "open minded," "reasonable" person unfettered by "too much history" in town. "There are people who want to keep the town in a time warp, but that's not realistic." Tim Bower was a realtor. He argued that he would be better able to comprehend and assess the complex technical data presented to the board by commercial developers. Abigail Arnold had summered in town her entire life, but only recently had become a full-time resident. Arnold came to help care for her aging parents. A Harvard MBA and career in corporate business gave her experience in "long range planning, financial analysis, capital budgeting, and negotiations." She asserted that this background would enable her to "reconcile the differences" among board members and project applicants. Arnold introduced into the campaign the phrase "controlled growth" and invoked the Master Plan of 1980. Her criticism of the current PB chair was direct. She warned that the prospect of having realtors hold four of seven Planning Board seats was unwise.

Arnold and Mottard won the seats with 300 and 316 votes respectively, to Bower's 200. Don Sipe won the one-year seat over Barbara Carbee but by only seven votes out of 499 cast. Their positions on growth and development sounded similar. Carbee had recently changed careers from education to real estate. Sipe saw a conflict of interest in having realtors making land use regulation decisions that could potentially work to their personal benefit. He called for consideration of the "rights of abutters" to be balanced against the ambitions of developers. Carbee pointed to her many years on town committees and service organizations that gave her a deep understanding of the town's history and its residents' concerns.

CAPITAL IMPROVEMENT PLAN

When the Planning Board reorganized itself after the March 1988 election, Abigail Arnold was elected chair, replacing Charles Eggert. Arnold set an ambitious work agenda for the board and came prepared to move forward in big steps at a rapid pace. Eggert resigned. His seat was filled by Scot Heath. Now the board majority was fully committed to creating a Capital Improvement Plan and less inclined to accommodate commercial development. The board set to work on a mountain of back-logged applications. By July the board unanimously approved a review of the 1980 Master Plan, and in September it adopted the first Capital Improvement Plan in the town's history. The Capital Improvement Plan for the next six years took an incremental approach given the downturn in the national economy. This Capital Improvement Plan would be the foundation on which the annual budget-building process would rely. The capital improvement planning rationale was that a town needed to anticipate and carefully sequence substantial expenditures. Scheduling major projects within six-year spans enabled successive town meetings to steadily build reserves to fully finance projects and avoid debt financing. Revenue expectations could be matched with scheduled spending so spikes in taxes could be avoided. Also, a CIP would provide a basis for growth management initiatives if any were deemed necessary in the future. The Planning Board stated, in their first CIP annual report, that current appropriations for roads were insufficient to meet the need for maintenance let alone improvement. A Road Improvement Program (RIP) subcommittee was formed. It included the road agent and members from the PB, BAC, BOS, FVFD and three other standing committees. The first RIP was presented in the 1990 Town Report. It sought to build the capacity of the Highway Department and to repair critically problematic roads. The 1995 Master Plan looked back on the early years of the RIP and concluded that "the process appears to have been reasonably well integrated in both planning and budgeting cycles and the program, itself, has on balance been successful.

Improvements have been more coherent and better and more consistently financed than they were prior to 1988; in addition, the quality of implementation appears to have improved and, with it, the credibility of the Highway Department."

DEVELOPMENT PRESSURE CONTINUED

Intense development pressure continued through 1989; the PB processed seven subdivisions representing 27 building lots. Development "fever" broke in 1990. The volume and pace of routine work for the Planning Board abated. This enabled the board and its subcommittees to focus more on capital improvement planning, particularly with respect to roads. In the work "bee" that took place in 1988-1990, several other projects were completed. New subdivision regulations were written with developer input. The PB in collaboration with the Conservation Commission authored a Water Resource Management Plan as directed by a 1989 Warrant Article. At the request of the PB, Town Meeting reaffirmed that building permits and occupancy inspections were required for new structures, alteration of existing structures, and septic systems. The Planning Board chair began sending out a quarterly newsletter to every home in town with an update on PB activities. This continued for several years and appeared to be helpful in reducing the degree of anxiety about growth and development issues as well as improving the credibility of the board with residents. Eventually, the newsletters came from the Planning Board, not just the chair.

HISTORIC DISTRICT COMMISSION FAILURE

The aspirations of the newly visionary Planning Board misfired on one initiative. A Warrant Article from the Planning Board came to Town Meeting 1991 to establish an Historic District Commission (HDC) aimed at fulfilling the Master Plan's call for "preserving community character" in the Village. Though initially accepted by voters, it proved to be unpopular. Proponents assured residents that the creation of this commission did not mean regulations would be written. However, many Main Street residents were suspicious that was exactly the intent; they doubted the plan was for a purely advisory committee and did not want to be told how their property should look or be maintained. The HDC was chaired by Alan Thulander. It drafted an ordinance and held hearings. Before an ordinance was brought to Town Meeting, a petition Warrant Article was presented in 1993 by Dr. Louis Wiederhold and Polly Freese to disband the Historic District Commission. Though the Warrant Article was only advisory and was tabled, it had an impact. No Historic District ordinance was ever brought to Town Meeting and the HDC was disbanded in 1999.

SAVINGS AND LOAN CRISIS BRINGS CHANGES

Through 1988 and 1989 the Planning Board continued to monitor the compliance of Tory Pines with the site plan, but larger forces changed the situation completely. The nation was going through a Savings and Loan (S & L) crisis in the late 1980s. Irresponsible and fraudulent behavior in this sector of the banking industry had led to many bank failures and was contributing to a recession in the economy. The Tory Pines project was built on successive loans from several banks. Due to the S & L crisis and recession, credit dried up. Fish was overextended. His primary lender foreclosed. He tried to declare bankruptcy but was refused Chapter 11 protection. In November of 1990, Tory Pines, with the hotel complex unfinished, was auctioned. It was purchased by a bank for $4.8m, though he owed that bank $14m. The silver lining for Francestown was that the bank then paid $165,000 in back taxes owed by Fish. The first of the hotel buildings, a 32-unit structure, was unfinished. It sat empty, a ghost town in the woods, until it was demolished in 2018. The cost of demolition exceeded the cost of construction.

The golf course business came out of bankruptcy under new ownership in the 1990s and remained solvent as of 2020. Throughout that stretch of thirty years, a half dozen owners maintained the 18-hole course, the pro-shop, restaurant-bar, and small hotel. Owners included a Japanese resort company, the Demoulas family who own the Market Basket grocery store chain, Terry Schnare of Bennington, and Shell Vacations. The golf course restaurant and bar, variously named the Snooty Fox, Malarkey's, and the Tollbooth Tavern, continued to operate even as various schemes for vacation rentals rose and fell. In 2011, Dan and Terry O'Grady from Massachusetts bought the complex and gained approval to expand the restaurant and banquet hall space. The O'Gradys' vision was modest and their business has been modestly successful.

By 1990, the Planning Board, led by Abigail Arnold, emerged from the instability of 1986-1987 to become the most influential entity in the town's governance structure. As tumultuous as the Planning Board's journey was through the late 1980s, the fundamental structuring elements for its work in the 1990s emerged from the storm: reaffirmation of Master Planning and the inauguration of Capital Improvement Planning. There were circumstantial factors involved in the rise of the Planning Board as well. The failure of Tory Pines and Ski Crotched removed two sources of conflict and preoccupation for the town. The recession, particularly in the home loan industry, dried up demand for subdivision and home construction. Beginning in 1989, and continuing through 1998, the number of subdivision and building permits were in single digits each year. Nothing like the sustained demand faced in 1984-1988 would ever occur again. In 1995 the Planning Board would draft a new Master Plan, and that plan informed town leaders' decision-making for the next two decades.

Conclusion

Through their strong leadership, persistent focus, and relentless work ethic, Scot Heath (from 1985 to 1991) and Abigail Arnold (from 1988 to 2000) were able to significantly influence the town's path forward. Heath instigated a movement for land preservation that eventually led to the protection from development of over 6,000 acres in town. Arnold was instrumental in setting the sails of the Planning Board on a course to fulfill its primary mission – long-range planning. Over the next decade, Arnold, working in concert with Alan Thulander (1992-2002), and David Jonas (BAC chair, 1990-1998), brought stability, efficiency, and foresight to Francestown's governance.

By 1990, the die was cast. Francestown would not be a resort town. Francestown would follow modern procedures for planning its growth and development. Land use in Francestown would be driven by a melding of the ambitions of the Conservation Commission and the Planning Board. While there would still be periodic disputes over specific projects and decisions, the overall trajectory of the town was set for the next 30 years.

CHAPTER 3

AN ERA OF GOOD FEELING

1990S

The years from 1992-2002 will be referred to as "the 1990s." This was a decade of consolidation for Francestown. In this decade the substantial changes introduced from 1976 to 1990 became the enduring structure of town governance. Capital Improvement and Road Improvement Plans shaped the budget on the Warrant each year. A new Master Plan was written in 1995. It echoed the values of the previous plan but was more ambitious in its detail and recommendations. The land conservation movement quietly built reserves in the ConCom's Conservation Fund. The young families who had moved to town in the prior decade expected the town to provide a robust recreation program. They were eager to volunteer and lead, but they expected town government support. That same energy pushed the school district to fulfill its promise to provide appropriate school facilities for each of the member towns.

The governance themes of the 1990s included steady modernization of the town's infrastructure, the permanent establishment of a system of carefully planned-for municipal financing, the maturation of a municipal recreation program, the building of a new town school, and the creation of more appropriate spaces for town officials to do business.

THE THULANDER DECADE

A question asked of every person interviewed for this book was, "Who are the individuals who made the greatest difference in Francestown's story between 1970-2020?" The person named most often, far more often than anyone else, was Odin Alan Thulander. Thulander is widely acknowledged for his singular devotion to Francestown. Though he is not eulogized with affection by all witnesses, there is generally unreserved respect for his dedication, hard work, and responsible management of town affairs. From the 1980s forward, "preserving the rural character of the community" became the mantra by which the town meditated on its future. Thulander had a clear vision of what that meant to him, and he pursued that vision with vigor. Described as "rigid" and "uncompromising" by some, few question his conscientious stewardship of the town's resources. The 1990s were the "Thulander Decade" in Francestown.

The Select Board was a well-oiled machine in the 1990s. Thulander's "side men" on the Select Board for most of the decade were John Jenkins and Bert McClary. Jenkins served three terms, and McClary two. All three of these men were generally conservative with respect to the scope of town government; they had lived in town for many years when the municipality's responsibilities were modest, and spending was parsimonious. They were comfortable with that. Jenkins and McClary came to meetings prepared, invested themselves in deliberation, but did not aspire to day-to-day administration of town affairs. Thulander did. He was the town's "administrator," and he pushed back against attempts to hire a professional town administrator. It is no accident that although the Master Plan of 1995 suggested that a professional town administrator would be advantageous, no such position was created during Thulander's time on the board.

Alan Thulander could be stubborn. For example, the *Monadnock Ledger* protested that the town was withholding the names of people who were arrested. Thulander would not relent so the *Ledger* sued. The town settled and subsequent police reports have included the names of those arrested by the Francestown Police. John Jenkins, Bert McClary, and Thulander served together until 1996 when Scott Carbee replaced McClary. In 1998 Paul St. Cyr took the open seat left by John Jenkins' retirement, and in 1999, David Jonas filled the open seat when Carbee did not run again. Thulander and St. Cyr were reelected in 2000 and 2001. Following her service on the Select Board, Betty Behrsing, who had been the town's administrative assistant in the late 1980s and first half of the 1990s, was honored when she retired in 1996.

Paul Lawrence succeeded Phil Ireland as moderator in 1994, out polling Dr. Wiederhold for the position. Lawrence presided at Town Meeting continually until 2019, an unprecedented run. At one point a new state regulation that disallowed judges from serving in elected office threatened Lawrence's tenure. Thulander used his influence at the state level to arrange a modification of that regulation and Lawrence's service continued.

NAMING ROADS AND ASSESSING PROPERTY

A 911 emergency phone system for the town became operational in 1995. As a step in the direction of introducing the 911 system, the town had to finalize the names and addresses of all properties. If official road names were to be agreed upon, town leaders decided this also was a good time to put up road signs. Decisions were made. Bible Hill Road not Quarry Road. Bible Hill Extension not Bradford Road. Stevens Road not Pratt Road. Ferson not Pherson. Ed and Frank Jones were consulted on the history of road names before the Select Board finalized the list of official names. "Lane" became the designation for a private road. Of course, there was significant deliberation over the aesthetics and cost of signage. Eventually, in keeping with Select Board parsimony, the Improvement and Historical Society was asked to pay for the new signs, and they did. Re-naming applied to elected positions as well. The title of the "Overseer of Public Welfare" was changed to "Public Assistance Administrator." More subtle and sensitive language for a more modern

Francestown. How modern? Even in the early 1990s the scope of town government did not include full responsibility for street signs.

The town's first completely professional, fully outsourced, assessment of property was conducted in 1990-1991. Town meetings financed the computerization of the tax cards and put in place a program of tax exemptions for elderly property owners. The revaluation held for the entire decade. The Select Board did not request another revaluation until the New Hampshire Board of Tax and Land Appeals (BTLA) ordered them to do so in 2001.

CAPITAL PLANNING – STEADY AS SHE GOES

In the 1990s, the Planning Board, Budget Committee, and Select Board were committed to a disciplined embrace of the Capital Improvement Plan (CIP). By sequencing major project, equipment, and operational expenses, spikes in the tax rate could be avoided. Additionally, all three boards embraced the idea that remedial planning was in order. Roads and bridges should be improved not just maintained. Towards that goal. the CIP process was designed for modestly increased spending which would be matched by steady growth in tax revenue but without jumps in the tax rate.

The resulting increase in town spending was dramatic. The town's operational budget in 1990 was $742,000. In 2002, Town Meeting approved the first million-dollar operational budget. In 1990 $64,500 was placed in reserves; in 2002 the figure was $168,000. In 2002, $257,000 was drawn from reserves compared to $47,500 in 1990. Total authorized spending, the budget plus other Warrant Articles, went from $888,000 to $1,710,000. The town had 300 more residents in 2002 with an additional 100 homes paying taxes. The town was gaining revenue through steady growth, albeit at a slower pace than in the "go-go" 1980s.

It appears that the CIP strategy worked. Overall, the budget-building process was disciplined and truly collaborative. On only a few occasions the Select Board advanced a Warrant Article not recommended by the Planning Board and Budget Committee or changed the level of an allocation. The 1999 Town Report captures the story of the first decade of budgetary planning, "This year marks the 11th anniversary of the CIP. Capital spending...for the six years prior to its inception averaged $68,000/year.... A total of $1.9 million was raised over the eleven-year period [$173,000/year] .... The CIP established reserves as the preferred method of financing large ticket items and the last outstanding debt issue was retired in 1998. As a result of CIP recommendations .... a number of new reserves – e.g. transfer station improvements, recreation land purchase/improvements and acquisitions – were created to bridge the gap between perceived needs/goals and their realization. The CIP was also the catalyst for a 6-year road improvement program, annual funding for which went from a $14,000 appropriation in 1989 to $100,000 per year in 1999. As a result of the gradual build-up of programs... [capital spending] went from 7.1%

of total net appropriations in 1989 to 10.9% in 1999 without creating volatility in the tax rate."

Abigail Arnold's extended leadership of the Planning Board and the CIP process cast a long shadow. Her expertise in town finance was valued and frequently drawn upon in the decade after she left the Planning Board. Occasional analytical articles in *The Francestown News*, and regular input at town meetings, led many residents to ask, "What does Abigail think about this?" She was well-armed with command of the details.

Within the CIP was the Road Improvement Program (RIP). Predictably, anticipating road projects over a six-year period was challenging. A road could deteriorate quickly. Too often the easiest way for the Select Board to respond to an emergency was to raid the RIP budget. After a decade of such gyrations in prioritization, by 1999 the RIP simply scheduled work on "other paved roads" rather than naming the targeted roads. Within a decade, the town may not have known which roads it was going to upgrade each year, but it increased its annual maintenance commitment from $50,000 to $100,000.

In 1996 the Highway Committee was assigned to study the operations of the Highway Department and make recommendations. They did a cost-benefit analysis of using town employees and equipment to do major road construction versus contracting for those projects. The committee recommended "to have a majority of the work on all CIP reconstruction projects be performed by qualified outside contractors, rather than by the Highway Department." Money would be saved because often the department had to lease equipment it did not own. The three full-time department employees could concentrate on preventive maintenance on town roads.

EMERGENCIES AND EMERGENCY PLANNING

The inherent problem in any long-range budget-planning scenario is that emergencies happen. They did. And citizens and their elected leaders can be impulsive. They were. These two factors combined at times. Ad hoc changes to the CIP by the Select Board became more common in the late 1990s, so much so that Arnold asked rhetorically if they intended to continue the CIP process.

The first emergency to present itself was the early closure of the Tri-Town Landfill, the next was when the chronically problematic dam on the Bixby-Creamery Pond failed. Though ConVal's vote to build a new elementary school for Francestown was not an emergency for the town, deciding what to do with the 1940 "Red School" was. The most troubling event, for the present and future of the Capital Improvement Plan, was a sudden interest in erecting a new highway department garage "right now!" Other smaller emergencies also led to adjustments to the CIP: a new library fire escape, razing the ski lodge, and purchasing computers capable of dealing with the anticipated disruption of "Y2K."

The decade opened with two unanticipated financial emergencies. The first was a national economic recession. This made the Select Board skittish about ramping up reserves and projects. Then, the state ordered the closing of the Antrim-Bennington-Francestown landfill by the fall of 1992. The bill for Francestown's share for de-commissioning the landfill was larger and due sooner than anticipated. The town had started a reserve for de-commissioning but given the expedited schedule the reserve was insufficient. By 1993, the payment due would exceed reserves by $100,000. Therefore, in both 1992 and 1993 the CIP had to be modified. Plans to fund other reserves were deferred. However, the plan to lease and improve the recreation area stayed on the schedule.

The town returned to full funding of capital reserves as called for by the CIP in 1994 and 1995. Then the dam broke, literally. The earthen dam built in the 19th century to create the Bixby-Creamery Pond had been repaired in 1974 and 1986. Again, leakage was detected, and repair was scheduled in the CIP. The Select Board decided not to contract out the repair, but to marshal local expertise. George Whipple, Kris Stewart, Rick and Steve Miller, and Phil Ireland were asked for advice on the project. When Whipple began the repair, the face of the 200-year-old earthen dam ruptured as did the expense. Thulander solicited Ed Gagnon, who had experience in re-constructing the dam in Bennington belonging to the Monadnock Paper Mill, to design a new dam structure. Gagnon's design for a concrete dam was approved by the state. In a dramatic day-long event in August 1997, over twenty concrete trucks lined up for a continuous pour that avoided seams in the structure. The pond was refilled by mid-October. Thulander acquired Federal Emergency Management Agency (FEMA) funds to cover much of the cost; the town's share was small, but the anticipation of emergency spending disrupted the CIP anyway.

Another potential financial emergency that could implicate future CIPs was looming. An assessment of the town's bridges was completed by the state Department of Transportation. Eight town bridges were declared "Structurally Deficient" or "Functionally Obsolete." The good news was that the state had a schedule for funding most of the cost of repair or replacement. The bad news was that some of Francestown's bridges might fail before their scheduled repair dates. There was a capital reserve account for bridge repair, but whether it was sufficient would depend on luck.

Red School Building

In 1996 school district voters approved a ConVal bond issue that paid for a new elementary school in Francestown. An ad hoc committee led by David Jonas recommended to Town Meeting 1997 that the town buy the "Red School" building for $115,000. The committee concluded that the town needed office space and off-street parking. The existing building was a better value than constructing a new one. The space was considered a key lot for the aesthetics of Main Street; the committee wanted the town to control it. The purchase was included in the 1997 CIP. Renovation expenses, nearly $200,000, were added to the CIP in 1998 and 1999. The school building purchase and renovation pushed back other planned spending. Thulander mustered his influence at the state level to exempt the Red School building from having to physically comply with the Americans with Disabilities Act (ADA). The town promised state authorities that it would service people downstairs if they could not use the front steps.

The building use committee's report included a recommendation that the town be the only tenant in the Red School. The report was accepted by Town Meeting on a 96-25 vote. Leaders of the Francestown Community Pre-School sought to use part of the building and submitted a petition Warrant Article to reserve space in the building for private organizations. That article was defeated 31-112. The move of town officials out of the Annex into the Red School took place in 2000. The move was completed when the huge safe holding historical town records was brought up Main Street in the bucket of the town's front-end loader.

Highway Garage Project

By far the biggest hiccup in the hope for a "steady as she goes" CIP process was the Highway Garage project. The idea of a new highway department garage was first mentioned in the Town Report of 1997. It was reported that the Highway Committee would "study...the size, location and cost of future buildings that will be required by the Highway Department." After his election to the Select Board in March 1999, David Jonas, who chaired the Budget Committee through the 1990s, became an ex officio member of the Highway Committee. He moved forward on research for a new building. Jonas, and committee members Paul Ellis and Scott Carbee, visited several highway departments' garages in neighboring towns and developed a profile of the many features that such a facility should incorporate. The Select Board brought in consultants from Management Resources, Inc. (MRI) who confirmed the committee's recommendations. Town Meeting 2000 adopted a Warrant Article funding pre-engineering, as well as surveying and water testing for a site behind the Fire Department garages. The committee's report stated that construction should not occur until late 2002, or 2003. Reserves for a highway department building totaled $190,000 by 2002.

The Selectmen's article in the 2001 Town Report states, "Plans for a new town highway facility are nearing completion and we plan to make a full report on this project at this year's town meeting [2002]." The CIP recommended a Warrant Article of $400,000 for the highway garage. Funds were to be diverted from "road improvement" to cover the gap between the project price and the reserve fund balance. The plan was recommended by the Planning Board, Budget Committee, and Select Board.

A "Bargain Price" Steel Building

Prior to Town Meeting 2002, Alan Thulander, David Jonas, and Charlie O'Neil located and purchased a prefabricated steel building. They bought the building with private funds but perceived their purchase as on behalf of the town. It had been configured for installation in Virginia but was on the market at what appeared to Thulander and Jonas to be a bargain price. The Warrant Article for Town Meeting 2002 would enable the town to buy the unit from Thulander and Jonas and have it installed in Francestown quickly. According to local architect Mike Petrovick, the building was "like an erector set." Customization would be necessary to meet the list of specified needs compiled by the committee.

The plan was presented to residents at Town Meeting 2002. Many questions were asked about how the structure would be finished and what was involved in preparing the site. Road Agent Junior Foote, tried to lighten the mood when he quipped, "I don't know what is so confusing about voting $400,000 to build Junior a new garage." As he listened to the barrage of questions and concerns from residents, Harry Varnum, who had served on the Highway Committee for five years, observed that the Town Meeting was not ready to decide on the Warrant Article given a myriad of questions posed by attendees. He moved to recess the Town Meeting to a later date solely for consideration of this Warrant Article. His motion was approved.

Town Meeting was scheduled to resume on May 4, 2002. In the intervening six weeks, Varnum and Petrovick collaborated to prepare a more detailed presentation. Varnum worked with Sanford Engineering to finalize site plan details. Mike Petrovick worked with the Select Board, Highway Committee members, and the new Director of Public Works to identify what would be done to finish the building after the erection of the prefab structure. When re-presented to Town Meeting in May, the expenditure of $400,000, about half of which came from the reserve fund, was approved unanimously. Town Meeting voted to suspend the normal bidding procedures to facilitate the unusual purchase arrangement. In September 2002, the Select Board voted to reimburse "the individuals" who purchased the garage kit on behalf of the town. The contract to erect the prefab structure went to a company from Hollis that specialized in such structures. Francestown Sand & Gravel hustled to prepare the site. Town Meeting 2003 was asked to approve another $275,000 to complete the project. By the end of the project, the highway garage cost $681,000.

Though it was widely agreed that the town needed a modern storage and maintenance facility for its larger and more up-to-date fleet, the process for achieving this goal proved controversial. David Jonas and his wife, Susannah, moved to Francestown in the mid-1970s and immediately became engaged in the life of the community. David was an independent, entrepreneurial businessman. His service to the town began on the Conservation Commission in 1976. He was the ConCom's representative on the 1980 Master Plan committee. Next, he chaired a committee that studied library funding and facility needs in the early 1980s and was elected as the town's representative on the ConVal School Board in the late 1980s. Through the 1990s he chaired the Budget and Advisory Committee. Jonas was well prepared to lead decision-making in town when he was elected to the Select Board in 1999. He and Alan Thulander worked well together; they shared a conservative approach to town finances. Their partnership in pushing the Highway Garage Project forward in the way they did reflects their self-confidence and entrepreneurial initiative. But according to one of the key participants, that same confidence may have led them "to get too far out ahead of Town Meeting when we put down a deposit on the prefab building." A definitive reading of the voters' minds isn't possible, but it appears likely that some voters' unease with how the project unfolded led to Jonas' twenty vote loss in 2002 in his bid for reelection. Local construction contractors were especially unhappy that erection of the prefabricated building required specialized personnel who were brought in from out of town.

Perhaps Thulander paid a price for the highway garage, as well. He was completing what he said would be his last term as a selectmen. It was his sixth term. In September 2002 he ran for reelection to the NH House of Representatives in a district re-drawn following the 2000 census. In the new, multiple-town district, he lost to his primary opponent. The loss he understood, but it was the uncharacteristically modest margin of victory in Francestown that disappointed him. Quoted in *The Francestown News,* Thulander said he believed there was a message to him from his hometown; as a result, he resigned as a selectman and from his other official roles in town. By the end of 2002, both principal authors of the highway department garage project were no longer in leadership positions in town.

Return of Francestown's Ski Area – Hopes Dashed

Some residents held out hope for a re-opening of the ski area on Crotched Mountain which would mean both a return of skiing and jobs. After the ski area folded several revival attempts were proposed but not completed. One attempt showed enough promise that FIHS made its Labor Day parade theme in 1995 "Welcome Back Crotched Mountain!" earning them a "Dewey Beats Truman" award. As the years went by without a re-opening the main issue shifted from a return of skiing to what would become of the hundreds of acres on the eastern slope of the mountain. The town was owed unpaid property taxes on the 300+ acres. Creditors of the bankrupt ski area proposed to swap ownership of the land for forgiveness of the un-paid taxes. The Conservation Commission recommended that the Select Board accept the offer. However, the Select Board wanted the tax revenue more than they wanted to own the land. Subsequently, the board pursued a strategy of putting a tax lien on the acreage which enabled them to seize it and try to sell it. Eventually, the land was auctioned and Cellular One became the owner.

In 2000, having failed to sell the land to a developer, Cellular One donated the 318-acre tract to Francestown. The Select Board had mixed feelings about accepting the property, but they were wary of a real estate development on the mountain. A Warrant Article passed at Town Meeting 2001 directed the board to accept the donation. A Warrant Article in 2002 spelled out the process by which the Select Board could dispose of the property, requiring a series of hearings and collaboration with the Planning Board and the Conservation Commission. The former ski lodge and other small buildings on the mountain were considered a liability; some were burned in training exercises by the Fire Department and the lodge was razed by a crew of volunteers organized by Francestown Sand & Gravel. The denouement of Francestown's ski area was a source of genuine regret for the men who razed the buildings. Several of them, or other family members, had come of age working on the Mountain. They had parked cars, groomed runs, operated and maintained lifts, and made snow.

In 2002 the Bennington ski area property, owned by Terry Schnare of Bennington and Don Hardwick of Francestown, was purchased by Peak Resorts of St. Louis. The new owners planned to re-open a ski area in Bennington. Although most of the new ski area was in Bennington, some of the runs were within Francestown's boundaries. Peak Resorts received Zoning Board approval only after extensive hearings and plan adjustments.

RECREATION EXPANSION

In 1989 a burst of energy came out of the RecCom aimed at improving the town beach, expanding programs, and improving the recreation area owned by FIHS. The town renewed the lease of the Scobie Beach property and added a shed for lifeguard equipment, a telephone for emergency use, and a portable toilet. The raft was rebuilt, and the terrain of the beach was landscaped and sanded. The Stewarts, Millers, Sandersons, Paiges, and Lanoies provided volunteer labor and equipment. The Little League program enrolled sixty children. An all-Francestown soccer team competed in a regional league. Skating returned to the Bixby-Creamery pond. Ballroom dancing lessons were offered by Jane Lawrence and Peter Bixby. The RecCom cooperated with the New England Cycling Club, the Spokes and Slopes Club of Peterborough, and Tory Pines to sponsor a mountain bike race.

In 1990, the CIP called for, and Town Meeting approved, a capital reserve account for acquiring and improving recreational facilities. The following year Kris Stewart and Paul Lawrence proposed that FIHS work with the RecCom to improve and expand the recreation facilities on FIHS land. Specifically, they proposed that the town lease additional recreational land from FIHS at Rt. 136 and County Road South. At that time the town was leasing only the baseball field and the two tennis courts. The RecCom's expansion plan included expanding the leased land to include a soccer field, a set of courts for basketball, roller blading, skate boarding, street hockey, and a parking lot.

At the FIHS annual meeting there was vigorous debate about whether such development on that site was appropriate. Abutters to the recreation area expressed concern about traffic, noise, and lighting. Stewart responded to the resistance by appealing for FIHS to "take a positive approach ... [and] simply find a way to do it." The RecCom pitch pointed out that there were 300 children ages 0-18 in town. Stewart had long been involved in promoting recreation for the town's youth. He had grown up in town as a participant and then became a coach and organizer. On several occasions, Stewart's excavation business traded a donation of labor and equipment on an FIHS project for the organization's support for recreation programming. The FIHS annual meeting approved the somewhat contentious proposal and donated $5,000 toward construction of the soccer field. Warrant Articles at town meetings 1992 and 1993 directed the Select Board to lease the property for $1.00. At Town Meeting 1993 a Petition Warrant Article was proposed by abutters to the Recreation Area. It directed the Select Board to study alternative locations in town that might be better sites for enlarged recreation facilities. Abutters' concerns were articulated in accord with the theme of "preserving the rural character of the community." The petition Warrant Article did not pass. In 1995, additional funds were approved for fencing and lighting of the new recreation fields and courts.

The town's lease of FIHS facilities completed a gradual transition from FIHS to the Recreation Commission as the organizer and funder of recreation programs. The finality of this evolution was memorialized at FIHS' annual meeting in 1993 when FIHS' recreation subcommittee was officially disbanded. FIHS continued to donate funds to recreation projects from time to time. The expansion project was completed mostly in the summer and fall of 1994. Extensive site work was done by local contractors mostly as volunteers. The list of individuals, organizations, and businesses who contributed labor, materials, and money was extensive, with especially substantial donations from Francestown Sand & Gravel, Miller Plumbing & Heating, D. H. Hardwick and Sons, George Whipple Construction, and Ronald Kullgren. The total value of the project was more than $92,000. The town contributed $36,000. At Town Meeting 1995, the Recreation Commission, and Kris Stewart in particular, were celebrated for leadership in organizing this community-wide project. The new recreation area's grand opening was held on Memorial Day weekend in 1995. For several years to come the project was commemorated with a Family Recreation Day.

Baseball dugouts, a storage shed, a walking track, a horseshoe pit, a swing set and jungle gym, and volleyball courts have been added to the recreation facilities since 1994. There have been periodic upgrades to the facilities, including lighting for the courts and water from the Village Water Company. In 2002, as a memorial for a young Francestown boy, Tim Samuelson, the RecCom started a springtime fishing derby. That annual event has continued for twenty years. For several years the RecCom kicked off baseball season with a parade on Main Street complete with blaring fire trucks. A lifeguard station was built at the Scobie Pond beach in 2003. Mary Jane Marsden continued to organize contra dances and dance lessons as she had in 1980s through the 1990s. Her commitment to contra dancing kept that Yankee tradition alive in town long enough that at a dance in 2002 three generations of her family were able to participate.

Over the past 25 years, when possible, the Recreation Commission has employed a paid director. Scott and Lorie Jenkins, Pam Delahanty, and Donna Noonan have served in that position. They supervised part-time staff including lifeguards, who are often certified to teach swimming, and a varying number of coaches and teachers who run special classes and summer camps. Historically, most recreation programs have been managed and coached by parents of participating children.

RECREATION COMMISSION LEADERSHIP

The history of the RecCom is a pattern of intense activity and support followed by a period of coasting. Compared to most town committees RecCom members are more hands-on. They usually coach, organize, and directly supervise activities. Often, RecCom members' involvement waned when their children got older. The longer serving members are the exceptions to this pattern. When leadership of the RecCom is detailed by who served and when, there are "generations" of leadership. B.J. Carbee (1979-1988) succeeded the original RecCom chair, Carol Prest. Paul Lawrence (1984-1997) and Nancy Rice (1982-1995) were a bridge from this first generation of leadership to the second. Kris Stewart joined the RecCom in 1989. His charisma, energy, and chutzpah were crucial in selling the idea of town control and expansion of the recreation facilities in the mid-1990s. Teaming with Lawrence, Rice, Peter Zahn, and Peter Bixby, Stewart was a force on the RecCom for 17 years. Among other second-generation RecCom members in the late 1990s, the efforts of Scott Jenkins, Larry Laber, and James Nealand stand out.

The third generation of RecCom leadership, overlapped with the second. In the early 2000s a revitalized RecCom included Kris and Lisa Stewart, Scott and Lorie Jenkins, Andrej & Stephanie Kokul, Pete and Michelle Kazanovicz, and Bub & Tracy Rokes. It was at this time that Bub Rokes began his long run as the heart of the town's recreation programming, much of that time in partnership with Donna Noonan. Some years it was just Bub and Donna keeping the programs afloat. Paul McGrath provided support for several years. Since Noonan and Rokes retired in 2017 and 2018, the backbone of the RecCom has been Mike Beisang and Dawn and Tom Kirlin. In forty-five years, forty-six residents of Francestown have been members of the Recreation Commission.

Waste Disposal, Recycling, and the Transfer Station

Francestown's waste disposal changed with the closing of the Tri-Town Landfill at the end of 1992. The Bennington site was "unlined" and did not meet ever more rigorous EPA standards. The transfer station arranged to haul rubbish further afield. For several years, the Waste Disposal Commission was just two men: Dud Parker and Scott Carbee. Parker was a founder of systematic, transfer-station-based recycling in Francestown. He led the Commission from 1977 until he died in 1992. Carbee joined the Commission in 1986 and followed Parker as chair until he stepped down when he was elected to the Select Board in 1996.

Participation in recycling waned in the late 1980s due to a weak market for recyclables and the ease of disposing of a broad waste stream in Bennington. However, with the increased cost per ton to transport non-recycled waste, motivation increased to pull recyclables out of the general waste stream again. This enthusiasm led Town Meeting 1990 to make recycling of paper and glass mandatory. Scott Carbee led the push for required recycling. He disseminated a guide to help homeowners sort their waste. Stickers were required for transfer station users and attendants were empowered to issues warnings and deny access to non-recyclers. Recycling refusers protested when they were denied use of the transfer station, but the Select Board held firm. For the next three decades residents were required to recycle. The materials included in that mandate expanded over time. Hazardous waste disposal days were held at least every two or three years from the mid-1990s through the early 2000s. In the Master Plan survey of town residents in 1994, the operation of the transfer station received positive reviews.

The transfer station's share of the town budget rose to around 7%, considerably greater than the few hundred dollars spent in the 1970s. About 70% of the material deposited at the transfer station was compacted and hauled to Peterborough to a Waste Management, Inc. facility. Recyclables were compacted before transport by volunteers who owned heavy equipment. A respected fixture of the transfer station staff, James "Jumbo" Mason, passed away in 1999; his primary partner on the staff, George Cilley who joined in 1993, continued his leadership of the crew up through 2020. In 2000, the station became part of the new Department of Public Works. After he left the Select Board, Scott Carbee returned to the Waste Disposal Commission and was its leader until 2007.

Conservation Commission in the 1990s

For most of the 1990s Jeff Gorton chaired the ConCom. During the decade town meetings allocated $60,000 to the Conservation Fund but land acquisition was not a priority. The ConCom implemented elements of the 1993 Town Forest Management Plan, including trail building, habitat enhancement, and interpretive maps for hikers and wildlife enthusiasts. It assisted the Planning

Board and ZBA with site reviews when wetlands were involved. An Open Space Management Plan was developed for the Master Plan. This plan included prioritized criteria for future land preservation projects. The Piscataquog Watershed Association asked the ConCom to partner in conducting a baseline survey of the flora and fauna in the river's flood plain for use in permitting future development plans along the river.

The ConCom did not avoid controversy completely during the 1990s. In 1992, a kerfuffle arose about the use of firearms on town forest land. Abutters to the Lord Town Forest objected to hunting on this land because of its frontage on Ferson Road, a school bus route. This was a challenge to the New Hampshire tradition of allowing hunting on publicly held lands as well as on un-posted private lands. Selectman Thulander questioned whether the Conservation Commission had authority over the use of town forests. Without resolving the jurisdictional question, a compromise was reached where hunting was still allowed in the Lord Forest but not with rifles.

In 1998, the ConCom was criticized when some members of the commission advocated for the ConFund to be used to buy Whiting Acres, a tract between Route 136 and Scobie Pond. The acquisition was motivated primarily to block a housing development. The purchase was not pursued. Later in the year additional acreage held by the Merrill Trust adjacent to the Crotched Mountain Town Forest went on the market. The Master Plan's Land Use section designated this land as a high value target. An overture was made by the ConCom in partnership with Francestown Land Conservation, Inc., but the asking price exceeded the available funds, and a state grant could not be arranged.

In the spring of 1998, two long-time veterans of the ConCom retired -- Jeff Gorton, chair since 1992, and Taisto Holm -- who had served since 1986. Select Board Chair Thulander celebrated these men's service by noting that "Jeff brought an evenhanded approach to the diverse problems which fall within the purview of the Commission [and]... Ty's wonderful work ethic and willingness to pitch in will be hard to replace. They both will be sorely missed." Betsy Hardwick, a name new to town committee service, volunteered to serve on the ConCom and was appointed.

CONSERVATION COMMITTEE CONTROVERSIES

Accompanying these ConCom membership changes, a small purge of the ConCom was instigated by the Select Board. The board and Fire Department wanted to develop a fire pond in a new area in town. Members of the ConCom argued that the site should be examined carefully because pond excavation could affect the Piscataquog River and the major aquifer under the site. At the same time the ConCom was reviewing a resident's plan to expand a pond that was part of a natural wetland. The ConCom consulted the NH Department of Environmental Services about both situations. The Select Board took exception to this. A ConCom member was singled out and accused of being "uncooperative" and was "deselected" from the Commission, probably as a shot across the bow. Thulander alleged that the ConCom's concerns "are not in the best interests of the town" and that the commission was "having difficulty balancing conservation interests with the needs of the town." Thulander expressed his hope that in the future the ConCom would create better working relationships with other organizations in town, specifically the Recreation Commission and the Fire Department. A member of the Fire Department was selected to fill the open ConCom seat. Letters to the editor published in *The Francestown News* commented on this event. One writer noted that "the Selectmen, who are not experts in the conservation field, [do not] seem to have the ability to work with one who is." Another added, "I don't understand the resolution to 'unselect' a member...from the group.... how about putting aside personal grievances for the good of the community?"

A year after the purge, a letter from the Select Board was published in *The Francestown News*. It appeared to be a peace-making initiative. In it the board praised the ConCom for their good works during the past year. Whatever uncooperativeness the Select Board perceived before was now water over the dam. Betsy Hardwick, appointed to the ConCom in 1998, became the chair in 1999. The board doubled down in their praise of the new leadership: "Chairperson Betsy Hardwick, and all participating members of the Conservation Commission...have given many hours to ensure that our expanding town-owned forests are properly managed and protected. Their dedication will not only be enjoyed by today's residents, but by our future generations." This commentary was also a response to a ConCom member who was actively challenging timber harvesting in the town forests, Dodi Finlayson. The Select Board supported the "new" ConCom in their implementation of the Forest Management Plan.

RENEWED LAND PRESERVATION?

Betsy Hardwick, a life-long resident of the town, the daughter of Sonny and Dot Hardwick, embraced the Hardwick family's deep attachment to Francestown as a genuinely rural community based on agriculture and forestry. She was still leading the ConCom in 2020. Perhaps ironically, though the Thulander-led select boards of the 1990s had not shown interest in land conservation, their support for Betsy Hardwick's leadership of the ConCom led directly to the most aggressive campaign of open space land preservation in the history of Francestown.

In the first years of Hardwick's leadership, money from the ConFund was used to purchase 17 acres of land at the junction of Route 136 and Farrington Road. The land was used as a trailhead parking area for town forest hikers and nature enthusiasts, a picnic area, a bird viewing shelter, and interpretive trails around a meadow and wetland. This was the first purchase of conservation land by the town since 1990. Tellingly, the Conservation Commission's write-up in the 2000 Town Report echoes the Master Plans of 1980 and 1995 and laid the foundation for a revived campaign for preservation of open space in Francestown. The ConCom stated in the Town Report, "The Commission continues to be concerned with the protection of open space. We continue to look into the potential purchase of land or protective easements to conserve vital resources. Open space will help maintain our state and our town as we currently know it. It protects our water and air quality, provides wildlife habitat and recreational opportunities, and is important to the economy of New Hampshire. It is the key to preserving the integrity and rural character of our town. Open space makes dollars and sense: studies done throughout the state show that on average, open space costs less than developed property and that income generated from developed property (taxes) is insufficient to support the associated costs to towns. Studies found that on average, taxes are higher in towns with a greater tax base and more taxable property. Taxes were found to be lower in towns with more undeveloped land per resident, regardless of whether or not property was publicly or privately owned. Your support is appreciated in our goal to protect open space." The gauntlet was thrown down. A crusade for open space preservation would re-commence and this would be its gospel. That campaign, a defining event in the town's story, is described in Chapter 5.

OUTGROWING THE RED SCHOOL

By 1992 enrollment in the Red School exceeded the capacity of the three classrooms. This occurred despite a reduction of grade levels. Since 1990 students in grades 5-8 attended Great Brook Middle School in Antrim. Two temporary, manufactured classrooms, not connected to the building, were installed at the Red School. In addition to being overcrowded, the school was generally substandard. Lunch was served in the upstairs hallway, which was also used for special education instruction, and eye and ear evaluations by a nurse. Three of the six teachers shared the role of principal. There was no all-school meeting space nor a gym or library. The Town Hall was used for indoor Physical Education. The septic system was over capacity. The school had a computer-to-student ratio of 1-to-22; both computers had been donated by the PTO and the Francestown Academy Foundation's board. School buses loaded and unloaded from the street, blocking traffic on Route 47. The PTO and other volunteers improved the playground and enriched the school's program by supporting cultural experiences, entertainment, and providing annual book gifts to each student. The class sizes were not inappropriate -- six classrooms for 110 students -- but the facility itself was. Additional growth in enrollment was projected.

SCHOOL FUNDING FORMULA DEBATE

Discussion about building new schools had been ongoing among district leaders for a decade, with no proposals being made to voters. In Francestown a new site would have to be chosen; the current land did not have sufficient space for expansion or parking and playfields. Jane Lawrence, Francestown's school board representative, was chair of the school board committee that was planning expansion. She was a vigorous advocate for building new school buildings. Finally, in 1995, the school board put an article on the district's warrant to build new elementary schools in the towns with the oldest and most over-crowded schools. The Warrant Article, which was a bond, did not pass. The failure of the proposal was caused by another issue challenging the school district, the "funding formula."

The question of financing had vexed the district since shortly after its inception as a "cooperative," multi-town, district. The original funding formula called for each town to pay an assessment from the district calculated with two factors: the number of children enrolled from the town, and the value of the property in the town. The ratio of the factors was originally set at 75% for the number of students attending from a town, known as "average daily membership" (ADM). The remaining 25% of the calculation was based on "equalized assessed valuation" (EAV). Towns with lower assessed value argued that the 75-25 ratio was unfair. They had to tax at a higher rate to pay their assessment than did towns with higher EAV. Francestown's assessment was generally in the middle of the nine towns. Increasing the weight of EAV in the formula would cause Francestown to pay a larger share of the district's expenses. As recently as 1994 warrant articles had been put forward to change the funding formula, but these were not approved due to weak support in Hancock, Temple, Sharon, Dublin, and Francestown, the small towns with higher EAV.

When the school building bond was placed on the warrant in 1995, towns eager to change the funding formula saw an opportunity to put pressure on towns that stood to get a new school but opposed changing the funding formula. Residents in Antrim, Bennington, and Greenfield were mobilized to vote against the building bond, unless Francestown, Hancock, Temple, and Dublin would support a change in the funding formula. Neither warrant article passed in 1995. Complicating the finance situation further, there were other newly proposed expenses that threatened to drive up the district's budget by a double-digit percentage. One proposal called for equipping classrooms with computers to achieve a 1-4 ratio of processors to students. A push for expanded vocational education options for non-college bound students at the high school, the Applied Vocational Technology Center, also had a substantial price tag.

CONVAL SB2 ORGANIZATION PROPOSAL

In addition to the dispute over the funding formula, there was a governance issue. To vote on the district's warrant, residents were required to attend the annual meeting in Peterborough on a winter night. Attendance was chronically low. Some residents questioned whether the single site district meeting represented authentic democratic consultation and approval. A proposal in 1996 would change the district to an "SB2" organization. If the shift was approved by voters, all warrant articles would be on a ballot that would be included in each town's annual March election. Some school board members and district administrators feared that such a move would make it difficult to pass ballot measures; low turnout at the annual meeting made approval of the board's Warrant easier. A district with rapidly growing enrollment, inadequate elementary schools in several communities, a dispute over how towns' shares of funding for the district should be calculated, a new union contract with the staff, and requests for funding for computerization and a new vocational building, was in a challenging position to persuade voters to approve any of the proposals.

THULANDER ATTACKS FUNDING PROPOSAL

It did not help that the "mayor" of Francestown was not an enthusiastic supporter of the public school district. Before the funding-formula vote in 1994, Alan Thulander wrote a blistering Op-Ed piece in a Peterborough paper decrying the unfairness of the proposal to force the towns with higher property values to pay a larger share. The Select Board joined their chairman and came out aggressively against the formula revision. A flyer was distributed by the Select Board with a list of eight reasons not to support a formula revision. The proposal failed. Another attempt in 1995 fell short as well. The school building bond was offered to voters again in 1996, as was another proposal for adjusting the funding formula. This time the school board set the alternative funding formula at a balanced 50-50, EAV-ADM. Thulander wrote another Op-Ed piece in a Peterborough paper. He suggested a counter proposal with 100% of funding for the school district to be based on student attendance and none on the valuation of property. Thulander accused the ConVal teachers of being over paid and the district of financial inefficiency. He argued that the true problem facing ConVal towns was not the acquisition of revenue, by whatever formula, but the un-controlled spending by the district. In the 1990s, per pupil spending by ConVal exceeded the state average by 14%. The Select Board withdrew their representative from the Selectmen's Advisory Committee to the school board, arguing that the SAC was ineffective. Subsequently, the SAC fell into dormancy; it was reborn in 2004 and still functions, with a Francestown Select Board member participating. Thulander may have over-played his hand. Resentment in other towns against his proposal and attack on the teachers and district may have lifted both proposals over the bar. In March 1996 ConVal district voters approved Jane Lawrence's comprehensive elementary school building proposal as well as the 50:50 funding formula. In addition, a petition warrant article to change the district to an SB2 structure passed. It provided for March elections in all nine ConVal towns for the school district's warrant.

Concern about ConVal's budgets was widespread in district towns in the late 1990s and early 2000s. Critics concluded that the school board alone was not an adequate defender of taxpayers' interests in controlling spending. Advocacy for more vigilant oversight led to the appointment of a Budget Committee consisting of representatives from the nine district towns. Charlie Pyle, who was serving on Francestown's BAC, was appointed by the Select Board and served for the duration of the committee's tenure. The existence of this committee reduced direct criticism of the school board's budgets. After several years, the committee was decommissioned.

New Elementary School Opens

The new Francestown Elementary School opened in the fall of 1997. Between the vote and the ribbon cutting there was rancor. Considerable debate took place about the building site. Residents complained about poor communication between the school board and the town. There was concern that building the school close to the Piscataquog River might adversely affect the river. Gordon Russell, president of the Piscataquog Watershed Association, a widely respected conservationist, assured residents that neither the construction process nor the building would pose a problem for the watershed. Alan Thulander was not done. During construction, Thulander told *The Francestown News*, that the school district was "cutting corners" on what they promised. Francestown's school board representative explained that Thulander's allegations were not accurate. Wood framing was replacing steel framing because no contractor would bid on the steel framing. Also, kitchen facilities had been reduced through "cost engineering" during the design phase, not as an ad hoc action after voters' approved.

School Fundraising Activities

Through the rest of 1990s into the early 2000s the community embraced their new school. Fund-raising by the PTO was ubiquitous. Most famously, the PTO sold Francestown Afghan blankets with the artwork of prominent structures in town. In 1998 a public meeting was held to discuss and plan for landscaping. FES received grants from the National Gardening Association and the National Wildlife Federation to landscape the front of the school. Additional funds were provided by NH Fish and Game. In 2001 the "Schoolyard Habitat" was completed at FES. Also, a team led by Cathy Gombas, Holly Stanley, and Cindy St. Jean, raised money for playground equipment and a team of volunteers installed it. FIHS and *The Francestown News* made major donations. The Piscataquog Watershed Association helped FES embrace its riverine setting by involving the students in a release of hatchery salmon. Based on an application written by Beth Wallace, FES was declared a national Blue Ribbon School, and was honored for its extensive parent volunteer program, including the initiation of a Lego League team and an after-school program led by Celeste Lunetta. Denise Glover and Andy Paul represented Francetown on the ConVal School Board from 1996 through 2004, followed by Stewart Brock's nine years (2005-2013).

BABY BOOM AND PRESCHOOL

The 1980s-1990s birth bubble in Francestown, and the cultural shift to mothers employed outside the home, led to increased demand for pre-school openings in the 1990s and early 2000s. The Francestown Community Preschool parent cooperative, founded in the 1970s, served children from forty families. Other pre-school/daycare options were Creative Kids daycare owned by Karen Couturier, and Eileen Rodier's Joyful Tikes. At their enrollment peak, FCP expanded their program in the lower level of the post office building by taking over the space used by Creative Kids. Creative Kids sought refuge in the lower level of the Community Church. In 2004, as its enrollment slipped, the FCP moved into the church's Vestry as well. When the number of young children ebbed, the town's preschools and daycare homes closed.

HOME SCHOOLING AND PRIVATE SCHOOL

Home schooling grew in the early 2000s and continued to be a popular option through 2020. The numbers have always been estimates because the local public schools need not be notified by homeschool parents. In 2002 the estimated number of homeschooled children in town was between 10-15. By 2015 that figure grew to more than 30. Some homeschool parents planned shared activities. The children's section of the library made a special effort to serve homeschool families.

A private school operated in town for a few years in the early 2000s. The New Holland Vineyard School offered a non-grade-leveled elementary and middle school program in a converted private home on New Boston Road. The school was the inspiration of Jane Gallagher Hooper. At one point it served over a dozen students. Hooper put together an advisory board including several notable educators.

A NEW MASTER PLAN

Between 1994 and 1996 a Planning Board subcommittee researched and wrote the town's second official Master Plan. The plan would have a major impact on the town through the following decades. Town Meeting 1994 authorized funds for a new Master Plan, and a Planning Board subcommittee quickly developed a survey of all town residents. One of the strengths of the 1995 Master Plan was the comprehensiveness of the survey, both its detail and the level of participation by town residents. The Master Plan Committee and a phalanx of volunteers went door-to-door to ensure that all citizens were encouraged to complete the survey. Abigail Arnold was the lead author of the 1995 plan. The plan addressed a broad set of issues and provided detailed information about the town's current situation and residents' views and wishes. Over the ensuing decade, and beyond, the Budget and Advisory Committee, the Select Board, and the Planning Board frequently referred to findings and recommendations made in the 1995 Master Plan.

Planning Board members are expected to refer to the current Master Plan while performing their duties, especially when they consider amending ordinances. The effectiveness of a Master Plan hinges on the extent to which the leaders of the town, and the citizens at Town Meeting, embrace the plan as "theirs." The authors of the subsequent Master Plan of 2015 paid direct tribute to the town's leaders' embrace of the 1995 plan when they stated: "In the past twenty years, since the last full Master Plan update, all of the 1995 recommendations have been addressed and most implemented...."

The Southwest New Hampshire Regional Planning Commission (SWNHRPC) provided technical assistance to the Planning Board in writing Master Plans of 1980 and 1995. Specifically, the Commission was useful in providing statistics, developing maps, and suggesting language. The Commission also developed regional planning documents as an information source for Select Board and PB decision-making. The members of the Planning Boards who wrote the Master Plan of 1995 were Abigail Arnold (chair), Ken Campbell, Mary Frances Carey, Sandy Ellis, Lisa Stewart, Richard Stein, Alan Thulander, and Peter Zahn. Data provided by the master plans have been used throughout this book

VOLUNTEERS NEEDED

The 1995 Master Plan asserted that the town did not have enough volunteers. From 1970 to 1995 the number of volunteers needed for town leadership or committee positions was consistently the same proportion of the town's population, about 10%. However, since 1970, several private or quasi-governmental organizations increased their need for volunteers. The programs of the FVFD, Fire Auxiliary, FIHS, OMH, the Water Company, and Recreation Commission expanded the number of positions to be filled. The RecCom's need for coaches or instructors grew substantially. The Master Planners observed that the willingness of residents to volunteer was not keeping pace with the number of positions on offer. The Master Plan survey showed that two-thirds of respondents did not volunteer. A degree of "scolding" came from the MP authors: "Obviously, the majority of households who are not carrying their weight cannot be excused by lack of need." In addition to that judgment, the Master Plan observed that the current stable of volunteers often filled multiple positions and were "overtaxed." Some volunteer positions required more time in 1995 than they had in 1970 due to increasing complexity: "Municipal volunteers now need to be conversant with an ever-increasing number of regulations and laws." Two-worker families had become the norm and some residents were working more than one job. Opportunities for children to participate in organized activities increased and so did the time parents spent driving them. New residents were less likely to volunteer and by 1995, fifty percent of residents had lived in town for less than ten years.

The Master Planners suggested that a contributing factor to low participation in decision-making and volunteering was insufficient communication from the government and organizations to residents. The Master Plan recommended "a newsletter devoted to town issues and activities." In 1996 *The Francestown News*, a monthly in-town newspaper, founded by Sarah Pyle, Ann Soper, Mary Frances Carey, and several other volunteers, began publication. Almost 300 issues were published by 2020. The Master Plan's jeremiad about volunteerism ended on an optimistic note. The level of response to the 1994 Questionnaire and the uniform vision of what the town should be like "suggest that there may be much untapped enthusiasm and commitment in the community." Since 1995, every few years, a "volunteer fair" is held in town by one of the town committees or organizations in an effort to promote opportunities for service to new residents.

Defining "Rural"

From the first Master Plan survey in 1979 to the third in 2014, there have been consistent assessments of what residents want the character of the community to be: rural. What do residents mean by "rural?" In 1994, 80% of respondents chose "rural lifestyle" as "very important" in their decisions to live here. By 2014, as the town moved even further away from its rural heritage, still more respondents, 90%, rated "rural lifestyle" as the most important characteristic of the town. In 2014, respondents were also asked to identify qualities that contributed to the town's unique character and quality of life. "Clean water" was deemed of greatest importance by 81% of respondents, followed by "scenic qualities related to forest and farm" (69%), "peace and quiet from open spaces" (68%), and "land/water for recreation" (65%). "Local economic base" received the fewest votes at 26%. The 1995 Master Plan authors addressed the question of rurality directly. Ninety-two percent of respondents wanted Francestown to remain "as it is now" (57%) or be "rural" (35%). Residents indicated that their "concerns about growth" included "loss of open, rural and forest areas" (52%), increased traffic (48%), school enrollment (45%), and decreased privacy (40%). It's clear that "rural" means "as little change as possible," especially if that change means fewer forested areas, less privacy, more traffic, and larger class sizes.

Another way to understand what residents mean by "rural" is to look at what they think about housing policy and commercial development. In 1994 and 2014, 44% of respondents felt the Zoning Ordinance with respect to housing was "just about right" with about 20% feeling it was "too restrictive." Sixty-four percent of respondents in 1994, and 66% in 2014, felt current dimensional residential requirements (lot size, frontage, and setbacks) were "just about right."

When it comes to commercial development, there has been a substantial shift in residents' attitudes between 1994 and 2014. In 1994, 63% of respondents opposed the creation of a separate commercial district. In 2014, opposition dropped to 46% and 64% of respondents supported the idea of creating a "recreational" district in the northwest corner of town near the mountain and golf course. The same percentage of respondents favored "establishing a commercial district, possibly on Main Street, where zoning regulations would be relaxed to encourage retail and small business development." Responses gathered from the 2014 survey and the 2016 Master Plan workshops suggest that public support is strongest for more permissive zoning in the Village-Main Street area, the least rural area in town.

FARMING FADES

One might think that a logical element of the definition of "rural" might include farms. The 1995 Master Plan observed, wryly, that "though the keeping of livestock is still permitted everywhere in town, the last cow living on Main Street left in 1968, and the last dairy farm closed in 1988." After Frank Jones closed his dairy, he continued to cut hay and raise a few beef cattle for the next twenty years. Several families in town maintained small numbers of sheep, cattle, and horses. As of 1995, commercial animal husbandry in town included a hundred and fifty sheep and llamas at Knot-A-Thought Farm on Poor Farm Road, a herd of sheep on Udall Road, an Angus herd on Bible Hill Rd, and a breeding program for Galloway cattle on Udall Road. Hay meadows were still widespread in Francestown. Raising produce commercially was nearly extinct. Green Truck Farm was a small organic produce operation on County Road South on land leased from the Kunhardts. It also functioned as a Community Supported Agriculture enterprise (CSA). Abbott Farms on the south turnpike ran a seasonal farm stand, specializing in sweet corn. Another farm stand, Theo's, sold vegetables on Poor Farm Road. Harvesting timber was still a vibrant business. D.H. Hardwick and Sons was the major logging outfit. There were several sugaring operations in town and a few certified tree farms.

The Master Plan of 2015 summarized the farming changes since 1995. Most of the commercial farms that existed in town closed or relocated in the 1990s and early 2000s. In 2008, an article in *The Francestown News* featured three farms producing beef: Donny and Linda Abbott's Lost Village Farm, Wayne LeClair's Rocky Meadow Farm, and Larry and Diane Savage's Green Ledge Farm. All three ranchers sell their beef locally. A 2007 article noted the farms raising specific breeds. Turcott farm on Greenfield Road has a small herd of Scotch Highland beef cattle. Abbott raises Angus, LeClair has Galloways, and the Savages raise Belted Galloways. Joe Valentine and Paula Hunter have Cotswald sheep and Oberhasli goats. The Neilleys had Cotswalds. Henry Kunhardt raised Suffolk sheep. By 2015 there were only two farms specializing in raising beef; only one is recorded with NH Department of Agriculture. Hay fields account for about 500 of the 1,500 acres of unforested land and is the main reason that Francestown's remaining meadows have not returned to forest. The boarding, raising, and training of horses is considered an agricultural activity, according to the NH Department of Agriculture. Equestrian farms present vistas contributing to "the rural character of the town." Many Francestown residents keep horses for private recreation for which they need open fields for grazing and hay. Apparently, Francestown can be "rural" without much agriculture.

If farming has largely died in Francestown, then the key "rural" feature is "open space" – undeveloped forested tracts and meadows with high "conservation value" containing ledge, rocky slopes, wetlands, brooks, pools, and trails, accessible primarily from Class VI, defunct, or abandoned logging roads. By the late 1990s "the rural character of the town" assumed a maximum amount of undeveloped forested land and well-set-back homes thinly distributed along thoroughfares.

1995 MASTER PLAN - FINDINGS AND RECOMMENDATIONS

The 1995 Master Plan saw no reason to believe the likely projected population growth would compromise the ruralness of the town: "there is clearly enough land to absorb the growth – most probably, given land characteristics, in similar dispersion patterns as at present." Though there was another four-year burst in home-building in 1999-2002, the slow rate of population growth and home-building for most of the 25 years following the 1995 plan proved this projection's prescience.

The 1995 Master Plan provided the following observation which communicates the authors' assessment of "rural," and how best to preserve it. The plan recommended that land use activities "be compatible...with the town's rural character, aesthetics, and lifestyle and with conservation/preservation of natural resources for the benefit of both present and future residents." The Master Plan recommended that the town's land use boards "ensure" that regulations "protect the town's natural beauty, rural character, historical assets and unpolluted resources." It recommended that support for Current Use legislation continue, and owners be encouraged to establish conservation easements on their land. It also recommended "recapitalizing" the Conservation Commission for land acquisition. "Land use change taxes" should be added to the Conservation Fund for purchase of open space or for conservation easements.

A major focus of each Master Plan is an assessment of community services, levels of satisfaction, and perceived areas of need. The 2015 plan compared residents' evaluations of various town services between 1994 and 2014. The highest rated services in 1995 were fire protection, the transfer station, rescue services of the FVFD, snowplowing, the library, and the Conservation Commission. These were rated 70% or better combining the categories of "Good" and "Very Good." Ratings of 60% or better were given to the Police Department, the Planning Board, town administration, recreational facilities, public schools, and the cemeteries. Satisfaction with roads increased substantially over twenty years with approval of road maintenance reaching 50%.

The Master Plan of 2015 reported that when asked if they wanted "more," "less," or "the same" of various public services, residents wanted "less" of everything, probably meaning lower taxes. The response for schools may be telling because it is by far the most expensive service for which voters pay, and in the 2000s the costs continued to rise each year despite steady decreases in enrollment. Residents wanted "less" from the public schools than they did in 1994. That is, they wanted to pay less; they did not want to receive lower quality education. They also wanted to pay less for police, roads, cemeteries, plowing, and the library. They did not want less from the fire department, the transfer station, or recreation. Most services received a preponderance of the keep-it-the-same ratings. Only three items had a higher rating for "more" than for "same" – those were "Environmental Services" (49% to 45%), "Road Maintenance" (50% to 46%), and "Wildlife Preservation" (48% to 47%).

More Growth Concerns

From 1990-1998 the town averaged five permits for home-building per year. In 1999 the number jumped to 19, followed by 17 in 2000, and 20 in both 2001 and 2002. The number dropped to back to single digits for the following 17 years. In response to this burst of activity, the Planning Board met with the Select Board to discuss the feasibility of a Growth Management Ordinance. Such a move had been discussed in the mid-1980s. Planning Board members Abigail Arnold, Ben Watson, and Sarah Pyle informed the Select Board that they contracted with a consultant on responding to growth. The consultant soothed the most strident worries when he reported that the Southwestern Regional Planning Commission's figures "showed no high level of concern." The Planning Board did prohibit construction on sub-standard lots in 1999 and asserted its willingness to control the scheduling of development projects in phases depending on the town's and school district's ability to provide services. In 2001, Town Meeting authorized the Planning Board to charge "impact fees" on developers. The most lasting response to this brief growth spurt was the campaign to preserve open space launched in the early 2000s. Though a "Growth Management Ordinance" was imagined, the real growth management strategy coming into focus in the 2000s was for land to be preserved through conservation easements, town purchases, or acquisition by land trusts.

When the ski lodge was razed and the land with the ski runs was donated to the town, the hope of some, and the fear of others, that Francestown would become Vail, Stowe, or Waterville Valley was gone. Hopes and fears that the town would become Bedford or Amherst also subsided when population growth ebbed. By the end of the 2002, the briefly re-kindled alarm from the 1980s – "the suburbs are coming, the suburbs are coming" – appeared to be under control. The possibility that development would "come up the hill" from New Boston and Weare to the east or from Amherst and Milford to the south no longer seemed to be a pressing concern.

In the twenty years from 1995 to 2015 the town's infrastructure was upgraded significantly. The town had a new elementary school, a refurbished library with nearly three times the usable space, a new highway garage and salt storage shed, new town offices in the renovated former Red School, a reconstructed Main Street with a new sidewalk, a new Heritage Museum, an almost entirely new highway fleet, several new fire trucks and, albeit in the works, fund raising to renovate the Town Hall.

CHAPTER 4

A BUMPY NIGHT

TOWN GOVERNANCE, 2003-2020

"Fasten your seatbelt, it's going to be a bumpy night."
Bette Davis as Margo Channing in "All About Eve" (1950)

Bette Davis' famous line could have been announced at Town Meeting 2002 and many of the annual meetings that followed, because the period from 2002 through 2015 was a "bumpy night" for citizens of Francestown who were engaged in town governance. The trajectory of municipal administration that was established in the late 1980s continued – long-range planning, more robust town services, and more attention to the regulation of land use including control of development. But an unfortunate pattern emerged during this time -- personality clashes among town decision-makers.

THE NEXT GENERATION

As the 2000s unfolded, many of the new leaders of major town institutions were next generation natives. From 1999 through 2020, Betsy Hardwick led the Conservation Commission, the most important actor in the ongoing land preservation campaign in Francestown. From 2008-2015 she served on the Select Board, and in the second decade of the new century, Hardwick joined the board of the ConCom's major partner, the Francestown Land Trust. Gary Paige, in his own estimation "half a Foote," became the road agent in 2006, maintaining a tradition of Foote family leadership of that department. Larry Kullgren moved into the chief's role with the Francestown Fire Department in 2008, and Pam Foote Finnell became the clerk and tax collector in 2014. Paige, Kullgren, and Finnell all continued in their positions through 2020.

Paige, Kullgren, and Finnell replaced older natives, but this next generation's assertion of leadership was not a given. Each position could have found its way into the hands of a non-resident or move-in, or these leaders could have easily found work outside of town. But each of these native leaders exerted an overt act of ownership, laying claim to a beloved town and its traditions. Hardwick's leadership of the Conservation Commission was a departure; her predecessors in the 1980s-1990s were move-ins. The emergence of native leadership of the conservation movement in town linked the present and future to the strong environmentalist women of Francestown's past: Pat Place, Sibby Kunhardt, Connie Bicknell, and Connie Varnum.

Two Vignettes Illustrate Challenges

Before proceeding with the story of town governance from 2003-2020, consider two vignettes that relate to the challenges of this period. At Vespers 1999, Sirkka Holm was the featured speaker, and she very straight-forwardly acknowledged the tensions that often underlie decision-making in town. She finished her address with a message of hope.

"An Address to the Congregation at Vespers, 1999," by Sirkka Holm.

Well, folks, here it is, Labor Day 1999, the last Labor Day of this millennium....
Tonight, we are celebrating our town, our Francestown and its continuity into the next century. But the name Francestown is not what's significant—what is significant is its people.
And, indeed, what a mixture of people we have. They fall into all kinds of categories. We have the native-born, those whose families have lived here for generations. Then there are the flatlanders who come from all over and are not considered Francestownians until they've lived here at least three generations. Of course, there are the summer folk who decide to live here once they retire and the other younger summer folks. We even have several kinds of political opinions, thank goodness.... There are Democrats, Republicans, Libertarians, a growing number of Independents and nowadays Reformers. And what about backgrounds? We have folks representing various ethnic groups and economic backgrounds, and there are children and senior citizens, teenagers, twenty-somethings going on up to fifty-somethings.
Then we have all those wonderful volunteers who keep this town going, like our firemen, the women's auxiliary, and the rescue squad. And what about the good folks who work on the various commissions and boards, historical groups, the Meeting House, recreation, and our newspaper. And of course, how many work hard and diligently on the Labor Day festivities. There is the church and its women's groups, and the ones who work at landscaping the school and activists in general as well as our theatre group. And how about the quilters, sewers, knitters, and painters?
Now, with all these varieties of folks and interests we also have differences of opinion. Seniors wonder why "younger folks" don't do more volunteer work because they feel that youth is needed. And the younger folks with children say, "How can we?" since both parents work, and they have to spend time with their children and their activities. Then we have those who are interested in animal rights and concerned about the protection of wildlife while, on the other hand, hunters figure they're entitled to have deer or bear or moose meat for after all, that goes back to the times of their ancestors. And, of course, we have folks who move in and right away want every convenience they had in the city, while others mumble and say, "if you move here, what you see is what you get," and "let it alone" and "don't mess around with Francestown!" There are some who want to develop Francestown to the nines while others are horrified at this and staunchly defend every single tree, bush, and meadow and want it to remain as is since there is a feeling of permanency that way.
The Town Meeting, a much-cherished New England tradition, is the place where our differences of opinion are unmasked. We have had some pretty lively ones. There is much tension when an issue involving the town comes up and much standing up and speaking and

counting and growling and dirty looks cast about. For instance, after a town meeting, some folks may not be talking to other folks, but, after a while, they cool down. Who knows, at the next town meeting on another issue, the ones who were avowed enemies may be allies. That's the way it goes, folks. Perhaps it's best if we keep talking to each other since we never know when we'll need each other.

In spite of all the differences, however, the people of Francestown have shown kindness, consideration and feeling in helping each other when their neighbors are in difficulties. There are some magnificent cooks here and it is traditional when there is an illness or death or a catastrophe, for cooks to bring dishes to feed a family that is having troubles. The community church and its parishioners get together to help those who need assistance. And folks do this throughout Francestown not making a big deal of it. It is this spirit of helpfulness and of sympathy for each other, when the chips are down, that gives Francestown its soul.

So, I say we are all fortunate to live here in this lovely town, and we certainly are fortunate to have each other. People may come and go — that is, they may move in and out; and new ones are born and some die, but the spirit of Francestown in helping each other lives on. This is handed down from generation to generation. That's a great way to celebrate this century's end and to celebrate the next century's beginning. That's where our happiness and security lie — in each other."

A second vignette that relates to the town's rancorous story from 2003-2015 was made public when a resident received a letter from a friend who heard that he was considering running for Selectman. The resident gave *The Francestown News* permission to print the letter. Here are excerpts:

"Have you had a lobotomy? Did you say you are thinking about running for Selectman...? It is a thankless job under the best of circumstances.... Under less than peachy conditions, about half of the town will think you are corrupt or an idiot because you don't agree with them. Expect people to just show up at your house on Saturday mornings wanting to talk to you for about four hours on end, non-stop, because the dump isn't open on days that are convenient for them. Expect all the experts to call you up at midnight and tell you what the snowplow driver is doing wrong and how they know better because they used to drive a plow truck back in the Hoover administration.

Besides the Monday night Selectmen meeting, as Selectman designee, expect to go to the Tuesday night Planning Board meeting, then the Wednesday night ZBA, then the Thursday night Firemen meeting [this pattern continues for the next seven nights] .... In your spare time you get to volunteer to lead the volunteers painting Town Hall.

At the same time, you are both too new in town to understand and accurately represent the real town residents, but you are also part of the good ole boys' club that's been running things (badly) forever.... As overseer of the poor, you get to see some heartbreak situations, and some ding-dongs you'd like to club with a baseball bat.

You get to treat them both equally. Did I mention the lawsuits where someone is suing the town over a ZBA decision? Win or lose in court, financially speaking you lost. Your police department is both too brutal and aggressive, and a bunch of wussy pansies who don't do anything except ride around and eat donuts. Both of which are your fault because you should just fire them all. Whenever you go to the dump, store, church, and are in a hurry, expect people to stop and tell you that their property taxes are outrageous and in the next breath tell you that they want more and better services.

God bless you, my son. Go forth and do great things."

SELECT BOARD – THE TUMULTUOUS YEARS

Select Board Members, 2003-2010
2002, Paul St. Cyr, Steve Brown, * Thulander *resigned*/Betty Behrsing
2003, Paul St. Cyr, Steve Brown, Steve Griffin
2004, Paul St. Cyr, Steve Griffin, Steve Brown *resigned*/Betty Behrsing
2005, Paul St. Cyr, Steve Griffin, Bill McAuley
2006, Steve Griffin**, Bill McAuley, St. Cyr *resigned*/Tom Anderson
2007, Steve Griffin, Bill McAuley, Tom Anderson
2008, Bill McAuley, Tom Anderson, Griffin *resigned*/Betsy Hardwick
2009, Bill McAuley, Tom Anderson, Betsy Hardwick
2010, Bill McAuley, Betsy Hardwick, Scott Carbee***
  **Brown elected over Jonas*
  ***Griffin elected over Anderson (re-count)*
  ****Carbee elected over Anderson*

The selectmen in the first decade of the 2000s were Paul St. Cyr, Stephen Griffin, Bill McAuley, and Tom Anderson. All were move-ins, good men with good intentions. However, during the time they served there was a series of disputes and personality clashes.

By the time he was elected to the Select Board in 1998, Paul St. Cyr had a native vibe. He came to town in the mid-1980s, served for many years in the Fire Department and for several years as the Building Inspector. Griffin, McAuley, and Anderson were much more recent move-ins. Their self-confidence to lead was grounded in their prior professional experiences. But as a native, long-time observer of town governance stated: "Those guys would have been better off if, before they began to pull the levers, they understood more of the culture of the town and the reasons things were done the way they were."

In 2002 two Select Board members changed. David Jonas was edged out for reelection by Steve Brown. In the fall, Alan Thulander resigned. The remaining Selectman was Paul St. Cyr; fortunately, he was unflappable. In the election of 2003 to fill Thulander's seat, only one candidate filed for the position, Stephen Griffin, who moved to town in the late 1990s with a background in professional municipal administration. Griffin faced a write-in candidate, but his margin of victory was comfortable. Since moving to town, Griffin had organized a group called "Voices for the Village." Voices focused on envisioning an improved town Common, one with a better traffic pattern and a more aesthetically pleasing New England feel. Voices held several public meetings to gather recommendations from town residents and to discuss possible changes: burying power lines, changing the junctions of the roads, and landscaping. At Town Meeting 2003, a petition Warrant Article was on the ballot which directed the Select Board to consider the recommendations of Voices. The Warrant Article did not pass, but its author was elected to the board.

Though Paul St. Cyr was elected to a third term without opposition in 2004, new faces characterized the Select Board over the next seven years. In the fall of 2004, Steven Brown resigned with five months left in his term. Retired Select Board member Betty Behrsing, who had completed Thulander's term in 2002, filled Brown's seat until the 2005 election. No one filed for the open Select Board position in 2005, but two write-ins offered themselves, James von Rosenvinge and Bill McAuley. McAuley won. McAuley was a professional engineer who moved to town in the 1990s and was active in the Old Meeting House, Inc., and the Water Company.

In March of 2006, Griffin faced reelection but was challenged by Tom Anderson, also a recent move-in. In an interview for *The Francestown News*, Anderson discussed his career in public safety and what had motivated him and his wife Kay, a nurse, to move from Pennsylvania to Francestown. Anderson described a "cautionary tale" about the rural town in Pennsylvania where they lived experiencing rapid suburbanization. In 2005 Anderson had joined Francestown's police department. The 2006 race between Griffin and Anderson was tight and required a re-count before Griffin was declared the winner. In April of 2006, Paul St. Cyr stepped down from the Select Board with nearly a year left in his term. McAuley suggested that Anderson ought to be appointed to the open seat due to the strong support he received in the recent election. Griffin was opposed and alleged a conflict-of-interest between serving both on the Select Board and as a town police officer. Anderson pointed out that he was currently the only resident police officer. After several contentious weeks, Anderson was appointed.

McAuley's and Anderson's relationships with Griffin were awkward. In May 2006, McAuley publicly accused Griffin of "various practices which raised some questions about his judgement," and stated, "I can no longer have confidence in his leadership." McAuley did not elaborate. Anderson and McAuley voted to replace Griffin with McAuley as Select Board chair. Some residents expressed frustration with what they found to be vague accusations.

In 2008 Bill McAuley was elected to a second term. This coincided with a turn toward even more personal conflict among the Selectmen. Based on tradition, the chairmanship for the coming year would rotate to Griffin. However, in the annual reorganization meeting in March, Tom Anderson publicly questioned Griffin's fitness to be chairman. Anderson cited Griffin's absence from the ConCom's ceremony celebrating the purchase of the Shattuck Pond properties and his failure to appear at two meetings with the town's attorney. Earlier Anderson had chastised Griffin publicly for not calling in from vacation during the flood emergency of April, 2007.

At the same meeting, Bill McAuley reviewed what was accomplished during his two years as chair. McAuley celebrated that in the past two years the Highway Department, Police Department, and Waste Disposal Commission had been re-organized and re-staffed, Fire Department upgrades led to improvement in the town's "municipal grading," and a cutting-edge geothermal HVAC system was installed in the renovated library. McAuley described being Select Board chair as a time-consuming responsibility, but he believed the next chair was in position to build on this "positive momentum." Griffin was elected chair. Soon after, the momentum to which McAuley referred deflated. The long-serving administrative assistant to the Select Board resigned, as did her assistant. Both women cited a bad work environment due to Anderson's way of communicating. McAuley defended Anderson, stating that "he holds people accountable." No other public comments were offered by any of the parties. One week later, Griffin resigned as Selectman, also without comment.

In late April of 2008, Betsy Hardwick was appointed to the board by McAuley and Anderson to fill Griffin's seat. Hardwick had been chair of the Conservation Commission for nine years and was widely respected and popular in town. When Griffin's term expired in March 2009, Hardwick was elected to the seat in her own right. She remained the chair of the Conservation Commission. Hardwick's membership on the board may account for a more circumspect and diplomatic tone in the Select Board's minutes in 2009 and 2010. McAuley was chosen to serve as chair of the Select Board for a third consecutive year.

Tom Anderson ran for a second term in 2010. That election featured full-scale personal politics. He faced off against Scott Carbee. Carbee won 62% of the vote following a campaign that was thorny and led to the largest turn-out of any election in town up to that time. This rivalry was not put aside when the election was over. Right-to-Know document requests aimed at Select Board activity increased dramatically in the years immediately following the 2010 election.

In 2011, Bill McAuley chose not to run for a third term. Abigail Arnold filed for the open seat and was easily elected. Since leaving the Planning Board in 2000, she had not held an elected or appointed position in town governance though she had actively kept track of town finances, regularly offering her analysis at town meetings. Arnold was active in the land acquisition campaign (Chapter 5) and was a member of the FLT governing board. 2011-2015 was the first, and only, time that two women served on the Select Board at the same time. Betsy Hardwick and Abigail Arnold were only the second and third women to serve as "Selectmen." After Betsy Hardwick was reelected unopposed in 2012, Bill McAuley attempted to earn a third term by challenging Carbee in 2013, but the incumbent drew 288 votes to McAuley's 199.

It wasn't until the second decade of the new century that a degree of stability returned. Those select boards featured a "native," two "summer settlers," a "move-in in the 1970s," and a "prodigal son:" Betsy Hardwick, Abigail Arnold, Brad Howell, Scott Carbee, and Henry Kunhardt. Though not always a team at ease with one another, they calmed the rambunctiously personal politics experienced for the first fifteen years of the 2000s.

During the period of frequent changes on the Select Board and personal unease between the members, the board faced several situations where they were required to make difficult decisions: concern with the management of the Police Department, a rebellion among the members of the Waste Disposal Commission, contentiousness over how to proceed with expanding the Bixby Library, and problematic decision-making by the long-tenured road agent.

POLICE DEPARTMENT

Native succession did not follow in the police department as it had for the road agent, fire chief, Conservation Commission chair, and town clerk. Peter Flood, after 25 years in the department, mostly as chief, was not succeeded by a local. It is inherently challenging to follow someone with whom the townsfolk have had a long-standing experience of stability and normality and it did not help that Flood's successor, Phil Woodbury was, according to several observers, "aloof."

Concerns were raised over Police Department management. Some residents were suspicious of whether increased budget requests by the new police chief were justified. At Town Meeting 2004, an amendment to the budget Warrant Article made from the floor called for a reduction in the police budget. It was approved 113-36. In 2005, conversations between the Select Board and the chief, whether in public meetings or non-public sessions, brought forth little detail about how operational decisions were made. The Select Board expressed its uncertainty about the state of police department administration by directing Chief Woodbury to hold regular public meetings to respond to questions from residents, and the board openly discussed whether "an outside firm to look at the Police Department" should be hired. Instead, the board appointed a "Police Study Committee." The committee focused on the accuracy of the chief's record-keeping, turnover of police officers, and how on-duty coverage was scheduled. Members of the Committee concluded that the chief was inflating the number of "service calls" that were logged.

Following St. Cyr's early retirement from the Select Board, and Tom Anderson's appointment, another committee to scrutinize the department was formed: a "Police Management Committee." The committee was directed to work with the chief to improve management of the department. Not long after the committee began to meet with Woodbury, he resigned citing the confrontational attitude of the committee and the Select Board. Officer Tom Thiebault, a veteran of two decades of policing in town, was appointed interim chief. The Police Management Committee recommended a full-time police chief, computer software for better record keeping, and more transparent communication between the police department and the community. After a few months, Thiebault stepped down as acting chief. He was succeeded by Officer Steve Bell. Thiebault remained as an officer until 2008.

An accompanying concern bubbled up. It was reported in the *Manchester Union Leader* that a member of the Police Management Committee, Jason Martel, had talked with the police chief of Bennington about the feasibility of merging the towns' police departments. This initiative was not well received locally. The offender said he was misquoted by the reporter, but nonetheless he apologized.

A search committee recommended Steve Bell be hired as chief. Bell served from mid-2007 until March 2015. Like his predecessor, Chief Bell did not willingly make public monthly reports on department activity. This led to close questioning of his budget and record-keeping at town meetings. However, in 2011 the Select Board showed confidence in the chief by raising his salary and awarding him a five-year contract. Select Board concern about the police department decreased over the next few years.

WASTE DISPOSAL COMMISSION

The Waste Disposal Commission (WDC) supervised operation of the transfer station. Scott Carbee led the Waste Disposal Commission for much of the 1990s. Carbee was an advocate for increased recycling and for keeping as much material as possible out of the trash-stream. From 1996-2001, Jeff Gorton was the WDC's chair. When Gorton stepped down in 2002, Carbee returned. By 2004 Carbee was the only member of the WDC. Following the creation of the Department of Public Works (DPW), the transfer station was folded into that department along with the Highway Department. The WDC was not listed in the annual town report for a few years. The commission was reconstituted after the DPW was dissolved in 2006.

Town resident Becky Moul tuned into the finances and operational practices of the transfer station during her service on the Budget Advisory Committee. She concluded that it could be managed more efficiently and at the same time do a more comprehensive job of recycling. Selectman Tom

Anderson shared her assessment of transfer station management observing that "The transfer station was disgusting; things weren't being recycled properly and were often just thrown in the compactor." Moul challenged the Select Board, "If you want this to change you need to create a committee and support it." She recruited volunteers to join the revived WDC. When the committee was reconstituted, Carbee, due to his long experience, again became the chair. There were personality and style differences between the new members and Carbee and this quickly led to conflict within the commission.

Commission members had the authority to change leadership, but it was the way this *coup d'état* took place that became a flash point. In September 2007, following several contentious meetings, Commission Member Becky Moul called for a non-public session to "discuss past and current tensions on the WDC." In the non-public session the commission discussed their conflict, including members' criticism of the chairman's leadership. When the commission came out of the closed session, they elected Moul as chair. Carbee pushed back, stating that this was an improper use of a non-public session, and the commission was acting inappropriately when they edited their minutes through email conversations. He took his objections to the Select Board. The town's lawyer confirmed that the non-public session was inappropriate and recommended that whatever had been talked about be re-discussed at the next public session. That was done and the resulting leadership change held. In keeping with his long commitment to the work of the transfer station, Scott Carbee remained a member of the WDC. Based on this experience, the Select Board chose to hold a "what you need to know about 'the Right-to-Know' law" training for all town board, committee, and commission members. An editorial in the *Ledger-Transcript* praised Francestown for holding such a training session. Scott Carbee was credited with raising the issue.

The lesson of appropriate use of email by committee members doing public business may not have been learned well enough by all elected or appointed officials in town. In 2009 a logging company sued the town regarding a dispute over a timber harvest on Bible Hill Road. It came to light that the Select Board had violated the Right-to-Know law by exchanging emails among themselves about the situation. A long *Monadnock Ledger-Transcript* investigative article in November 2010 told the story of the dispute that was resolved by the town paying to settle the suit.

Overall, the battle of the Waste Disposal Commission exacerbated the level of personal animus that was washing into the politics of town governance in the first decade of the new century. Moul and Tom Anderson were allies in reforming the transfer station and in directly criticizing prior management, and Kay Anderson was a member of the new WDC. When Carbee challenged Tom Anderson for his Select Board seat in the 2010 election, and BJ Carbee faced off with Kay Anderson over the position of Supervisor of the Checklist in the same election, personal politics were clearly at play.

For the next several years, the Waste Disposal Commission (WDC) pushed for dramatic improvements in the amount of recycling and for reduction in solid waste haulage. The Select Board supported the WDC, and the transfer station staff bore down on following appropriate procedures. The crew of George Cilley, George Morgan, Sr., and Heather Ayers was in place for most of the next decade. New residents who were enthused about recycling joined the revitalized WDC.

From 2007 to 2008 the town increased its recycling by 61 tons as the rate of recycling rose to 43%. Revenue to the town from recycled material was up significantly. The amount of material being compacted and transferred to a landfill decreased reducing the town's expense for landfill use. Furthermore, electronic items left at the transfer station no longer were placed in the compactor; residents paid a fee for their disposal. The WDC began publishing a quarterly newsletter, "Talking Trash," that was distributed to town residents to inform them of changes in transfer station policies and procedures and to provide education in appropriate disposal of waste. Though substantial procedural improvement was made, some proposed policy changes discussed by the WDC were not adopted, such as requiring see-through trash bags to ensure that residents were not putting recyclables in the compactor. However, such proposals showed that anything was on the table if it might lead to lower expenses or greater revenue.

In 2009-2010, Francestown received recognition from the New England Regional Resource Recovery Association for having the highest rate of recycled materials, "weight per capita," in New Hampshire. The town's recycling rate passed 50%. The transfer station's management was stable and drew little attention from the Select Board for the next ten years.

BIXBY LIBRARY EXPANSION

In the first decade of the 2000s, the town's library also provided some drama involving personal politics. The Master Plan of 1995 definitively assessed the situation of the George Holmes Bixby Memorial Library (GHBML). Nothing had changed by the early 2000s. "Computerization for library record-keeping and Internet access are challenges facing the library... Also, the building is not handicapped accessible, and the space is crowded. There is a very small capital reserve fund ear-marked for future expansion. Expansion is problematic given that the lot has limited additional space and the building can only legally be used as a library-museum. There is no provision in the 1996-2001 Capital Improvement Program (CIP) for any substantial facility improvements." By the turn of the century, the State Fire Marshal ordered the second floor of the building closed due to lack of an adequate fire escape.

The GHBML Trustees of the early 2000s were ambitious to remodel the existing structure and to create an addition that harkened to the past but facilitated the future. The trustees, and Director Joan Hanchett, shared their vision with a professional architect, who drew up a plan for a $1.3m addition. The proposed structure looked like the barn that was adjacent to the Titus Brown house (now the Bixby Library) in the 1800s. The design provided abundant space for computer use and meetings. Under the leadership of Trustee Chair Mary Frances Carey, a campaign was launched. The trustees guaranteed that the town would not have to pony up any money for the addition. Seed money for the project came from Esther Hill, who left nearly $400,000 to the library in 2003. A variety of fund-raisers were launched, from an Artisan Cheese event at the Inn at Crotched Mountain, to the famous – infamous? – "Naked Calendar" of 2004.

The plan was beloved by some; others were appalled. The design was criticized for not matching the neighborhood. Constructing a three-story addition would dwarf the existing structure as well as the other buildings on that part of Main Street. While supporters were excited by the new public meeting space, other residents couldn't imagine demand for library services would justify that much new space, let alone the cost. Some questioned whether libraries would continue to be valued in the digital age. Long-time residents, Dr. Louis and Betsy Wiederhold were deeply opposed to the plan. Betsy served as a library trustee in the 1970s, and in 2003 ran for the board, but fell substantially short of election. Soon after the election, a trustee seat opened. The remaining trustees suggested a preferred appointee to the Select Board. Instead, the Selectmen chose to appoint Wiederhold. The already divisive issue became personally uncomfortable for the now mis-matched trustees until the next election. Wiederhold lost that election as well. In the meantime, she argued that the deed restrictions on the Hill donation of the property to the town would prevent the planned addition and legal research had to be conducted to clarify this.

At Town Meeting 2004, voters approved a request from the library trustees to use town land adjacent to the current structure for an addition. An amendment to the request gave the library trustees full authority regarding an addition without approval of the Select Board. Coincidentally, that year the Planning Board conducted a survey that was to be the kick-off for a new Master Plan. In that survey the idea of adding library space was endorsed. Town Meeting 2004 had passed a Warrant Article, by a single vote, requiring the library trustees to hold a series of public meetings presenting their plans. Three well-attended meetings were held.

In the summer of 2004, the Wiederholds attempted a different approach. They volunteered to donate open acreage on the north end of Main Street for the construction of an entirely new library structure. When the library board turned down their offer, the Wiederholds ran a full-page ad in the *Monadnock Ledger* with a graphic of the planned addition and a copy of both the donation letter and the rejection letter from the GHBML Trustees. In the same paper a long legal opinion from a Peterborough lawyer clarified that the Library Board had almost total control over the library's business and that the Town Meeting vote in March 2004 was definitive.

Though full-scale *sturm un drang* accompanied this project for almost two years, its ambitions withered quietly in the absence of sufficient financial support. By 2006 it was clear that private donations and available grants were not going to be enough to launch the project. Heidi Dawidoff, the new library trustee chair, announced that the Library Board was re-considering the design for expanding the library. The board was imagining a more modest addition that would facilitate better use of the existing Bixby building. There was enough money in the library's building fund, along with the donation from the Hill family, to get a more modest project done.

New Library Board Member Mike Petrovick, an architect, suggested the smaller and less expensive approach. The plan had two phases, first an addition to the northside of the building housing a circulation desk, stairwell, bathrooms, and an elevator to permit handicapped access. A second phase could be an addition to the back of the current structure, for extra reading space and computers. Phase one would bring the facility into full ADA compliance. The current building would be updated to ensure that all floors could carry the weight load of books, and insulation would be added to the roof and basement. By November *The Francestown News* reported that the Library Board had put out a Request for Proposal (RFP) to more than a dozen architectural firms. Town Meeting 2008 approved a Warrant Article to release the Capital Improvement Plan (CIP) funds that had been reserved for a library project. The plan for library renovation provided for temporary quarters for the staff and books to be in Town Hall.

The heating system for the GHBML had been problematic for years. In response to several individuals' advocacy for the installation of a geothermal heating and cooling system in the library, the Select Board added it to the project. This decision led to frequent finger-pointing in the decade after its installation. Cost overrun for the installation was the first taste of dissatisfaction. Over the following years, glitches and breakdowns and frequent repairs characterized the system. Advocates contend there is nothing wrong with the concept, that the problem has been its execution. At least twice, Town Meeting has been asked to double-down on its bet on the geothermal system. Expenses for repair have exceeded the initial installation costs. Several consultants have offered advice but with only modest improvement.

While the renovation plan unfolded, legendary Director Joan Hanchett became ill and took a medical leave. In mid-2007 she passed away. Carol Brock, the children's librarian, who had stepped in as interim director, was hired as director. Mary Farrell became the children's librarian. Brock's first year as director involved a complete move of the library materials to the Town Hall during construction. The library project – summer 2008 to summer 2009 –

involved a big move out, and a big move back. Dozens of volunteers were involved on both ends of the project. A temporary storage space was built in the basement of Town Hall to house books. The staff worked out of the old post office area on the first floor, which in the 2017 renovation became the bathrooms and an elevator. For the library staff in 2008-2009, there were no bathrooms and no heat, but great community appreciation. The return to the library by the fall of 2009 meant a revival of library book discussions for adults organized by Elizabeth Hunter-Lavallee, sufficient space for Mary Farrell to roll out a summer reading program for kids in 2010, and resumption of Heidi Dawidoff's long-standing movie night series.

ROAD AGENT AND SCENIC ROADS

The *pièce de resistance* of issues with a strong personal edge facing the Select Board during this period was the fate of the long-serving road agent. No one involved in this event came away with a good feeling. Since 1987 Clayton "Junior" Foote had been the road agent in Francestown. His appointment at that time was a return of "the family business" to a Foote after an experiment for a few years with an out-of-town boss. He and his family truly were sons and daughters of Francestown. Foote's knowledge of road maintenance and road building was extensive. In 1999, he earned his Master Roads Scholar designation from the University of New Hampshire. Foote perpetuated several traditions of the road crew: a fierce independence, a facility for getting a lot done with barely serviceable equipment, and a reputation for "tree hating."

Most of the mileage of town roads in Francestown are dirt and gravel tracks lined by stone walls and towering forests. Trees shade the roads, extending their spring and fall muddiness, and they encroach on the space needed for a plow to throw snow back across the walls. It is easy for a road worker to see the trees along the road as unfriendly. Men who worked for Junior attest that as a long-time veteran of road care in Francestown he viewed roadside trees with disdain and passed this along to his staff. In an earlier era, that would have been accepted. But in the Francestown of the 1990s and the years following, increasingly committed to conservation and to the quaint aesthetics of rural life, the day was past when the road agent could cut trees as he saw fit. This was especially true as the town, like villages across the state, designated many of its roads as "scenic." By law, trees on a Scenic Road may only be cut after a public hearing.

As early as 1989 the Select Board had said to the road agent, "Put away the chain saws." If only it had been that easy. The Select Board minutes from the 1990s feature a litany of complaints against the road crew for unapproved tree cutting. A cavalier attitude to disturbing stone walls was also evident. In 1997 *The Francestown News* published a plea for better Select Board supervision of the road agent with respect to tree cutting on Scenic Roads. One example was the cutting of a huge maple on Mountain Road that brought angry abutters to the Select Board. In each instance, Foote was openly unrepentant.

In 2000, a Department of Public Works was superimposed over the Highway Department and the transfer station. This created a level of supervision between the Select Board and the road agent, a Director of Public Works. Tom Plourde, previously a road maintenance supervisor from Mont Vernon, was hired and tasked with supervising Junior and his road crew. Plourde knew much less than Foote did about the town's roads and their maintenance, and as his tenure lengthened it became clear that he was not fully invested in his role. The added supervision did not lead to much change. In 2002 former Planning Board Chair Abigail Arnold, filed an official complaint with Plourde regarding tree cutting the road crew had done, without prior approval, on Old County Road South. She demanded that the Select Board enforce the Scenic Road law. Plourde's response was to publish the Scenic Roads list and re-emphasize the procedures his staff were told to follow. The road agent received some support, indirectly, from Public Service New Hampshire (PSNH), the power company. PSNH identified Francestown as one of the least well-trimmed towns in this region of the state.

In January of 2006, without Select Board permission or a Scenic Road hearing, twenty-one trees were cut and chipped. The chips were blown into a wetland. A permit from the NH Department of Environmental Services is required before anyone can legally put material in a wetland. Only three trees had been designated to be cut when the project began. Foote had worked for the Highway Department for 36 years, and at age 69 he was less than a year away from being vested for his pension. He had two formal reprimands in his file for similar actions. The Select Board – St. Cyr, Griffin, and McAuley – decided that this incident was grounds for termination. Foote requested a public hearing.

Several residents came to Foote's defense and spoke up for him at the hearing. These included Kris Stewart, owner of Francestown Sand & Gravel and road agent in 1980, Conservation Commission Chair Betsy Hardwick, Chris Danforth, a resident who was a wetland scientist, and Dan Cyr, a resident who was a forester. Foote stated that most of the trees cut were not even "statutory trees," that is, they were small in circumference. He said that his crew had cleaned the chips out of the wetland after they were blown in. Some who spoke up contested whether the area where the chips were blown was a wetland. The owners of the trees that had been cut stated that they did not want the wood, so there had been no misappropriation of anyone's property. Plourde came in for criticism; it was alleged that his instructions to the road crew had been vague. But, when asked if he recognized that what he had done was wrong, Foote stated, publicly, "I would do it again." Though members of the Select Board may have hoped to choose a different outcome following what was presented at the hearing, Foote's statement led to a 3-0 vote to terminate.

He was offered the opportunity to resign but declined. Later in the year, Tom Plourde was terminated; the DPW experiment was over. Plourde, and Tony Roberts, the out-of-town road agent in the 1980s, had the look and demeanor with which this generation of town leaders was more comfortable, but they did not bring the level of expertise and depth of knowledge that the Foote men had.

By the end of 2006 the Select Board was successful in courting Gary Paige to step into the road agent position. Paige, Junior Foote's nephew, had begun working for the town in 1985; he was a life-long son of the town. He split his time between the transfer station and Highway Department for a couple of years until he began full-time service on the road crew. Paige learned his skills from his families, the Footes and Paiges, who had been caring for the roads of Francestown for generations. Paige had come into the department during the era of Army surplus, second-hand equipment that was prone to need repair as often as it was available for work. He was able to see that times had changed and that the residents' and Select Board's expectations were not those of the 1970s-1980s. "Tree-hating" would not continue under his leadership. Some key developments in the second decade of the 2000s include the reconstitution of the Highway Safety Committee, the Select Board approving an omnibus snow removal and ice control plan from the Highway Department, and the three-year rebuild of the east side of Bible Hill Road. Except for a squabble between Paige and the Fire Department in 2008, the Paige era of leadership of the Highway Department has been careful and efficient.

OTHER PROJECTS IN THE EARLY 2000S

A focus of the Select Board in 2003-2005 was completing the highway garage project and preparing the town for the state's rebuild of Main Street. The highway department garage project continued to be controversial. At Town Meeting 2004 an "overwhelming majority" of voters postponed any expenditure on completion of the highway department garage and salt shed until the Select Board presented "firm numbers on actual bids" for the work. Eventually in 2005, voters approved completion of the project.

A long awaited rebuild of Main Street by the state Department of Transportation was began in 2005 and finished in 2006. The Main Street project instigated extended discussions at town meetings about sidewalks. They were in severe disrepair, but the Select Board hoped that the basic sidewalks installed by the state would be satisfactory. Some Main Street residents aspired to a more stylish installation. Folks who don't live on Main Street find the Villagers' complaints fussy at times. A tangent to sidewalk aesthetics was another chronic concern -- sidewalk snow removal. Town Meeting overruled the Select Board by approving highway department plowing of the sidewalks. The brightness of the streetlights on Main Street became an issue in 2010. The Select Board's concern was that streetlights in the Village area cost the town several thousand dollars per year. Coincidentally some residents of Main Street complained that street lighting was too bright. In 2008, a budget saving measure approved by Town Meeting allowed the town to shut off some streetlights. A brouhaha resulted. Main Street residents unhappy with the loss of brightness expressed concern about the safety of walking the street in the new level of darkness. The Select Board responded by asking Public Service New Hampshire to reinstall some of the lights, but PSNH said that a re-installation was not possible. Instead, the town purchased three new lights. The net result was only a small amount of savings. *The Francestown News* parodied the situation in the next April Fool's issue with a Photoshop picture of Main Street with an abundance of elaborate light fixtures.

HIRING A TOWN ADMINISTRATOR

Abigail Arnold was elected to the Select Board in 2011. With Arnold's ascension to the Select Board, the board's leadership in budget development was reasserted. Through 2002 the budget process had been dominated by three figures: Selectman Alan Thulander, BAC Chair and Selectman David Jonas, and Planning Board and CIP Committee Chair Arnold. With the departure of these figures from budget development leadership, the series of Select Boards from 2000 to 2020 were uneven in their teamwork with the BAC, though up to 2011, the BAC and the Select Boards usually partnered closely in the budget development process. Charlie Pyle served on the BAC from 2000 to 2020, and beyond, most of that time as chair. Pyle's reports include instances when Select Boards utilized BAC expertise that went beyond budget preparation, including BAC participation in the creation of the Department of Public Works (DPW), hiring a DPW Director, and a study of health insurance costs and options. In that study the BAC interviewed insurance providers and ultimately recommended a new employee insurance plan. When veteran town finance hawk, Arnold, joined the Select Board, the BAC was often kept "at an arm's length" according to a BAC veteran of that era. The BAC was not involved in the run-up to hiring of a town administrator. Although, once a town administrator was hired, consultation with the BAC increased.

Recommendations to hire a town administrator had been made in the 1990s and early 2000s. The Master Plan of 1995 suggested that the town would profit from professional administration. That was not going to happen with Alan Thulander serving both as a Selectman and as the unofficial town manager. In 2003 the Select Board appointed a "Study Committee" to review how the town's business was administered. That committee reported that Francestown's Select Board was responsible for many more administrative functions than in comparable towns. Like their predecessors, the committee recommended creating the position of town administrator. Instead, the Select Board hired a clerk to assist their administrative assistant.

In anticipation of another effort to bring a professional town administrator on board, former Selectman Paul St. Cyr at Town Meeting 2012 moved to decrease the executive line of the budget by an amount that would prevent a town administrator from being hired. St. Cyr had been on the Select Board that turned aside the 2003 recommendation. At Town Meeting he asserted that administration of the town "has been run just fine" in prior years without a professional administrator. Select Board member Betsy Hardwick rejoined that without a professional administrator the town had missed out on substantial tax revenue and had not optimized grant applications. She asserted that the position would pay for itself. Another resident contended that the tradition of volunteer, amateur selectmen administering town business was not up to the challenge of the increasingly complex business of a multi-million-dollar municipal government. St. Cyr's motion to amend the executive line of the budget was not approved.

St. Cyr believed that small town democracy was being well served by traditional volunteer administration by the Select Board. Three years prior, he had taken the initiative to promote democracy by overturning established tradition. In 2009, St. Cyr proposed a petition Warrant Article to switch Francestown to an "SB2" town meeting system. Under such a system, the Warrant Articles voted on by in-person voters at the traditional Saturday Town Meeting instead would be presented on a paper ballot at the Tuesday town election. St. Cyr argued that such a change would enable more residents to vote on all the Warrant Articles. At that time, an average of 150-200 people typically attended the traditional Saturday in-person session of Town Meeting, whereas an average of 250-350 people voted in the traditional Tuesday election. Those who opposed changing to an SB2 format argued that a New England tradition of direct democracy would be lost. Articles in *The Francestown News* and the *Ledger-Transcript* argued the merits of the two positions. A public forum was held in February before the March vote. St Cyr spoke in favor of a change to SB2, but no one else did. To some extent this made his point. None of the folks who supported his petition Warrant Article attended the public forum. Most of them do not participate in Town Meeting because they aren't available, or they don't feel comfortable in that setting. If only a portion of the electorate attends the Saturday business session of the Town Meeting, claims of "democracy" ring hollow. On the floor at Town Meeting the vote was 145 to 276; a switch to the SB2 format was rejected. Interestingly, 145 is a fair estimate of the number of people who vote in elections but don't come in person to the Saturday session. Paul St. Cyr believed, in principle, that small-town democracy would profit from more voters and retention of volunteer management. Neither position won the day.

In August of 2012, Mike Branley, a professional town administrator, was brought in as a temporary employee from Municipal Resources, Inc. He was titled "Administrative Coordinator" and could not be a full-fledged "town administrator" until action was taken by Warrant Article at Town Meeting. Branley set to work building the 2013 budget as a full-fledged town administrator would be expected to do. He served until 2015 before moving on to administer a larger town. In his short tenure he impressed even some of those who did not want the position created. Observers of town governance describe Branley as smart, efficient, creative, and humble, a fast learner with a useful degree in Public Administration. A selectman who was not involved in the hire subsequently described Branley as a "perfect hire for the town at that time."

In addition to moving toward a future with more professional management, the town took steps to enter the digital age in presenting itself to residents and the outside world. Several residents created an unofficial town website as early as 2004. By 2008 the town had a professionally developed website. However, the means to get this done was "old school" Francestown. *The Francestown News* paid the website developer. If there was a complete reversion to the 1970s, FIHS would have paid the bill.

The Select Board's office, prior to the hiring of a town administrator, had two clerical employees, an administrative assistant and a clerk. In the four years following the 2008 resignation of the administrative assistant, turnover was frequent. There was some controversy. In the absence of an administrative assistant, Abigail Arnold stepped in to serve until a new person was hired. Two short-term hires didn't work. During these stumbles, Arnold sometimes served as a volunteer, and at other times she was paid. Over the prior decade, deferential trust in the Select Board had eroded, and some residents criticized Arnold's paid role as a conflict of interest. After pointed criticism, the board voted to no longer pay a Select Board member who assumes administrative duties.

EARLY BRIDGE REPAIRS

Following Gary Paige's appointment as road agent, roads were less of a preoccupation of Select Boards. But roads cross bridges. Bridge issues elbowed their way to the attention of the town and its Select Board as the 2000s unfolded. Bob Foote, road agent in the 1960s-1970s, had learned bridge-building as a SeaBee. The type of bridges SeaBees built were just large culverts that could be installed with a bulldozer and a backhoe. Every significant bridge in town was repaired or rebuilt in this fashion from the late 1960s through the 1980s. Eventually a metal culvert degrades and is no longer structurally sound. The only other support for the bridge deck are the rocks piled on either side of the culvert, but in few cases in Francestown were those supports structurally independent of the culvert itself. In the late 1970s, the Select Board began insisting that an engineering consultation and fee be included in major projects, but the involvement of a local engineer added little longevity to the lifespan of these SeaBee bridges. The last major traditional bridge repair, the Poor Farm Road bridge, was completed in 2004 by the Millers and Kris Stewart.

The next major bridge replacement was done with concrete reinforced abutments independent of the culvert. The Russell Station Bridge over Rand Brook with a price tag of over $800,000 was the largest bridge construction ever undertaken by the town. Flooding in 2007 had washed out the old bridge's support system. The new bridge was completed in October 2011. On this project the town served as general contractor employing Francestown Sand & Gravel (FS&G). FS&G worked with a local environmental consultant, Chris Danforth, to balance construction imperatives with conservation concerns. Danforth arranged DES and Fish and Game permits. A diversion channel was used during construction. Though there were cost overruns, the project received positive reviews and laid the foundation for having the town superintend subsequent bridge construction projects.

TURNPIKE BRIDGE REPLACEMENT

In December 2012, the next domino fell. A state inspection of a "red-listed" bridge south of the intersection of Cross Road and Woodward Hill Road on the Second New Hampshire Turnpike led to the posting of a weight limit. Because the weight limit excluded school buses and other large vehicles from using the bridge, the Select Board felt compelled to close the bridge. A bridge on Woodward Hill Road in Clarksville was closed as well. The state moved the turnpike bridge's replacement date up to 2014 on its calendar for state financing. The CIP had anticipated the replacement of four failing bridges, so some reserves were available.

The Select Board sent a press release to town residents acknowledging the inconvenience caused by the closing of the bridges but stated that "we really have no choice.... The town is currently exploring all reasonable options to reopen these bridges in a timely manner.... A state inspection report indicated critical bridge deficiencies, stating that the bridges are 'in need of complete replacement or extensive rehabilitation to carry all legal loads.'" A temporary repair on Woodward Hill allowed it to be re-opened, but the turnpike bridge was to remain closed until it was replaced. The Select Board judged that repairing it prior to replacing it was "not cost effective." A detour was identified but it provoked concern for some residents, especially the dangerous intersection at Rt. 136 and Red House Road. There also was concern about having ski area traffic on Francestown backroads.

Lively discussion ensued about the prospects for a temporary repair of the bridge. The Stewarts of Francestown Sand & Gravel met with the Select Board in January and presented a repair option that would keep the bridge temporarily open with one lane of traffic. They estimated the temporary repair price as around $70,000. The Select Board chose not to put a temporary bridge option forward as a Warrant Article, but they said such an option could be proposed as an amendment from the floor to the proposed town budget. At Town Meeting 2013, Kris Stewart took the floor with an easel and graphics and intoned a line many residents remember: "I come here today to sell you a bridge." Stewart explained his plan for a temporary bridge, which was followed by a three-hour discussion of the pros and cons of the proposal. The proposed amendment to add $70,000 to the budget passed, 90-78. Some of those who were present at that Town Meeting say they voted for Francestown Sand & Gravel to do the job. Others contend they voted for a temporary bridge without regard to how it was to be accomplished. And 47% voted against a temporary bridge without regard to who built it.

Given the budget amendment, the Select Board considered how best to pursue a temporary bridge. This led to a fierce dispute over whether the project should be bid. Selectman Scott Carbee and others held that the Town Meeting voted for Francestown Sand & Gravel to do the project. A case was made that the situation was an emergency and therefore no bidding was necessary. Select Board members Hardwick and Arnold believed the project should be bid due to rules established by earlier town meetings. Kris Stewart made it clear that if the project were put out to bid, Francestown Sand & Gravel would not bid on it.

The Select Board asked Road Agent Gary Paige, and local engineer Henry Kunhardt, who served on the Budget Committee, to work with the town's engineering firm, CLD Engineering to create a plan and a bid package. They directed this team to answer two questions: "Can the project be done for $70,000 and if so, how?" Paige and Kunhardt were given a March 28 deadline. The proposal Stewart had presented called for the town to buy a set of 40' beams to support the bridge deck. Once the permanent bridge was built, the temporary beams and decking would be available as a "kit" for future use. Paige found that NH DOT was willing to rent the town some very long beams, 62 feet. This was the key element in the Paige-Kunhardt design. Longer beams reduced reliance on the degraded stonework on either side of the failed culvert. The foundation for the long beams would be solid blocks of concrete setback from the culvert by up to 12 feet. The shorter 40' beams would have to be close to the current water passage. Paige and Kunhardt proposed that the town serve as the general contractor, as it had with the Russell Station Road project. The town would rent the long beams. Bids would be let for the erection equipment and the decking lumber. Paige and Kunhardt estimated the cost of this design to be $55,000. Both the state's bridge personnel and CLD Engineering endorsed this plan.

On April 8, the Select Board accepted the Paige-Kunhardt plan by a 3-0 vote. Later, Scott Carbee moved to reconsider the vote, but the board majority did not agree. The Select Board advertised the bids and requested qualified individuals to apply to be "Clerk of the Works," coordinating the project for the town as general contractor. Applicants were interviewed, and Henry Kunhardt was hired as clerk. A letter was sent to all residents on April 22 from Town Coordinator Mike Branley explaining what had transpired since Town Meeting. Branley credited Kris and Lisa Stewart for valuable input and for the "momentum to move forward." He also thanked Paige and Kunhardt for their work developing the plan that was approved. Bids for the bridge lumber and equipment were awarded on April 25 on 3-0 votes.

The project was completed in mid-June. Carbee reported to his colleagues that he received positive feedback from residents about the completed bridge. Planning began for permanent replacement of the turnpike bridge in 2014. The price tag was about $1m though 80% of the funds came from the state. The town used CLD Engineering for design and hired a bridge building company. The new bridge was completed by September of 2014. A series of bridges were replaced between 2014 and 2020, including bridges on Scoby Road, Woodward Hill, Juniper Hill, and South New Boston Road. When the Old County Road North bridge failed, a temporary bridge was installed that can be saved and recycled.

Criticism and Grievances

Abigail Arnold was reelected in March 2014. Those residents dissatisfied with decision-making by the Select Board regarding the turnpike bridge mobilized to make the town election of 2014 a referendum on how that event was handled. Over six hundred voters cast ballots, breaking the record set in 2010. Arnold was challenged for re-election by Lisa Stewart but prevailed 342 to 256. In addition to the bridge kerfuffle, Arnold was criticized for her "attitude," which Stewart contended was not respectful. A consequence of the infusion of personal grievances into the politics of town governance was that around 2009 several residents began to attend Select Board meetings regularly, aggressively critiquing board members' decisions and behavior. Initially the lightning rod was Selectman Tom Anderson. By 2012 dissatisfaction focused on Abigail Arnold and Betsy Hardwick. It may not have been a coincidence that the first Select Board with two female members faced the most intense scrutiny and criticism of any board between 1970-2020.

A set of grievances accumulated. One critic called for the Select Board to adopt an "ethics ordinance," suggesting some Select Board actions were unethical. The road crew was criticized for driving town equipment to Greenfield to eat lunch at the Harvester Market. The owner of an auto repair business faced sustained push back from the Select Board because they contended that he had not followed the proper permitting process for his garage. In 2012 when he needed the town's endorsement to operate as a state-licensed auto inspection station, the Select Board temporarily blocked his application. In 2013, the town's new property assessment company called for the Francestown Village Water Company to pay property taxes on its land. The

President of the Water Company, Dennis Orsi, appealed to the NH Board of Tax and Land Appeals, which sided with the Water Company. A citizen angry about work on Pleasant Pond Road alleged that trees had been improperly cut on this Scenic Road and that he was not treated properly when he complained. He directed his ire at Betsy Hardwick and brought up an old issue about whether Hardwick should be held responsible for the maintenance of Cressy Hill Road and its bridge. Cressy Hill Road was mostly a Class 6 road and Hardwick was the only resident on the road.

This steady drip of grievances continued through 2014. At that point a group coalesced around the issue of Cressy Hill Road. At Town Meeting 2014, a petition Warrant Article was proposed to prohibit the Highway Department from doing maintenance on the road. At Town Meeting the retired fire chief, the former road agent, and a former Select Board member stated that the road has been maintained by the town for as long as they could remember. The Warrant Article was defeated with a 75% "no" vote, but the issue remained a topic of conversation.

POLICE DEPARTMENT RESIGNATIONS

On the eve of Town Meeting 2015, residents with grievances were given another bone to chew. In October 2014, the Select Board contracted with MRI, Inc. to review the Police Department's management practices. The consultant met with Chief Bell and reviewed documents and procedures followed by the department. Two days before Town Meeting 2015, Chief Bell submitted a letter of resignation to the Select Board. On the Monday following Town Meeting, the MRI consultant presented his findings, which included an absence of professional standard-operating-procedures and problematic evidence documentation and storage. Following Bell's lead, the other officers in the Francestown Police Department resigned.

The Select Board acted quickly to stabilize the situation. The board arranged coverage by police from neighboring towns. By March 23, Fred Douglas, a retired police chief from Milford, and Steve Campbell, the current police chief in Bennington, agreed to serve as interim chiefs. A public forum was held to brief residents on the status of the department and to receive questions from residents. Douglas and Campbell hired additional officers. A search for a permanent police chief was conducted by the NH Police Association, which led to Fred Douglas being hired as chief. In 2017, Mike Dowd, a retired Milford policeman, joined the department and served as chief in 2019-2020, with Douglas as one of the officers. Three sworn officers were serving the town in 2020.

LAWSUIT FILED OVER SELECT BOARD MEETINGS AND MINUTES

In the summer of 2015, five residents filed a lawsuit against the town alleging that some board meetings with Selectmen from neighboring towns had been posted improperly and they contended that closed session minutes from three meetings of the board had been sealed incorrectly. The five residents -- Dennis Orsi, Prescott Tolman, Betty Behrsing, Lisa Bourbeau, and James Gann – alleged "right to know" violations for the misposted meetings and the incorrectly sealed minutes. The Superior Court ruled that the Select Board did err in how they chose to seal three sets of non-public meeting minutes and did not properly post meetings of the Select Board of Francestown with other towns' Select Boards. The court ordered that the minutes in question be unsealed. Those minutes contained information about MRI's investigation of the police department and some Cressy Hill Road discussion. But nothing startling was revealed. In his ruling the Superior Court judge stated that the Select Board "did not purposely or maliciously violate the law." He characterized the violations as "minor" and ordered the town to unseal the three sets of meeting minutes. The plaintiffs appealed, seeking some sort of punishment, but the judge dismissed the appeal asserting that the suit was unnecessary and that the plaintiffs should have worked with the town to resolve their concerns. The court characterized the lawsuit as "the airing of grievances," an "omnibus collection."

STABILITY RETURNS

The five years of political life in Francestown following the closure of the lawsuit was a period of stability and relative quiet. In 2016, Henry Kunhardt replaced Scott Carbee on the Select Board. Kunhardt, the son of George Kunhardt, a renowned sheep breeder, grew up on Starrett Farm on Old County Road South. His mother, known as Sibby, was a fixture in town, chairing both the Library Board and Conservation Commission in the 1960s-1970s. Henry returned to Francestown in the early 2000s. An engineer professionally, Kunhardt revived Starrett Farm as a sheep operation. His preparation for the Select Board included a decade on the Budget Committee and as a trustee of the trust fund, as well as clerk of the works for the turnpike bridge project in 2013. During his two terms on the Select Board, he supervised the Town Hall and police station renovation projects and provided perpetual care for the geothermal system at the library.

Kunhardt joined two other Baby Boomers with Francestown roots. Betsy Hardwick had not run for a third term in 2015. She was succeeded by retired lawyer Brad Howell. Howell grew up summering in Francestown in the 1950s-1960s and continued to visit Francestown over the next forty-plus years. He faced Dennis Orsi, a leader in the lawsuit group, for the open select board seat, which he won 354 to 173. Howell was reelected in 2018. Orsi lost again in the 2017 Select Board election to Abigail Arnold, who served three consecutive terms ending in 2020. In that year, Marsha Dixon was selected as the fourth female Select Board member to serve the town.

By 2016, Gary Paige and Larry Kullgren were well-established and respected leaders of the highway and fire departments. They were joined in service to Francestown by another scion of long-time settled families, Pam Foote Finnell. In 2011, Finnell was appointed deputy to Elaine McClary. McClary retired after 23 years as the town clerk and tax collector in 2014, and Finnell stepped in to complete McClary's term. She then was elected in her own right in 2015.

OTHER DEVELOPMENTS

Meaningful, though not earthshaking, developments in town governance were a feature of the period from 2016-2020. Until Town Hall was renovated, town meetings were held at the elementary school and elections took place in the lower level of the Town Offices. The Select Board chose, for the first time, to include in the Town Report the vote of both the Select Board and Budget Committee for each proposed warrant article that had a budget impact. This occasionally showed "split votes" for Warrant Articles. Beginning in 2015, *The Francestown News*, assumed responsibility for the annual Candidates' Night after the Oak Hill Grange, its long-time sponsor, dissolved. By vote of Town Meeting, Select Board meetings were streamed online and recorded for viewing, though in the first three years of recordings only 16 out of 89 were viewed. In 2016, the Select Board ended a long-standing practice and ceased to publish the names of residents who had not paid their property taxes to the town. Town Meeting 2016 brought closure to the Cressy Hill Road controversy; attendees overwhelmingly approved that the town maintain the road and the bridge. Pleasant Pond Road was repaved and a donation of land across the turnpike from Cemetery #3 was accepted. In 2018, in a close standing vote, a Warrant Article authorizing the town to buy a digital ballot counting machine failed to pass by a slim margin at Town Meeting. Traditionalists preferred to continue having ballots counted by hand.

A significant step forward in budgeting quietly took place in 2017. Fire vehicles are on a thirty-year replacement cycle. Therefore, the 1989 Pierce Pumper was due for replacement in the 2000-teens. The replacement cost was estimated at $670,000. However, in 2018 Fire Chief Kullgren told the Budget Committee that the FFD could move forward without replacing this pumper. This was a huge savings to the town as well as a responsible and thoughtful move on the part of the FVFD.

PLANNING BOARD IN THE 2000'S

During the decades of the 2000s, aside from the Select Board and the Conservation Commission, the most active theatre of town governance and politics was the Planning Board. Leadership of the Planning Board and Zoning Board was in the hands of "move-ins" throughout the 2000s. Their work was strongly influenced by the mantra articulated and embraced by Francestown's emergent majority: "to preserve the rural character of the town." "Rural" meant "less developed" and "conserved."

In the early 2000s, a consultant to the Planning Board from the regional planning commission told the board that the town had a problem -- it was not perceived as friendly to development. A Planning Board member responded, "This is not a problem; we *are* unfriendly to developers, *on purpose.*" The struggle for the town's identity with respect to land use and managing development continued through the 2000s (Chapter 5). Parrying development, and prioritizing the preservation of open space, was the dominant ethic. That does not mean, however, that the debate quieted down. Residents of the town who wanted to prioritize individual property owners' freedom from regulation, continued to assert their preferences. Several of the elections for Planning Board seats were referenda on whether the Planning Board should be monolithically skeptical of development and at-the-ready with regulations to preserve the rural character of the community, or whether there should be a spectrum of differing opinions within the board's membership. One decidedly libertarian critic of the growth-management majority said, with a resigned sarcasm "We don't have a Planning Board in Francestown, we have two Conservation Commissions."

The changing membership of the Planning Board tells this story. In 2000, under Chairman Stewart Brock, all board seats were held by growth management/preserve-the-rural-character aficionados. But in 2002 and 2005 the election of Lisa Stewart and Linda Kunhardt infused a degree of diversity in perspectives. From 2011-2013, new members Henry Camirand, Bill McNeill, and Mike Tartalis brought skepticism of "excessive regulation" and a greater degree of openness to development. Camirand and McNeill left the board in 2014, but Lisa Bourbeau and Guy Tolman were elected. Both were outspoken in their disapproval of "too much regulation." The 2014-2016 Planning Boards were chaired by Larry Ames, with Linda Kunhardt, Bob Lindgren, Lisa Bourbeau, Guy Tolman, Sarah Pyle, and Lisa Stewart. Abigail Arnold was the *ex officio* Select Board member. Those were diverse boards. In some elections voters were given clearly differing choices. In 2013 Lindgren and Pyle were elected over Tolman and Tartalis, while Tolman and Bourbeau were easily elected in 2014. Hardwick and Pyle won over Bourbeau and Tolman in 2017. Consistency was not a hallmark of voter sentiment. Often the last decision the Planning Board made cast a long shadow.

From 2017 onward, membership was stable, with a preponderance of board members holding a growth management perspective. Karen Fitzgerald chaired the boards of 2017-2020 which included Lindgren, Pyle, Hardwick, Gerri Bernstein, and ex officio Arnold, alongside Kunhardt and Stewart. As of 2020, Bob Lindgren had served on the Planning Board and Conservation Commissions for a combined 43 years – 22 years on the ConCom and 21 on the Planning Board. Other long-tenured PB members over the 2000-2020 period were Sarah Pyle (18 years), Linda Kunhardt (16 years), Lisa Stewart (13 years), and Abigail Arnold (9 years as *ex officio*).

The 1990s ended with a spike in permits for home building which continued for three years. This led to another wave of anxiety about creeping suburbanization which fed the open space preservation movement of the next two decades (Chapter 5). The Planning Board was the primary theatre where tightening of the Zoning Ordinance played out. Regulation empowering the Planning Board to "phase development" was approved. Non-conforming lots were not permitted for housing starts, and in 2001 the Planning Board discussed adopting a developer impact fee. The board completed full reviews of subdivision regulations in both the first and second decades of the 2000s. The board exercised strict scrutiny of proposed subdivisions; some applications were rejected. The Planning Board and ConCom openly discussed mutual adoption of "smart growth" concepts. For example, "form-based zoning" was an oft-discussed concept from 2012-2017. Zoning changes were frequently on the ballot through the 2000s, and usually they easily passed.

COMMERCE ON MAIN STREET

In 2005, Sarah Pyle, owner of Country Brokers Real Estate, applied to the Planning Board and Zoning Board of Adjustment for the approvals she needed to move her real estate office to 169 Main Street from its location just off the Common. Both Pyles owned the Main Street house. The delicate nature of the request was that Sarah Pyle was chair of the Planning Board and her husband, Charlie Pyle, was chair of the ZBA. Both Pyles recused themselves and did not participate in the hearings held by the respective boards. The boards approved the permit applications. A group of abutting neighbors protested, suggesting bias on the part of the respective land use boards, and then, officially alleging that the abutters had not been properly notified about the hearings. The concerned abutters formed the Village Association (VA). The VA's general assertion was that having a business office on Main Street would change the character of the neighborhood by adding non-resident parking, increasing traffic, and changing the look of the family residences on the street. Over the years there have been home-based businesses on Main Street, but this would be a business office, not just a residence out of which a business was operating. Articles appeared in the *Monadnock Ledger* and the *Peterborough Transcript*. Coverage by *The Francestown News* (TFN) was handled delicately, given that Sarah Pyle was editor of TFN. When neither the PB nor ZBA was willing to reexamine their decisions, the Village Association filed suit in Superior Court. Resolution came in 2007 with the Superior Court upholding the decisions of the ZBA and PB. Country Brokers was allowed to open their Main Street office, which operated for several years.

NIGHT LIGHTS AND POTPOURRI

In the 2000s the Planning Board addressed a *potpourri* of issues not related to growth management. The Planning Board and ZBA spent significant time examining plans for new cell towers on Crotched Mountain and off Dennison Pond Road. The Zoning Ordinance that applies to animal breeding and kenneling was tightened when an unlicensed breeder failed to comply with reasonable requests from neighbors. A dispute over pollution from Crotched Mountain Ski resort's night-skiing lighting dragged on for several years. Night skiing was a key part of CM's business model. The bright lights mounted on their slopes were a source of complaint in Francestown and across the region as far away as Nelson. The Select Board, Zoning Board, and Planning Board faced different parts of this ongoing disagreement. The town was able to apply its lighting ordinance only to the night-skiing lights within Francestown. An engineer was hired to study the intensity of the lighting and what could be done to mitigate its impact. His report called for shields to be added to the light fixtures. Peak Resorts, Crotched Mountain's owner, was slow to comply with the resulting Select Board order but eventually they did. Considerable board time was spent developing a more permissive sign ordinance that was "content-neutral" and thereby did not violate First Amendment rights. Each time the issue of whether building permits should be issued for new homes on Class 6 roads appeared to be resolved, it wasn't. In 2005 the concern was focused on Scobie Point Lane and whether new camps, not year-round homes, could be built. That same year, Donnie Hardwick wanted to subdivide property accessible from the Class 6 section of Campbell Hill Road. The Planning Board could not approve the subdivision until the Select Board reclassified part of the road to Class 5.

The second decade of the 2000s ended with contentious hearings between the Planning Board and the Shattuck family. These hearings illustrated the ongoing struggle over what "preserving the rural character of the community" means and how much and in what way town residents want the Planning Board to regulate individual property owners' freedom over their land. The 2016 hearing, described in Chapter 5, was followed by hearings in 2019-2020 that resulted in the board denying a subdivision permit. That decision was appealed to the new state appeals board which ruled against the town. A dispute in 2020 over the rights of the owners of "home businesses" to park or store equipment on their property led to the proposal of competing amendments to the Zoning Ordinance. The question of what, if any, regulations would apply to such businesses was actively debated as the century's third decade began.

THE 2015 MASTER PLAN

The Master Plan of 1995 had a lasting impact over the following twenty-five years. Most of the impact was in the initial decade following its completion. As the 2000s began, enthusiasm for an update to the Master Plan was strong among members of the Planning Board. The process that produced the Master Plan that is referred to as the 2015 Plan was different than its predecessor. The Master Plan of 1995 was researched and written in a tight time frame, from start to finish less than two years. Whereas the process for an update to that Master Plan was started in 2002, re-started in 2004, and then re-started again in 2012. Given that the world digitized between 1994 and the mid-2000s, the nature of surveying was different; data for the 2015 plan was gathered largely through online applications. The various chapters of the 2015 update were written sequentially over several years. For example, the Land Use section was written in 2016, and the Water Resources Chapter came more than two years later. The 2015 Master Plan reflects conversations that have been taking place in town through the last two decades with respect to protection of resources and management of growth. A discussion of the results of the Master Plan survey from 2014, in comparison with the equivalent 1994 survey, was included in Chapter 3.

IN OTHER NEWS

Building Inspector or Code Enforcement Officer?

In the 1980s, the Select Board began hiring building inspectors. The building inspector's role was to review construction plans and determine if a building permit should be issued. Inspections followed to make sure that construction conformed with the approved plan. The town used the NH state building code. In 2006, for the first time, the Select Board appointed a "Code Enforcement Officer." It is not clear how the Select Boards from 2006-2016 were empowered to expand the scope of responsibility of the building inspector and to use the title code enforcement officer, but they did. Based on the Select Board's meeting minutes, the code enforcement officer was to function as a building inspector, but also was directed to check on whether existing buildings conformed to safety codes and setbacks. Two men served in this capacity from 2006 to 2015. They functioned more as inspectors than officers in that they alerted the Select Board to an issue of non-conformity so that the board could choose to respond or not. In 2016, the Select Board returned to use of the title "Building Inspector" when they appointed John Kendall to the position. He recommended whether the Select Board should issue a building permit. That changed in 2020 when the building inspector was empowered to issue permits without prior approval from the Select Board.

Police Department Office

Town Meeting 2017 approved funding for a renovation of the Police Station in the Town Hall Annex. The amount allocated was increased at Town Meeting 2018. Since the FIHS Historical Rooms moved to the Beehive in 2017, the entire space in the Annex was available as a headquarters for the Police Department. PRIMEX, the risk management firm serving the town, did not consider the space an acceptable environment for professional police personnel. The project was completed in 2018 for about $170,000. The police officers hosted an Open House-BBQ for the public to celebrate the new facility. Donny Abbott, who has served as the Animal Control Officer since 1983, retired from that position in 2020.

Waste Disposal Commission

The WDC continued its trajectory of stability up to 2020. A long-term trash hauling contract with Waste Management, Inc. was approved. The commission chose to continue to segregate recyclable materials instead of adopting a single-stream approach. Town Meeting 2016 approved a new transfer station recycling ordinance that was disseminated through a "Recycling Guide" published by the Waste Disposal Commission. Francestown's recycling rate continued to exceed the goal set by the state, though the rate slipped at the end of the decade. A new employee office was built at the transfer station.

Library

Carol Brock served as the director of the George Holmes Bixby Memorial Library until 2019 when she retired. The library computerized its record-keeping in 2014. Residents were issued library cards and the card catalog was put online. Some traditionalists chafed at such modernization, but practicality and diplomacy eased the transition for most users. Long-time Children's Librarian Mary Farrell retired in 2017. From 2017-2020, library trustees substantially remodeled and updated all areas of the facility. The library's HVAC system continued to be temperamental.

Recreation Commission

RecCom's hyper-activity in the 1990s was followed by an ebb and flow of Commission leadership in the next two decades. By 2005, leadership of the Recreation Commission was in the hands of Bub Rokes, who was joined a couple of years later by Donna Noonan. This duo led the commission until they retired in 2018 and 2017, respectively. Mike Beisang provided support, particularly for the baseball program during this period. Dugouts were built at the Underhill baseball field, and it was regraded in 2020. Dawn and Tom Kirlin helped reenergize the Recreation Commission after Rokes and Noonan stepped away. They initiated a weekly Community Market in the horse sheds beginning in 2018 that continued through the months of the COVID emergency.

Francestown Friends

From 1985 to 2005, years, Barbara, "BJ," Carbee was the town's public assistance administrator. In New Hampshire, towns have statutory responsibility to assist people in financial need. The laws are specific about what assistance is permitted. Carbee was succeeded by Phyllis Naegeli, who established written guidelines for public assistance decision-making. To address residents' needs that could not be met with town funds, Naegeli established Francestown Friends with members of the Community Church. She worked with Town Administrator Mike Branley to develop a set of guidelines for a volunteer work program for those receiving assistance, as well as a house inspection protocol if a recipient was receiving rent assistance.

Emergency Management

For many years, in addition to his leadership of the Select Board, Alan Thulander served as the town's Emergency Management Director (EMD). Before that title was developed, the position had been Civil Defense Director. Paul St. Cyr served in the position in the early 2000s and developed a Hazard Mitigation Program to address, among other things, the risks presented by flooding, and a protocol for unified command and control during disaster situations. This plan worked well during the severe weather events of 2008-2009. Kevin Holdredge became EMD in 2010 and worked with police, highway, and fire leaders during Hurricane Irene in 2011, led renewal of the Emergency Management and Hazard Mitigation plans, and coordinated COVID transmission mitigation procedures in 2020.

Variable Milfoil

An invasive weed that is found in ponds and lakes across the United States, was first identified in Scobie Pond in 2003. It has not been found in Pleasant Pond. The infestation in Scobie was started when plant fragments or seeds were attached to a fisherman's boat that had been in an infected lake. Town Meeting, through warrant articles, funded mitigation efforts through 2020. The treatments used have included removal of the weeds by professional divers or herbicide applications. Herbicide treatments have been most effective. The cost of treatment each year has been covered by a combination of town money and grants from the Department of Environmental Services (NHDES) which supervises treatments. The Scobie Pond Preservation Association (SPPA), a group of abutting owners of pond frontage, have worked with the town and DES over the years to assess the extent of the infestation and to observe the effectiveness of the treatments. For many years, the presumption was that the weed could be totally eradicated, but from 2015 onward DES was clear in communicating that control of the spread of milfoil was the most that the town and pond users could expect. A new herbicide was applied in 2018, which kept the pond clear for two years.

The Pleasant Pond Association (PPA) abutters worked with the town, the New Hampshire Lakes Association, and NHDES to create a Lake Host Program. This program pays volunteer boat inspectors during peak boat-launching hours. The hosts examine watercraft put into the pond to spot aquatic invasives and remind boaters of cleaning protocols. As of 2020 there has not been an infestation in Pleasant Pond.

Cemetery Commission

Through most of the 2000s the Cemetery Commission members have been Betsy Wiederhold, Polly Freese, Linda Kelly, and Ethel MacStubbs. During these years Cemetery #3 was expanded. Ethel joined the commission in 2001. Her mother, Lois MacAdam, implored her to "replace that damned fence in my memory!" MacStubbs fulfilled her mother's wish when the rusty chain-link fence at Cemetery #3 was replaced by a stone wall.

Village Water Company

The Water Company became aware that its water had a higher than recommended level of arsenic. In 2009 filters were installed to achieve acceptable levels of arsenic and lead and to mitigate radon. Prior to the Route 47/Main Street reconstruction by the New Hampshire Department of Transportation, water lines were extended to some residences on the north end of Old County Road South and to the Recreation Fields. During the Main Street construction, additional fire protection service was added for the library. Later improvements included deepening and hydrofracking of one of the company's two wells, remodeling the control and blending building, adding new electronic controls, and upgrading piping. The company services 60 residences in the immediate village area and provides hydrants for fire protection. In 2014 the NH Board of Tax and Land Appeals found the company to be a not-for-profit organization exempt from property taxation.

Lakehouse LLC

In September 2016 neighbors became aware that a single-family home located on Scoby Road across from Scobie Pond was operating as a "sober living" therapeutic home for young adults with addictions. It was known as Lakehouse LLC. A group of abutting residents expressed concern to the Select Board, arguing that the owners had not applied for a variance or a special exception for a business to serve transient residents in a residential home. For several months the owner of the business and town authorities conducted a back-and-forth communication about the nature of the business, its legal status, and whether it could be required to appear before the Zoning Board. Ultimately, it was determined that New Hampshire law did not empower towns to regulate this type of business. The Select Board was advised by legal counsel that Lakehouse LLC must be treated as a single-family home not as a business facility. The business lasted about a year before it folded.

Schools in the 2000s

At the beginning of the 2000s, the Francestown Elementary School building on the Turnpike was new but had a strong tradition of parent involvement and support. In 2004-2005, the Parent Teacher Organization (PTO) raised funds for playground equipment. Substantial donations were made by *The Francestown News*, FIHS, and the NH Charitable Foundation. As usual, local contractors and tradesmen brought their equipment and donated their labor to complete the project. The PTO organized after-school programs for students with a diverse array of options and supported all-school learning projects. Fundraising was continuous, from pre-town meeting pancake breakfasts to selling discount ski area passes.

Andy Paul represented the town on the ConVal School Board until 2005. In 2006, Stewart Brock began nine years as the town's board member. Brock distinguished himself as a persistent and copious communicator. He held monthly office-hours at the library for parents and citizens who wanted to ask him questions or communicate their thoughts. During his service Brock faced several challenges at the district level. Taxpayer concerns over the rising cost of schooling led to volatility in school district governance through the 2000s. Many taxpayers were troubled by ConVal budget increases that averaged 2-3% at a time when student enrollment and staffing were down by around 20%. In some years, the district's budget rose by 5-6%. Several district budgets proposed in the 2000s were rejected by voters. Taxpayer sensitivity also led to voters' rejection of several proposed teachers' contracts. For four years in a row teachers' contracts were not approved, dropping teachers' pay to 107th place among New Hampshire school districts. Francestown's voters sometimes supported the proposed contracts and sometimes contributed to their rejection. For several years there was a general tension in the district between teachers and administrators, administrators and the school board, and voters and their elected representatives.

In 2011, the district formed a district Model Study Committee (MSC) which was charged with considering how to reorganize the ConVal schools given steadily declining enrollment. The MSC report presented options for dealing with the structure of the district. The plans varied from consolidating into four school buildings from the current eleven to no changes but more spending so that art, music, physical education, and nursing services are available in all eight elementary buildings. Two school board members brought one of the proposals forward as a petition Warrant Article in 2012; the proposal failed. A Warrant Article was proposed in 2013 that would have enabled the school board to close individual schools, but it did not get the super-majority needed to amend the district's Articles of Agreement. Francestown supported the school closing amendment, 272-196. But only in Peterborough and Antrim did the measure receive the two-thirds approval needed.

During Brock's three terms, declining enrollment led to issues at FES. Enrollment at FES dropped from 115 in 1995, to 94 in 2000, to 59 in 2008. The steep decline in the number of Francestown students in ConVal schools was reflected in the enrollment in 2007. That year there were 104 Francestown students in four grades at the high school but only 69 in four grades at FES. By 2019 FES had fewer than 50 students. Declining enrollment led to cost-saving measures at FES. Multi-age classrooms were implemented in 2009. Brock provided detailed explanations in *The Francestown News* of what this concept would mean for students. This new organizational scheme was well-received by some parents but was met with skepticism by others. Parents whose children wanted, or needed, greater academic rigor or enrichment, perceived the multi-age classroom as an obstacle. Administrators emphasized "equity," which some parents saw as aiming for "the middle of the road" at the expense of the needs of more advanced students. During this debate, FES parents and community members formed rival committees. The district created a committee of parents and staff to propagate understanding of and support for the new curricular approach, while a committee of parents critical of the program at FES formed, as well. School administrators and board members met with the skeptical parent group to hear their concerns. The meetings were lively. Board Representative Brock played an active role in facilitating civil conversation. In 2010 the principal at FES was also responsible for schools in Hancock and Greenfield.

During the 2000s, homeschooling gained in popularity in Francestown. The laws of New Hampshire require little reporting by homeschool families. As a result, estimates of the number of children participating are approximate. Around 2010, a reliable estimate was that 20 children were homeschooled; by 2015 the number rose to 25-30.

In 2012, at a board meeting when Brock was not present, the board voted to reduce FES' kindergarten from full day to half-day. Brock protested vehemently both about the process and the impact, but the decision stood. In 2019, during a discussion of future budgeting, a motion was made to close FES due to low enrollment. Parents and community members complained about the board's discussion and the following board meeting was held in Francestown to enable dialog between the board and Francestown residents. The meeting was well-attended. In March of 2020, the town's two-term board member was defeated for reelection in the wake of concern over his role in consideration of closing FES.

In March of 2020, at the beginning of the COVID emergency, the school board voted to close in-person schooling but to offer all students remote instruction online. Some in-person schooling resumed in May of 2020. During the 2020-2021 school year "hybrid" instruction was provided. It combined in-person teaching with remote instruction. Special federal funding sources enabled the district to implement virus transmission mitigation strategies without hemorrhaging the district's budget.

The COVID Pandemic in Francestown

In February of 2020, cases of the COVID-19 virus began to proliferate in the United States. In March daily life changed substantially. However, the town election on the first Tuesday in March was held just before the most jarring changes took place. There was discussion among town leaders about re-scheduling Town Meeting until a time when more was known about the spread of the virus. But a decision was made to proceed in case it became impossible to meet later. At the time few persons knew that no meetings of this kind would be held again for many months and when they were we would be wearing masks and sitting uncomfortably distant from one another.

The week following Town Meeting, daily routines began to change. The ConVal schools ended in-person instruction and began teaching "remotely" online. The Select Board limited public access to the town offices to people with urgent issues, and soon after closed the offices entirely. When Town Offices re-opened masks were required for the next year. The Select Board met with the leaders of the police, fire, transfer station, and highway departments to discuss mitigation measures. Francestown's emergency management director called for all town vehicles to be sanitized regularly. Mask wearing was required at the transfer station. The library closed to in-person patronage; users arranged to pick up materials in stapled brown paper bags. The Select Board continued to hold its weekly meeting in-person, but public access was through the online streaming service. Zoom meetings became standard practice for other committees and boards. An executive order of the governor closed the museums. The Recreation Department canceled many programs including the Tim Samuelson fishing derby, lifeguard supervision of the town beach, and summer camps. The Friday evening Community Market continued albeit requiring masks. The first publicized case of COVID in Francestown involved a patron who had been at the Community Market but contact tracing did not detect virus transmission at the market. The town's health officer, Kay Anderson, worked with the Community Church to identify people who needed help with shopping and transportation. FIHS cancelled the annual Labor Day celebration, though an online raffle was held. Normal daily, weekly, or seasonal socializing, with family or friends, was delayed or lost entirely for months on end.

The Select Board anticipated a loss in tax revenue and implemented budget constraints. The town accepted Federal CARES Act money as well as funds from the Governor's Office for Emergency Relief and Recovery (GOFERR) to compensate for COVID related expenses. As a result, the town ended the year with a surplus.

The state's primary election in September and the general election in November were both conducted in Town Hall but with major procedural modifications to reduce the risk of COVID transmission. The state modified requirements for voting by absentee ballot, enabling those who feared the risk of COVID transmission to vote by mail. All voters received a letter from Pam Finnell, town clerk, explaining the absentee ballot procedures. Votes by absentee ballots were five times the normal amount.

As the town began planning for its 250th birthday celebration in 2022, it experienced the most abnormal period since World War II, or the pandemic of

1919. Small towns can be a good haven, and Francestown was a good place to hunker down for many residents.

CHAPTER 5

PROJECTS THAT DEFINED THE TOWN
2000-2020

Two aggressive, sustained campaigns dominated the town's story in the first two decades of the new century. These two campaigns are the culmination of changes in town governance that began to take shape in the late 1970s, came to life in the late 1980s, and were consolidated in the 1990s. The first initiative was the preservation of a substantial percentage of the acreage in town as permanent open space. The second was a million-dollar renovation of the Town Hall.

THE CONSERVATION CAMPAIGN

Land acquisition by the town and promotion of conservation easements on private land was on the back burner in the 1990s. That changed with the ConCom's statement in the Town Report for 2000. "The Commission continues to be concerned with the protection of open space. We continue to look into the potential purchase of land or protective easements to conserve vital resources.... Your support is appreciated in our goal to protect open space." This declaration by the Conservation Commission to the townspeople represented a gauntlet being thrown down.

The Master Plans of 1980 and 1995 had etched into granite the mantra that "preserving the rural character of the community" should be the primary goal for good public policy in Francestown. While there was near consensus in town about the importance of preserving the rural character of the community, there was not agreement that this would be accomplished by blocking the development of open space. Proponents of open space preservation viewed it as the key to preserving rurality. Undeveloped land would protect the environment and foster naturalistic recreation; it would be an aesthetically and culturally desirable alternative to housing construction or business siting. As such, master planners promoted it in both their Recreation and Land Use sections. Open space was viewed as a Recreational Facility and a Natural Resource.

The 1995 Master Plan noted that "arguments by opponents to future ... land acquisition include: the town already has enough town forest, conservation lands are a discretionary expense item the town cannot afford, and protected land whether purchased by the town or by private [land conservation] organizations ... reduces the value of the tax roll." Planners acknowledged a companion argument that preserving land reduced the opportunity for new housing that would increase the tax base. These counter arguments to open space preservation have been advanced through the 2000s.

A response to this skepticism that gained currency around the turn of the millennium was based on detailed analysis of economic data. There was evidence that development of land for residential housing was expensive for towns. New housing seldom provided enough tax revenue to cover the costs incurred by towns and schools. The costs of development included per pupil spending for public school students, the need to open seasonal roads for commuters, school buses, and commercial traffic, increased costs of waste disposal, and new residents' demands for a variety of enhanced public services. Examples of such service demands included more hours at the dump, better road construction and maintenance, more comprehensive policing, a more robust library, more hours for municipal officials, additional recreational programming, and enhanced emergency services. The argument included the observation that in a town such as Francestown, where 80% of the property was in Current Use status, any incremental loss in tax payment when it moved from Current Use to Conservation status was small. In short, taxes from new housing did not cover the costs to a municipality that new housing brought.

At times, in the heat of an argument about land use planning and regulation -- and those arguments were frequent -- the accusation was made, quoting from a Planning Board debate, that "conservationists seem to care more about land or wildlife than they do about people." The implication was that land use regulation decreased the freedom of individuals to use their land as they saw fit; a frustration for some that was as old as government itself. Conservationists and land use regulators saw themselves making decisions that benefited most residents, though specific individuals were inconvenienced. Often, proponents of land use regulation justified their stance by invoking "protection of the interests of future generations."

Skeptics of more acquisition of open space land by the town argued that the town forests were sufficient for recreation. The Master Plan of 1995 noted that "most property owners either do not know there are town owned forests or do not know where they are located." Additionally, the authors observed that most of the town-owned forests were remote and unlikely to serve the day-to-day recreation choices of most residents. Some of those who favored town or land trust acquisition of open space were not driven primarily by concern for wildlife habitat or protection of natural resources. They were openly "anti-development" and showed their hand by advocating for "protection of...*more visible tracts*" along the town's major roads, whether those lands had conservation value or not.

THE OPEN SPACE LAND PRESERVATION STRATEGY

As the millennium approached, a strategy for open space preservation was coalescing for Francestown conservationists. The strategy was to preserve –

through purchase and/or easements -- unfragmented blocks of backlands, water resources, and critical natural features. Although Francestown's 81 miles of roads seem extensive, in fact most acreage in town cannot be readily accessed from town roads. Large pockets of unfragmented backlands lie between widely spaced roads, behind the developed frontage. There are five particularly sizable backland areas that form a contiguous arc around the town from the northwest to the southwest. These unfragmented areas, which are part of even larger and environmentally important blocks extending into other towns, are relatively remote, sparsely populated and characterized by limited access. Much of this backland area contains important natural features and critical water resources.

Five targeted areas were identified in the early 2000s. Much of this acreage came under protection by 2020.

Area 1: Approximately 2,800 acres of unfragmented land lies on the shoulders of Crotched Mountain. This area is defined by Mountain Road, Campbell Hill Road, Greenfield Road, and the westerly town line. Sixteen hundred acres of this block were preserved as open space by 2020.

Area 2: Approximately 1,000 acres of backland are in the area defined by Wilson Hill Road, the Second NH Turnpike North, Old County Road, and the northerly town line. The state's 2015 Wildlife Action Plan identified the northernmost tier of this area, with its wetland complex, brooks, and vernal pools, as being "highest ranked habitat" in NH. By 2020, approximately half this acreage was conserved. Three hundred plus acres constitutes the town-owned Dinsmore Brook Conservation area, and most of the rest is private land under conservation easements.

Area 3: Eleven hundred acres of "highest ranked habitat" acreage is circumscribed by Old County Road North, Pleasant Pond Road, and the northerly town line. Separating this area from the next unfragmented area is Pleasant Pond and the development surrounding it. By 2020, approximately half this area was conserved, most of it in the town-owned Shattuck Pond Conservation Area.

Area 4: The northeast corner of town, the area between Pleasant Pond and Dennison Pond has approximately 1,200 acres of backland. Approximately 450 acres of this is conserved.

Area 5: An area in the southwest corner of town lies within a larger unfragmented block extending into adjacent towns. Within and extending out from this area, almost 1,000 acres is conserved along Rand Brook, Brennan Brook, and the south branch of the Piscataquog River. This includes the riparian corridor along the Piscataquog River and tributary brooks. Preserving the lands immediately adjacent to the river and its tributaries is justified by the importance of these water resources for people as well as wildlife.

These backland and riverine areas, and lands linking them, were the primary targets of the campaign orchestrated by the Conservation Commission and its private allies in the years following 2000. Almost three thousand additional acres in town came under protection by 2015. How these land acquisitions were paid for was a substantial public policy issue in the first decade of the new millennium. But paid for they were. town meetings allocated $425,000 to the Conservation Fund between 1987 and 2010, and added a $1 million bond issue in 2005. The Conservation Fund was created for the purchase of land and easements on privately held land, but it also served as "seed money" for acquiring grants.

Additional revenue came by vote of Town Meeting 2001. Fifty percent of Current Use land change fees were placed in the Conservation Fund. Proceeds from timber harvest in town forests went to the Con Fund. Government and private foundation grant sources were essential in the ConCom's land acquisitions. These include the Land and Community Heritage Investment Program (LCHIP), the Aquatic Resource Mitigation Fund (ARM), and the Land and Water Conservation Fund (LWCF). Complementing aggressive acquisition by the town, several private conservation organizations protected substantial acreage in Francestown through outright purchase or by holding easements. The primary private preserver was the Francestown Land Trust (FLT, originally known as Francestown Land Conservation, Inc.). The Piscataquog Land Conservancy (PLC, formerly the Piscataquog Watershed Association) and the Russell Foundation also played significant roles.

Betsy Hardwick took over leadership of the Conservation Commission in 1999. Hardwick grew up in the town's largest extended family. She was shaped by her family, and her years at the Grange, 4-H, Community Church, and Red School. Her grandfathers were a legendary shepherd and a much-admired carpenter. Her father farmed on the mountain and kept the ski area running; her mother raised eight children who never strayed far from town. Today that extended Hardwick family exceeds 100 when they gather for family events on the mountain. Farming, logging, and construction – pastures, forests, and skilled, manual labor -- are the foundation of the Hardwick's moral economy. Devotion to family and to Francestown are key characteristics of being a Hardwick. When the time came in mid-life for Hardwick to step forward and lead the Conservation Commission and later the Select Board, she had well-grounded beliefs of who Francestownians are and what was the best future for the town. Not everyone in town sees eye-to-eye with that vision, not even everyone in her family, but no one can seriously question her bona fides to lead the town.

The first major decision facing Hardwick's Conservation Commission was implementing the Forest Management Plan adopted by the ConCom in 1993. That plan called for appropriate timber harvests in the town forests. For the most zealous conservationists, proponents of a wilderness notion of forestry, even selective tree cutting was an anathema. This was Dodie Finlayson's view; she was a member of the ConCom when Hardwick became chair. Finlayson mounted a personal campaign to try to block the timber harvest, portraying the loggers as mechanized destroyers of the forest. Hardwick responded with articulate moderation. Her reasoned explanations were grounded in a genuine understanding of forestry and of sustainable logging practices, and most important, knowledge of the true nature of the forests growing in Francestown.

A petition Warrant Article was proposed at Town Meeting 2001 that would ban all timber harvesting in the town forests; it was rejected by voters 39-94. The initial harvest went forward, and harvests subsequently continued. The proceeds from timber harvests enable the ConCom to appropriately care for their holdings. The ConCom enhanced the Forest Management Plan by adding a thorough Stewardship Plan that included expanding the use of the Crotched Mountain Town Forest to recreation for novice hikers as well as veteran naturalists. The ConCom purchased 16 acres at the junction of Farrington Road and Greenfield Road. This provided areas for trailhead parking and picnicking. New trails were built, logged areas were reseeded, and wildlife habitat improvements were made. The commission sponsored several special volunteer work crew days to improve trails and habitat. The Master Plan of 1995 observed that most people in town didn't know where the town forests were; this acquisition enabled clear identification and easy access. The work at Farrington Road was supported by several other grants. As an Eagle Scout project Nate Sanderson mapped the Crotched Mountain trails. As this project proceeded the ConCom began work on a natural resource inventory as a foundation for promoting public awareness of the town forests and other natural areas to help build support for conservation.

The ConCom continued its more routine activities. The team reviewed subdivision proposals and wetland applications and monitored easement properties. Several grant-funded projects were aimed at supporting access to town forests, including improving trail maintenance, sponsoring hikes, and updating trail maps. ConCom members led hikes for elementary children and continued the tradition of distributing tree seedlings to school children each spring. Members educated themselves by attending workshops. They learned about landowner responsibilities under the new Shorelands Act and then proceeded to publicize the impact of this new law for abutters and users of the lakes in town. The timing of attention to the health of the great ponds in town was serendipitous. In 2003, Variable Milfoil, an invasive plant that spreads quickly, was found in Scobie Pond. The Conservation Commission had warned about the danger of invasive species and had launched a campaign in the late 1990s against Purple Loosestrife. The ConCom's timely education about the dangers to the ponds posed by invasives encouraged Town Meeting's willingness to fund mitigation efforts.

The knowledge of wildlife conservation advocates in town was enhanced by their participation in a program offered by UNH Cooperative Extension, and the departments of Fish and Game and Forests and Lands. The "Coverts Project," named for the British term for a thicket that shelters animals, kicked-off in 2002. Over the next eighteen years, no town in New Hampshire had more residents participate in this three-day wildlife habitat conservation training event than Francestown.

Meanwhile, a sleeping giant-to-be was awakening. FLC, Francestown Land Conservation, Inc., had slept through the 1990s, but life was breathed into it in 1999 by a new leadership team. They bought into the strategy of targeting "backlands-unfragmented corridors-water resources," and proceeded to aggressively raise funds, write grants, and build partnerships with the ConCom as well as with other fledgling conservancies, such as the Piscataquog Watershed Association. FLC got lucky. Don Hardwick was the owner of D.H. Hardwick and Sons, a premier regional logging company with large holdings. It was a leading advocate for sustainable forestry. Hardwick owned tracts in Francestown. He wanted perpetual protection against development for these lands. He made 220+ acres along Rand Brook near the confluence with the Piscataquog available to FLC at a below market price so it could be enjoyed recreationally for generations to come. The tract is highly valued wildlife habitat as well. Don was Betsy Hardwick's brother. This was FLC's first major land purchase, a "coming out" of sorts. Much more would follow.

The fear of suburban development coming up from the lowlands to the hills of Francestown was re-kindled during 1999. Part of the sales pitch to donors solicited by FLC for the purchase of the Rand Brook Forest was not just wildlife and water resource protection, it was anti-development. An FLC promotion stated "One important benefit of this purchase is that it helps stop the spread of housing developments which is sweeping this way. A second important feature is the abundance of diverse wildlife which are attracted to this beautiful land, and the pristine Rand Brook." For members of the FLC Board in 1999 a key motivation was to promote "smart growth" and to "control sprawl." FLC followed the Rand Brook acquisition with the purchase of the Normandin forest parcel at Russell Station Rd and French Rd.

U. S. Cellular tried to sell off 318 acres it owned on Crotched Mountain, much of which encompassed the old ski area property. No potential buyers followed through. As a result, USC made a gift of the land to the town, reserving 1.5 acres around their tower as well as a right-of-way to access the tower property. A potential jurisdictional tussle between the Select Board and the Conservation Commission over the future of this donation was avoided by passage of a Warrant Article at Town Meeting 2003. That Warrant Article authorized the Select Board to acquire and sell land without the need of a Town Meeting vote. But it also required the Select Board to seek the advice of the Conservation Commission and Planning Board regarding any transaction. The article excluded from the Select Board's jurisdiction "land donated to the town for community purposes." That last phrase targeted the tract donated to the town by U.S. Cellular.

While some residents saw the potential for housing on the mountain, many wanted a guarantee there would be no development. Several ski area buildings on the property, including the once grand but now derelict ski lodge, were decaying; they represented a serious liability as attractive nuisances. Contracting for professional demolition appeared expensive. One selectman opined that "the gift could be a $200,000 liability." Instead, a volunteer crew was organized by Francestown Sand & Gravel, and the lodge was demolished. The Fire Department burned some of the smaller structures as a training exercise. "It was sad. A lot of the firefighters who were there that night had worked or played at the ski area earlier in their lives. You could see the emotions on their faces reflected in the light of the fire," observed Jenny Fritz, FVFD reporter. This land, eventually, was conserved and part of it was added to the Crotched Mountain Town Forest.

In 2003, another large tract of land on Crotched Mountain was added to the town forest. In the late 1980s, Scot Heath had encouraged the Tamposi family to conserve a 200+ acre tract on the mountain. Donnie Hardwick continued Heath's effort to encourage Sam Tamposi to donate or sell the land. He did. The town bought the land at a bargain sale price. Fourteen years after Heath's first overture the land was donated to the town. This tract connected all the parcels of town-owned land on Crotched Mountain.

Forest Society Campaigns

In 2001, the Society for the Protection of New Hampshire Forests (SPNHF, The Forest Society) began publicizing research about the public finance implications of preserving undeveloped land; it was branded as the "Dollars and Sense of Open Space." Speakers and editorial page newspaper articles spread the news of research findings that when open space is conserved --withdrawn from development -- the tax dollars saved due to public services not being needed, more than offset any loss in tax revenue from houses not being built. This initiative was followed quickly by two complementary campaigns encouraging towns to conserve land and natural features: "New Hampshire Everlasting" and "Saving Special Places."

SPNHF held seminars to prepare local conservation advocates to make the case for setting aside open space in their towns. They recommended that every town should protect 25% of its land. Acreage targeted should have "significant ecological importance" such as productive forests and farmlands, upland buffers, and lands that feed water to existing and future water supplies, habitats for native species, and lands that connect to regional greenbelts. The 25% target combined privately and publicly conserved lands. SPNHF prepared and distributed a manual for use by local conservation commissions, planning boards, and private land conservation organizations. By 2003, a statewide campaign was in full swing, and the Francestown conservationists were on board.

"2010 BY 2010"

In 2003 Betsy Hardwick had published two articles introducing readers of *The Francestown News* (TFN) to the activist role that the Conservation Commission planned to embrace with respect to land preservation. The first article explained the role the ConCom could play in expanding the protection of open space. It was followed in the December TFN with a primer on how timber taxation works.

The 2003 articles laid a foundation for the month-by-month campaign that unfolded in the second half of 2004. At that time four advocate-authors began publishing a series of articles designed to educate the town's residents on the value of preserving open spaces. The articles and advertisements appeared in *The Francestown News*. The campaign, chiefly a brainchild of Abigail Arnold and Betsy Hardwick, began with the July 2004 issue. A half-page advertisement was titled "Saving Our Special Place for Future Generations." It featured a high-quality photograph of children and an adult fishing in a brook from a wooden hiking bridge deep in a forest. The photo was of Cole Eby and Joel and Forrest Barwood; it was taken in the Crotched Mountain Town Forest. Underneath the photo the ad directed the reader to contact three organizations to find out how to help: the Conservation Commission, Francestown Land Conservation, Inc., and the Piscataquog Watershed Association. For the next eight years and beyond, more than one hundred similar ads appeared promoting the work of these three organizations. Each ad was unique, with a different photo of a beautiful natural phenomenon – wildlife, forest, wetland, or a riverine scene. If collected, they would be a handsome set of postcards or calendar photos celebrating the natural environment of Francestown. The article accompanying the July 2004 ad also noted that Francestown Land Conservation, Inc. was being re-branded as the Francestown Land Trust, or FLT.

The August 2004 issue of TFN included a page one article about an event jointly sponsored by the Planning Board and the Conservation Commission, a public forum "focusing on natural resources and how our community can protect these resources through zoning, planning and other efforts." It reported that a representative from SPNHF "will be making a presentation on the benefits of conservation and the importance of open spaces to our economy and quality of life." Representatives of the Francestown Land Trust (FLT) and the Piscataquog Watershed Association (PWA) would be present to participate in the discussion: "The future of our town is strongly dependent on how we manage growth and act to preserve our water resources, forests, and farmlands." The title of the August ad was "Saving Special Places," echoing SPNHF's statewide campaign slogan. The photo in the August ad was of a young hiker kneeling next to Rand Brook below the old bridge.

In September, the ad text stated "Shattuck Pond is one of the few wild lakes left in New Hampshire. It is the heart of a critical 500+ acre conservation campaign led by the Francestown Conservation Commission." The commission began to focus on Shattuck Pond in early 2003 "as a priority for natural resource protection." The undeveloped backland area around Shattuck Pond featured several "unique and exemplary natural communities" according to the New Hampshire Preservation Alliance. The ConCom aspired to protect as much land abutting the pond as possible. Hundreds of thousands of dollars were required. In September of 2003, the ConCom had purchased acreage adjacent to the pond from Tom McDonnell and Tom Curren with help from an LCHIP grant and a federal grant (LWCF) totaling $380,000. Many grants hinged on the town's willingness to invest its own funds in the project. The idea of a "big bond" began to take shape.

An article accompanied the September ad. It was titled "Dollars and Sense of Open Space," again, a Forest Society slogan. In a companion article, Sarah Pyle reported on the presentation made by Dijit Taylor, Director of the Center for Land Conservation Assistance at the Forest Society, at the August town forum. The October, November, and December advertisements for "Saving Special Places" were accompanied by articles from Betsy Hardwick, Abigail Arnold, Sarah Pyle, and Elizabeth Hunter Lavallee. These articles made the case for "Wildlife at Risk," "Development on the Doorstep," and "Conservation Groups ID Critical Lands."

The November advertisement introduced a new, entirely local, campaign branded "2010 by 2010." "The Conservation Commission and Planning Board are advocating that Francestown keep 25% of the town in permanent conservation/outdoor recreation/agricultural land. To realize this goal, we are launching an ambitious campaign to save 2010 acres by the year 2010 – roughly an acre a day." The message was blunt, this was the time for residents to get on board. "There is no time to lose... Be a promoter: spread the word to your friends and neighbors. Join a local land trust. Plan a fundraiser or educational event. Donate money, an easement or land. Support the conservation warrants at town meeting. Together, we can do it!" In 2004, 2500 acres in town were protected from development; an additional 2010 acres would bring open space protected to about 25% of town acreage.

The December article included a boxed message from Arnold, Hardwick, Lavallee, and Pyle: "We have been getting a lot of positive feedback from readers, about this series of articles on protecting open space which has run in the last few issues of *The Francestown News*. As we continue to delve into this critical topic, we hope everyone, including us, will become more knowledgeable about both the threats and opportunities. We thank you for your encouragement, and for your involvement. Together, we can preserve and protect a vital part of what we all love about our community."

THE BIG BOND

The campaign of articles and ads stretched to eight months by Town Meeting in March of 2005. The January 2005 issue of TFN explained that the

Conservation Commission would propose a bond for land purchase at Town Meeting and opined on "Financing Francestown's Future." The ConCom held a public hearing in February to solicit commentary on the proposed bond and the land acquisition plan. An expository article in the March issue, "Bond to Save Open Spaces," asserted that "The bond will have no impact on taxes in 2005... [In 2006] for a $300,000 property, [it] amounts to $170 a year – or less than $15 a month, or 50 cents a day... the financial impact of the bond is offset by the economic advantages to the community of open space (e.g., forestry jobs and relatively lower costs imposed on a community by open space as compared to residential development that might otherwise occur)."

At Town Meeting 2005, attendance was much greater than usual. The Warrant Article passed, 264 to 44, and when the vote was announced, the meeting erupted in cheers. The advertisement in the April 2005 TFN said "Congratulations Francestown" and announced three celebratory hikes. Awaiting the bond approval was a stockpile of $786,000 of matching donations and grants that were available to the town. Later in 2005, the Planning Board discussed cooperation with the ConCom to map "significantly important lands" in town and to adopt "smart growth" policies.

The 2010 goal was achieved by the fall of 2010. A 2008 report at the "halfway" mark, celebrated various conservation easements either donated to, or purchased by, the town or private conservancies. One example was a "neighborhood collaboration" along Red House Road where five neighboring families teamed up to conserve close to 200 acres of forest, wetland, and farmland. Another coalition of neighbors set aside lands in the Whiting Brook drainage from the Candlewood-Kingsbury Hill area. Other steps toward 2010 acres included a tract on the eastern slope of Bradford Hill, and a thousand feet of river frontage and a riparian plain along the Piscataquog. Across the north side of town between the Turnpike and Old County Road North easements were donated which preserved almost 250 acres linked to the Dinsmore Brook Conservation area. The ConCom bought an easement on a property at Russell Station and Cressy Hill roads which was owned by the PWA. An easement was donated on one of the few remaining unprotected tracts of land on the south slope of Crotched Mountain contiguous with the town forest.

The role of willing local landowners to conserve their properties was essential, but the availability of government and private agency grants was critical. It was somewhat serendipitous that robust funding was available in the early 2000s from an array of sources including a program administered by a new Francestown resident. The federal Land and Water Conservation Fund (LWCF) was administered by the NH Division of Parks and Recreation. Other important sources of funding were LCHIP, the Aquatic Resource Mitigation Fund (ARM), the Forest Legacy Program, and the Farmland Protection Program. A key individual in the coalition of Francestown's ConCom, FLT, and PWA (PLC) was Gordon Russell. Russell's personal generosity, his encyclopedic knowledge of the land and water resources of the region, and his charisma carried a lot of weight in the land preservation campaign. Russell had been in the group that founded the PWA, which included two women from Francestown, Pat Place and Connie Varnum.

Funds from the bond were combined with almost a million dollars in grants and donations to purchase or protect over 1000 acres around Shattuck Pond, to be known as the Shattuck Pond Conservation Area. In a 2007 article in TFN, Hardwick explained that almost 90% of the conserved acreage was open to the public for hiking, snowmobiling, cycling, and riding. "Every lot conserved so far has inspired and motivated an abutting landowner(s) to add to the core habitat area."

Another backland area with important water source implications was the Dinsmore Brook-Collins Brook area on the northside of town. This area became the focus of the "Headwaters Project" in 2007. The ConCom called a special hearing to take comment on the possible acquisition using Con Fund dollars of more than 200 acres of this watershed property. Protecting this watershed created a wildlife corridor extending from the Deering-Francestown line to the Shattuck Pond Conservation Area, and on to the Crotched Mountain Town Forest. Another motivation was a rumor that this land, close to the golf course and ski area, was being eyed for housing development. Those who spoke at the ConCom hearing were enthusiastic about the Headwaters Project. Subsequently, in cooperation with the Russell Foundation and the Francestown Land Trust, the ConCom acquired land from the owners of the golf course. Conservation easements were arranged on areas abutting this purchase including substantial acreage from George Sanderson. Later, a documentary film about the Headwaters Project was made by Francestown's Hilary Graham, with the support of Gordon Russell, the PWA, FLT, and the ConCom.

After more than two years of effort by a coalition of landowners and several area land trusts, over 1000 acres that drain into three tributaries of the Piscataquog River -- Cold, Rand, and Brennan Brooks – were conserved. This area between the south slope of Crotched Mountain and the northside of Rose Mountain, includes some of the richest wildlife habitat in the state. The three brooks have excellent water quality and a diversity of aquatic life.

In 2010, with the goal in reach, 52 acres along Russell Station Road at the Rand Brook confluence were purchased by the ConCom with the easement held by FLT. Also, large tracts were protected in the Bullard Hill-Brennan Brook area, in the Old County Road South National Heritage District, and at the far end of Old County Road North. Using an LCHIP grant more land was added to the Dinsmore Brook Conservation area.

In October 2010, the ConCom and FLT announced the campaign had reached its goal. Approximately $6 million of land in Francestown was protected. Most of the conserved land was part of one of three blocks: the Shattuck Pond-Dinsmore Brook area, the Rand Brook-Piscataquog River confluence area, and Crotched Mountain. Several celebratory hikes were held on November 6, 2010, followed by a dinner at Town Hall.

In 1994 town forests totaled 712 acres, almost all of it acquired from 1987 to 1990. By 2012 town-owned conservation land encompassed 2120 acres, most acquired between 2005-2010. The ConCom also held easement responsibilities on over 800 additional acres. By 2020, between FLT and the ConCom, fee-owned lands and properties protected by conservation easements total about 6,000 acres in Francestown, well-above the 25% goal recommended by the Forest Society in the early 2000s.

A Pause to Reflect

In 2011 the ConCom chose to pause its land protection initiative and check with town residents regarding future activity. The commission held four community forums with help from the Monadnock Community Conservation Partnership, NH Fish and Game, and UNH Cooperative Extension to begin creating a new conservation strategic plan. If the public wanted to move forward on the same trajectory, the ConCom wanted to know which specific areas of town should be targeted for protection. The new strategic plan was completed in 2013. The plan called for a slowdown in land acquisition by the town. The ConCom would focus only on the highest priority areas such as the Dinsmore-Collins Brook Headwaters. From 2014-2020 most of the primary land protection activity in Francestown was advanced by FLT and other private conservancies.

The slowdown was not a stop. Momentum had been generated by the 2010 by 2010 campaign. Even as the ConCom's plan was being developed, the land preservation coalition – ConCom, FLT, PLC – worked with landowners to create two memorial forests in 2014. The owners made their lands available to the local conservation coalition at below market prices. One of the new memorial forests included the upper reaches of Brennan Brook and Brennan Falls. That tract completed a 2,600-acre block under the protection of the ConCom and four land conservancies. The other memorial forest was a large acreage off Old County Road North with 1300 feet of frontage on Collins Brook. It joined a block of more than 2000 acres that included the Dinsmore Brook and Shattuck Pond conservation areas.

The Conservation Commission marked its 50th anniversary in 2015. In the last half-decade prior to 2020, the ConCom focused on management of its holdings. A typical ConCom year included the annual roadside clean-up for Earth Day, distributing tree seedlings to FES kids, monitoring easements, hosting hikes in town forests, and offering workshops for town residents on conservation topics. With the presence of Emerald Ash Borers in town, the ConCom educated the community on ways to mitigate spread of this tree-killing invasive. The ConCom assisted the Planning Board by following up on ZBA applications for variances in shoreland and wetland districts, as well as formal complaints submitted to NH DES for violations of shoreland and wetland regulations. A Natural Resource Inventory was completed, and the Planning Board adopted it during the Master Plan process. Management Plans are periodically updated for town forests and conservation areas.

Motorized vehicle use of town lands has been controversial over the last twenty-five years. Many residents use ATVs/ORVs recreationally. For several years in the early 2000s, the Select Board approved residents' requests for ATV/ORV use of Class VI roads on a case-by-case basis. In 2014 the board withdrew all prior permissions given to use town roads. However, the ConCom worked cooperatively with snow sled organizations to maintain trails in Shattuck Pond and Dinsmore Brook and Crotched Mountain conservation properties.

Conservation advocates held sway over land use policymaking in Francestown for the last thirty years, although there were periodic disagreements about how the Planning Board and Zoning Board administered land use regulations. An example from the latter days of the 1970-2020 era came about in 2016 when the Planning Board held a hearing on Ron and Melissa Shattuck's subdivision of their property along the river near the junction of the turnpike and Cross Road. The hearings illustrated the ongoing struggle in town to define what it means to "preserve the rural character of the community."

In the hearing, the Conservation Commission provided a report recommending that the Shattucks consider a "cluster type" of housing development. A cluster subdivision brings the structure built on each separate lot into closer proximity, leaving a greater amount of undeveloped open space. The ConCom's suggestion initiated vigorous discussion by the board about the appropriate balance between applying the land use ordinance in a manner that maximizes the property owner's right to use their land as they see fit, and a desire to preserve as much open space as possible. A Planning Board member spoke in favor of "trying to keep development as far away from the river as possible" to preserve the "wildlife corridor" along the river. Another asserted that "it is imperative upon us to be stewards of our river in Francestown to benefit the remainder of the people" in the watershed, "it is important to retain the coolness of the river...and the canopy...for the wildlife corridor to function." Countering this sentiment, a member of the board spoke in favor of not compromising the rights of private property owners, "Francestown's subdivision regulations are, in effect, a complete bridle upon a property owner's ability to do with his property pretty much what he wants to do." He added, "I see an effort to impose upon them the god of conservation. What right do we have to tell somebody that they need to do cluster housing?" While acknowledging the value of conservation, several board members embraced the position that the job of the Planning Board was to make sure the land use regulations are followed but not "to tell someone to do something with their land that is outside the scope of our Master Plan." One board member objected to what she saw as prioritizing the rights of wildlife over human rights.

The Shattuck family and the Planning Board reached an agreement which called for the family to create a conservation easement along the river. The Planning Board chair summarized the effort to find balance when he stated, "People have rights for what they do with their land as long as they are not adversely affecting our environment."

FRANCESTOWN LAND TRUST

In 2004, Francestown Land Conservation, Inc. (FLC) changed its name to the Francestown Land Trust (FLT). FLC was born in 1986 with the hope that it could be a useful partner to the Conservation Commission in its initial campaign to preserve open space in Francestown. In 1987, Scot Heath, then chair of the Conservation Commission, teamed up with several conservation-minded residents and founded FLC. A local attorney drew up the incorporation papers. FLC's initial foray into easements was bumpy. The ConCom wanted to accept an easement donation, but the Select Board blocked it. Conservation easements were a new concept at the time and were not well understood by town leaders. The Harris Center in Hancock accepted the easement pending the creation of FLC; the easement was then transferred to FLC in 1989 becoming its first tract of protected land. As a registered 501(c)(3) tax exempt organization, FLT can hold and monitor conservation easements, negotiate land transfers, and, with public support, purchase sensitive properties. FLT is a completely volunteer organization that relies on private donations for its work and is legally separate from the town's Conservation Commission.

For the next 10 years the land trust was dormant. The ConCom's role in acquiring and protecting new acreage downshifted and the funding atmosphere in New Hampshire was lean. In November 1998, an article was published in *The Francestown News* with the headline "Francestown Land Protection Organization Seeks New Members." It was a pitch for the Francestown Land Conservation's (FLC) re-awakening after a decade of somnambulance: "Today, with growing development pressure spreading out from the Manchester-Nashua corridor and evident in new developments in New Boston and Lyndeborough, there is a renewed need for an organization such as FLC... At its 1998 annual meeting...an entire new board of directors was elected to 'reinvigorate' the organization."

The time was ripe given the ConCom's revived interest in land preservation, new fears of suburbanization, and the state's initiation of new conservation grant programs. Serendipitously, the new FLC board was presented with the opportunity to buy the Rand Brook tract. The purchase was accomplished in 2000. The initial 223 acres were purchased with money raised from 153 individuals. By 2020, several additional parcels acquired or in easements brought the preserve to 581 acres, most of which has additional protection of conservation easements held by the PLC and SPNHF. The Francestown Land Trust manages the Rand Brook Forest to protect critical water resources and habitat that supports biodiversity. They encourage educational and recreational use of the area.

Momentum built as more and more landowners in Francestown became enthusiastic about permanent protection of undeveloped land. A "flywheel effect" kicked in. By 2011, technically the 25th anniversary of the organization, the FLT Newsletter reported that "more than 400 individuals and 10 foundations and government agencies have worked [with FLT] to protect over 1,425 acres. This is in addition to 1000+ acres of land protected by 'partners' in Francestown over the last decade." Chair Dennis Calcutt observed that "We have arrived at our 25th anniversary having grown from a small core of concerned and dedicated citizens to a concerned and dedicated community partnering successfully with other organizations. Our accomplishments have been the work of many for the benefit of all. Our strongest asset may be our vision of the common good." For most of the last twenty years the FLT Board has been led by Chairs Dr. Greg Neilley, Dennis Calcutt, Chris Rogers, and Larry Ames. A few stalwart board members have served more than twenty years: Neilley, Ben Haubrich, and Dr. Barry Wicklow. Research within the watershed by Wicklow, a wildlife biologist, was critical to FLT's grant applications. Wicklow's enthusiasm and outreach to owners of high value conservation land was a decisive factor in many FLT projects. Herb Bromberg and Abigail Arnold held seats for more than ten years. In 2010, Arnold received the Gordon Russell Award from the PLC for her work on conservation in Francestown.

During Neilley's term as chair of FLT, protected acreage doubled and FLT began publishing a twice-yearly newsletter, initiated an annual fund campaign, and contributed an educational article to each month's *Francestown News*. The board began advocating for a "headwaters strategy," protecting environmentally sensitive acres along Cold, Brennan, and Rand brooks which feed into the Piscataquog River. The "2010" coalition of FLT, PLC, and ConCom, in cooperation with the Russell Foundation, Monadnock Conservancy and SPNHF, executed the headwaters preservation plan. This eventually led to the conservation of 1,000 acres of land in the watershed formed by the south slope of Crotched Mountain and across the valley to the north slopes of Rose Mountain where Lyndeborough, Greenfield, and Francestown converge.

In 2011, FLT launched a "Rand to Avery Brook" campaign to continue to build a block around the confluence of Rand Brook with the Piscataquog and along the river itself. The trust received a substantial Aquatic Resource Mitigation (ARM) grant to conserve and restore the Avery Brook catchment area. The local conservation coalition collaborated to protect 500 acres in Francestown through six projects including a 180-acre easement from the

Millers in the Avery Brook watershed with Piscataquog River frontage, and an easement from the Tenneys.

The protection of the upper reach of Brennan Brook was noted earlier in this chapter. The FLT Newsletter from 2013 explains the significance of this land: "Brennan Falls and the area behind the village ... has been a recreational area for townspeople since the 1800s. The 1895 Town History made note of the 'remarkable fall of 20 feet, oft visited by ramblers and romance-lovers' ... In terms of cultural and historical significance, the property also contains the summit of Oak Hill, the general area northwest of the village which was the earliest settlement in Francestown proper (1767) .... Brennan Brook, is one of the most important headwaters to the South Branch of the Piscataquog, a state protected river."

Acquisitions of fee-owned land and conservation easements continued steadily from 2014 to 2020. An agricultural easement at the "gateway to Francestown" on New Boston Road was donated to FLT. A large acreage that became part of the ConCom's Collins Brook and Dinsmore Brook Headwaters Project was purchased by FLT with an LCHIP grant. A family donated almost 70 acres lying between Journey's End Road and Scobie Pond as a memorial forest. FLT bought 100 acres off Wilson Hill Road with an LCHIP grant to add to the Collins Brook Headwaters preserve. A life-long resident sold FLT an easement on forty acres of prime agricultural land along the turnpike, and two families donated a total of 51 acres off Cross Road and along Route 47, respectively, in 2019.

A unique project began in 2018 which combined a private conservation-recreation-historical preservation initiative with the ongoing land protection efforts of the ConCom and FLT. It had long been a stretch goal of conservation-minded individuals in Francestown to conserve several land parcels around Route 47 on the north side of town that sit between the Crotched Mountain Town Forest, the Shattuck Pond Town Forest, and the Dinsmore Brook Conservation Area. This area was considered important to connect a "green corridor" across Francestown. In 2018, this conservation goal began to take shape by becoming linked with a personal vision of Jim and Cindy St. Jean to create a network of mountain bike and walking trails in Francestown. In 2018, they worked with the ConCom and many volunteers to build the first mountain bike trail in the Fisher Hill Town Forest. In 2019, the St. Jeans acquired the "Huberman tract" along the Turnpike north of the village, which abuts the Fisher Hill Forest, and donated a conservation easement to FLT. They expanded the network of mountain bike trails onto this land. That tract also has substantial historical significance, including a retired section of the original 2nd NH Turnpike, Signature Rock, the Fisher family homestead, 18th century cellar holes, and a reputed site of one of the town's early schoolhouses. Later, the St. Jeans assisted FLT with the purchase of the Aires land across Rt. 47, which had long been an FLT target parcel. Finally, the St. Jeans acquired the remaining two adjacent parcels to complete the green corridor, working with FLT to secure conservation easements. This combination of town, FLT, and St. Jean properties consists of over 180 acres devoted to conservation and recreation. "Turnpike Trails" not only provides an extensive mountain bike and walking trail system for public recreational use, it also serves as an important wildlife corridor. Additionally, the project's plan calls for the St. Jeans to work with FIHS, the Heritage Museum, and local historians to document and recognize the history of the families who originally lived on these parcels.

By 2020, FLT held 1,209 acres of fee-owned land, and 1,749 acres of conservation easements. The Land Trust maintains a website, publishes a semi-annual newsletter, leads hikes through its properties, and has provided financial support for an environmental education program run by the Harris Center for Conservation Education in the Francestown Elementary School. It also partners with the Francestown Conservation Commission, *The Francestown News,* and the George Holmes Bixby Memorial Library in the Joan Hanchett Nature Series.

The ConCom paused its aggressive land acquisition and took the temperature of the town's residents with respect to open space preservation. However, FLT and other conservancies continued to buy and accept easements on a steadily increasing amount of acreage. The Planning Board has been vigilant in applying land use regulations to proposed development. Community residents continue to repeat the mantra of "preserving the rural character of the community," with rural understood, essentially, as the way it is now, and has been for several decades. The "2010 by 2010" campaign defined Francestown by insulating it from substantial development and preserving the aesthetic, cultural, and socio-economic nature of the town for the foreseeable future.

TOWN HALL RENOVATION

The significance of the Town Hall renovation of 2017 is a measure of change in how residents view town government's scope of responsibility. By the mid-2000s, the Yankee tradition of limited government authority and budgetary parsimony had waned. This project illustrates the extent to which residents want their municipal government to act boldly, and their willingness to pay for it.

The Francestown Academy building housed a private high school until the 1920s when it was donated to the town. It was renamed Town Hall. From the 1950s until 1982, the Select Board had an office in this building where they stored the town's official documents and met weekly to administer town business. The facility was used for town meetings, elections, Grange meetings, and indoor recess and recreation for Red School students. It was also used by FIHS for board and membership meetings and other events such as the rummage sale and the FVFD's ham and bean dinner on Labor Day.

Periodically, the Select Board would approve its use for basketball with first floor the windows covered, and backboards set up. When the Recreation Commission began sponsoring dance and exercise classes, they were held at Town Hall, as were Mary Jane Marsden's weekly Contra dances in the summer. Once the new Fire House on the turnpike was built, the Select Board moved to what became the Town Hall Annex. No official town business was conducted in Town Hall apart from elections and Town Meeting, or an occasional special public meeting where attendance was anticipated to exceed fifty people.

Like several of the older buildings in town – the Meeting House, the horse sheds, the Community Church – regular care and maintenance was expensive and never ending. These buildings received enough maintenance to keep them going, but nothing more. During the 1970s-1980s, the heating of Town Hall often was shut down during the winter. Private donations for maintenance projects were received from time to time. In the late 1960s, FIHS, the Fire Department, and the Grange replaced the curtains on the stage. In 1972, money was raised by FIHS to have a new eagle built for the top of the cupola; the original eagle was saved and is now on display in the Heritage Museum. When the Community Theatre group began using the building for their productions in 1990, they donated their proceeds to repair the stage.

The chickens began to come home to roost in 2000. The state Attorney General rejected use of the building for elections due to accessibility issues and voting was moved to the Town Offices. By 2003, the second floor of the building was closed by order of the fire chief. He found the floor to be "spongy." A structural engineer was called, floorboards were removed to expose the joists, and every joist examined was seriously split. Where there had been concerns in the past about the soundness of the second story, it was addressed by the installation of yet another layer of flooring. Eventually, when demolition took place, three separate floors had to be removed.

HERITAGE COMMISSION

In 2002, an ad hoc committee "to review Town Hall" was formed. That Town Hall Study Committee reported to the Select Board in 2005 recommending a "phased renovation of the building." Coincidentally, at Town Meeting 2005, a Warrant Article was approved creating a Heritage Commission (HC). State legislation encouraged towns to establish Heritage Commissions to recognize, manage, and protect historical and cultural resources. The statutory duties of Heritage Commissions were extensive.

Members in the Commission's initial years included Diane Curran, Charlie Curran, Roon Frost, Jan Griffin, Stephen Griffin, Kay Severance, Peter Bixby, Joe Ludwig, Silas Little, Mary Lindstrom, Ann Stewart, and Bobby Abbott.

Initially, the HC focused on surveying historic sites and structures and applying for official designations. As early as 1980, a section of Old County

Road South and adjacent roadways had been designated as an historic district by the National Register of Historic Places. This included nine houses, from the baseball field south to Starrett Farm, including homes on Birdsall Road and Stevens Road. The commission began the process of getting recognition for Main Street, Mill Village, the Common, and other individual structures. A consultant told the commission that federal designation, though the most prestigious, was difficult to achieve. He encouraged them to seek state historic designation for most of the targeted structures and places. In 2008 and 2010, the Main Street and Mill Village districts were added to the NH Register of Historic Places, along with the Town Hall/Francestown Academy, the Butterfield Block/Beehive, the Moses Eaton home on Bible Hill, the Samuel Nutt-Joseph Kingsbury farm, and the Caleb-Weston House on Oak Hill Road. In July 2016, the Francestown Common was added to the National Register of Historic Places.

The official condemnation of the second floor of Town Hall brought the structure onto the Select Board's agenda in 2007. The board turned to the Heritage Commission to investigate options and to seek grants for renovation funds. The commission applied for grants for emergency repairs. Its first grant, $4,000, was obtained in 2010. That fall, the commission held a public meeting where residents shared their visions of the future of Town Hall. Shortly after that meeting, Maureen von Rosenvinge became chair of the Heritage Commission. This was an important step. She had a passion for the project and brought a great deal of energy and drive.

Mike Petrovick, a Francestown resident and architect, and Ted Fellows, a structural engineer, produced a comprehensive Architectural and Structural Report on the building. They concluded that structural supports for both floors were inadequate and unsafe. Their report led to the closing of the building for meetings of any kind until repairs were completed. Other deficiencies were also identified. The roof structure was stressed due to failing trusses and joists. The addition built in the 1930s was poorly constructed and separating from the main building. Heating, electrical and plumbing were inadequate and not code compliant. The building did not conform to the Americans with Disabilities Act (ADA).

Glenn Dodge, a member of the New Hampshire Timber Framers' Guild and an experienced renovator of timber framed buildings, was brought in for immediate truss repair. The commission was able to get an emergency grant from the New Hampshire Land and Community Heritage Investment Project (LCHIP) for the structural work. Dodge repaired the queen truss and added first floor supports in the basement to make the floor safe for public use. As he made these repairs, Dodge discovered that the bell tower was in danger of collapse unless steel beams were added for support. Dodge's work expanded to include the entire roof truss system and continued through 2012. The cost rose to $100,000. Town Meeting 2012 approved payment for these repairs. This represented an important threshold for the project's future. Town residents, for the first time, committed a large amount of tax revenue to preserving the building. Francestown resident and engineer, Henry Kunhardt, was contracted to oversee and coordinate all Town Hall renovation work.

Von Rosenvinge and the Heritage Commission put out a Requests for Proposals (RFP) based on the Petrovick, Fellows, and Dodge assessments of the building's needs. The RFP went beyond emergency repairs and included future renovations and architectural plans for that work. Von Rosenvinge reported to the Select Board that continued emergency repairs called for another $58,000 in 2013 and estimated that $550,000 would be necessary to make Town Hall "a functioning building." Later in the year at a public meeting two general plans for renovation were offered. The overall project estimate expanded to $900,000.

Town Meeting 2013 approved more funds for structural repairs to the basement and first floor. In addition to town funds, Pleasant Pond resident and philanthropist Andrew Houston donated $25,000, and LCHIP approved a grant for roof repair. In 2013, the Heritage Commission held an Activity Day/Volunteer Fair in the horse sheds with LCHIP personnel in attendance. The purpose was to demonstrate to LCHIP that the community was embracing the project. Town Hall designs were available for public examination. This event coincided with the dedication of the Heritage Museum.

The Heritage Commission recommended that Town Meeting 2014 approve a bond for a town contribution to the renovation project. The bond would be issued only if other funding sources were not obtained. The Select Board and Budget Committee were not unanimous in support of the bond proposal, but it did go forward to the Warrant. Von Rosenvinge explained that a future LCHIP grant would depend on whether the town supported the project. Essentially, the bond would serve as "seed money" to attract grants.

SKEPTICISM

Before the vote at Town Meeting, and in the public meetings that followed that spring, some residents expressed skepticism about whether a full renovation of Town Hall was necessary. They sought assurance that the building merited a $1 million price tag. A native resident described his skepticism. "Those who have moved into town in the past couple of decades or so have a different view of the role of the Town Hall than long-time residents have. Newer residents see Town Hall as a town center, but it has never been that. It was an auxiliary building not a primary building. It just wasn't used that much. It was one thing for a private organization to rehabilitate the Meeting House, which had been a key building in town, as the town's original, architecturally beautiful church. But the Town Hall is a worn-out, cast-aside school building with no architectural merit. Keeping the building from collapsing is probably worth doing, but it should not be treated as if it is an architectural treasure. A few hundred thousand dollars would have made the first floor useful." Given that renovation plans for the project and a proposed bond were coming forward at a time when the town was facing the need to repair or replace several bridges, some residents questioned which was a more important priority. The Select Board explained that while there were fifteen town bridges in need of work, and nine were on the states' "red list," state aid would finance the cost of most bridge work. Neither the Select Board nor the Budget Committee recommended the bond to voters. The BAC was split. Yet, Town Meeting 2014 approved a $350,000 bond by more than two-thirds, 132-46. The overall estimated project cost at this point was $880,000.

Two public meetings were held in May and June of 2014 to solicit citizen input on the draft designs. Between the two meetings, Maureen von Rosenvinge passed away. This was not a propitious time for new leadership; von Rosenvinge had been an important champion of the project. In these meetings, Petrovick described what must be done to make the building code compliant for public assembly. He reported that architectural historian James Garvin had assessed the building and identified the character defining features that ought to be preserved. At these meetings it was clear that LCHIP funding was going to drive the direction of the project. The top priority for LCHIP to provide funding was ADA compliance. New, accessible bathrooms were essential. In December, a large LCHIP grant was approved.

Once LCHIP funding was announced, the town hired an owner's representative, a project management firm, and a general contractor – MacMillan. By November of 2015, the estimated cost of the project rose to $999,000. The balance in the building fund was $713,000. This included the town's bond, the LCHIP grant, Heritage Commission funds, pledges, and grants applied for but not yet received. In December 2015, a "face the facts" meeting was held between the Heritage Commission, the Select Board, and the project's "Working Committee." The Working Committee combined representatives from the Heritage Commission, the architect, and the contractors hired for the project. Fundraising had stalled. MacMillan's representative clarified that fundraising had to be completed before the project could begin.

Frustration bubbled up from members of the Heritage Commission. Fingers were pointed. One member of the commission asked that "the record note her comment:" "We were promised the final numbers in September, now we're in a position that we have eleven days to raise over $300,000." Others rejoined that for a year and a half the architect had been saying that the project would run between $950,000 to $1,000,000, so a price tag of $999,000 shouldn't come as a huge surprise. A lengthy discussion ensued regarding what the original plan was, what was voted on at Town Meeting, who was responsible for fund-raising, the Select Board's role, the possibility of a second bond, and how the project could go forward if funding fell short. The Select Board announced on December 21, 2015, that the project would not be launched in 2016.

With some "cost engineering" the price of the project was scaled down to $955,000. Andrew Houston donated another $100,000. It was a matching grant and drew in several thousand more. An array of events was held to raise more funds. As they had in 2015, the Brocks held another Halloween costume party-dance fundraiser. Town Meeting 2017 approved a Warrant Article contributing $125,000 from the town's Undesignated Fund Balance. Following Town Meeting 2017 the contract with MacMillan was signed, work began and continued into the fall.

A dedication ceremony for the newly renovated Town Hall was hosted by the Heritage Commission in November 2017. The first event held in the new structure was a Veterans' Day celebration hosted by the Patriotic Purposes Committee. For the first time in many years, Town Meeting and elections were moved back into Town Hall. The project received a Preservation Achievement Award from the NH Preservation Alliance. In 2017 the Friends of Town Hall undertook a "Quilt Project," initiated by Ruth Behrsing, to improve both the aesthetics and the acoustics of the auditoriums. The following year, Bev Abbott, a life-long daughter of Francestown, donated new stage curtains. In 2020, the town re-roofed the building, while the structure of the horse sheds was being shored up.

The significance of the Town Hall renovation project is that the town took responsibility for it. That is a measure of just how far the town had come in providing a full range of municipal services and embracing a greater scope of municipal government responsibility. This would not have happened in 1970, 1980, 1990, or, probably, 2000. Between 2010 and 2020 the town's evolution from Yankee parsimoniousness to a more cosmopolitan sensibility was evident.

CHAPTER 6

KEY ORGANIZATIONS

One of the benefits of living in Francestown is the opportunity to join and play an active part in the "associational life" of the town through service organizations and affinity groups. This chapter profiles several essential town organizations. Two of the organizations are "quasi-governmental." That is, they perform functions that in larger towns or cities would be done by the municipal government or they act as an auxiliary: the **Volunteer Fire Department (FVFD)** and the **Improvement and Historical Society (FIHS)**. The FVFD is a department of the town government. Its facilities and equipment are owned by the town, and its budget and capital spending are authorized by Town Meeting. Yet it is self-governing to a substantial extent. For example, the volunteers elect the fire chief. Other organizations that have been meaningful to many residents are service organizations like the **Community Church (CCF)**, the **Old Meeting House, Inc. (OMH)**, and the **Oak Hill Grange (OHG)**. Most of the local clubs are affinity groups, bringing together people with a common interest. The Garden Club and the theatre troupes fit this description. Often these organizations provide an educational function. They relay information and teach skills. Scouting and 4-H are examples.

The four principal organizations featured in this chapter – FVFD, CCF, FIHS, and OMH -- have been pillars in Francestown society through the fifty years from 1970-2020. The two museums in town are profiled as well. They are recent "spin-offs" of FVFD and FIHS and are key connectors between the town's future and its past. The last section of the chapter includes short descriptions of smaller organizations. Not all residents are engaged in associational life, but for many, participation has defined their life in Francestown.

VOLUNTEER FIRE DEPARTMENT AND THE FIRE AUXILIARY

In 1937, Bob Cutter, Tommie Stewart, Royal Cleaves, and Arthur Lord organized the volunteer fire department. There were fire fighters prior to this new organization but previous efforts were more *ad hoc* than dependable. The vestigial Village Fire District, which had no practical existence after 1937, turned over its assets to the town in 1970: eight fire ponds, a hose carrier, and an antique hand-tub pumper. The "hand tub" was rehabilitated and is on display in the Heritage Museum. In the 1970s-1980s, the FVFD participated in regional parades displaying the antique pumper. In June of 1976, for example, at the Wilton Old Home Days parade, the Hand Tub crew included Deputy Chief Lawrence Kullgren, Ron Kullgren, Jay Irwin, John Paige, Joel Behrsing,

Rick Miller, Steve Miller, and the team's mascots – the Kullgren twins (Larry and David), then age 4.

The FVFD's founders recruited young Norman Stewart who went on to serve as chief for 25 years, from 1947-1972, and Clifton Foote who joined at age sixteen. Clifton Foote was Norm Stewart's deputy chief beginning in 1957. He became chief in 1973 and served until 1987. Don Abbott joined the department in the 1970s and succeeded Foote as chief from 1987- 2008. His leadership was followed by Larry Kullgren – one of the twins -- the son of former Deputy Chief Lawrence Kullgren. The chief and other command officers are elected by the membership. Compared to any other institution in Francestown, FVFD's continuity of leadership says a lot about the institutional strength of the organization and the dedication of its leaders. For many years, the leaders of the FVFD were also leaders on town boards, committees, and commissions. In the 1970s, Clifton Foote, Lawrence Kullgren, Robert Cutter, Dick Leavitt, Harry Varnum, Charles Brien, Louis Wiederhold, Alan Thulander and Don Hoyt were not just FVFD leaders, they were also elected or appointed leaders in town government. By the 2000s, there was more specialization and less overlap.

At the annual Town Meeting election, voters select "Fire Wards." Their responsibility is to oversee the FVFD's budget, to review how funds are spent, and to ensure that the department operates within financial procedures established by the town. The elected fire wards have always been members of the FVFD.

In the booklet he published to commemorate the 50th anniversary of the FVFD in 1987, Alan Thulander observed that from its inception, and particularly in the years after 1970, the FVFD has sought continual improvement of the town's firefighting and rescue equipment. In 1962, the decrepit former schoolhouse on the Common was demolished and a fire station was erected. It included a meeting room on the second floor dedicated to Paul Bradbury, a highly respected member of the FVFD in the 1940s-1960s. The Village Improvement Society contributed to the creation of this space and for years the Bradbury Room was where town committees and organizations met. The FVFD eventually outgrew the small structure. A study committee, chaired by Willis Fluhr, recommended that a new fire house be built. At special sessions of Town Meeting in 1980 voters approved the recommendation and the town bought land on the NH Turnpike South. The new firehouse was completed in 1982 at a cost of $100,000. A new meeting room was constructed by Don Hoyt and Al Van Cleave and outfitted with donations from the Oak Hill Grange and the Ladies Auxiliary.

By the late 1970s, like the rest of town governance, the trajectory of the FVFD was modernization in equipment and service delivery. A Rescue Squad was formed using an old Army ambulance. A capital reserve account was started to facilitate regular replacement of fire apparatus. Some equipment was purchased with the assistance from the proceeds of the FVFD's Labor Day Ham and Bean dinner. For many years, members of the FVFD went door-to-door prior to Labor Day collecting food contributions and soliciting pie donations. Chief Foote encouraged training to increase the department's professionalism. Sunday mornings at 10:00 a.m. were the weekly training sessions, which coincided with the start of the Community Church's service. Coincidence? Many couples in town divided their attendance with the wife attending church while the husband expressed his devotion to fire service. Under Donny Abbott's and Larry Kullgren's leadership, as new and more sophisticated equipment was added, training took on an even greater emphasis.

Fire Department Growth

For most of the 1970s, the data available on fire "calls" is sketchy. Based on the encyclopedic annual reports in subsequent years, it is fair to say that activity varied considerably from year to year. For example, in 1980 there were six structure fires, while in the preceding three years combined there had been five. The FVFD in 1980 had 25 volunteers who were equipped with a 1969 pumper, 1958 and 1947 tankers, a forestry truck, a generator unit, a tractor, the old rescue van, and a resuscitator. There were dry hydrants and fire ponds at various locations throughout the town. Rescue calls and chimney fires made up half of the 81 calls to the FVFD that year. In 1999, FVFD received over 100 calls for the first time.

In 1994 the FVFD voted to remain an entirely volunteer organization, rather than hiring paid staff. Increasingly, the number of volunteers employed locally decreased, which meant there were fewer personnel available to respond to a daytime fire. Because of this, mutual aid calls for assistance from the fire or rescue crews of adjacent towns grew in importance. The Master Plan of 1995 observed that the need for more volunteers had no easy solution. Those moving to town have been less likely to volunteer due to their work situations -- their commute, the number of hours they work -- or their prior experience of how fire services were provided. In 2000, there were about 25 active members. The FVFD reported that "volunteer pride and spirit remain strong." By the late 2000-teens, more than half of the FVFD volunteers had lived in town for more than 20 years, and 80% for more than 10 years. The intensive training requirements deterred membership for men and women with young families.

The Master Plan of 1995 reported that a capital reserve program was established to fully fund the replacement of vehicles. Each major vehicle has a useful life of 30 years – 15 as a first line vehicle and 15 as a second line. Admiringly, the Master Plan added that "despite significant inflation in the cost of fire equipment, fire department expenditures as a percent of total town spending declined from 16% in 1980 to 8% in 1990." Although other department's budgets had grown, careful maintenance of equipment and private donations from the Mount Crotchet Firefighters' Association and the Women's Auxiliary kept the Fire Department's costs down.

The Mt. Crotchet Firefighters' Association (MCFA) was organized by Alan Thulander and chartered as a not-for-profit in 1992. Thulander believed if the FVFD wanted better equipment it would need supplementary funding through donations and grants. He understood that the Select Board and Town Meeting were frugal. Grants written by the MCFA helped FVFD obtain an emergency generator, a rescue boat, and a new rescue vehicle. After Thulander reduced his participation in the MCFA, Mark Pitman became the primary grant-writer.

Known originally as the "Ladies Auxiliary," this organization was officially founded in 1971. Betty Stewart and Debbie Adams, Norm's wife, and daughter, were an unofficial auxiliary providing coffee and cookies. When Clifton Foote became chief, Liz Foote started the official Auxiliary alongside Joan Kullgren. In 2020 the organization was still exclusively female. It has outgrown the adjective "ladies," though the women of the Auxiliary certainly are that. Initially, leadership fell to the wife of the chief, and the wives of other command personnel served as officers. In 1974 a report by Town Historian Connie Dodge stated "the members think of themselves as an 'arm' of the FVFD, rendering assistance in times of fire or other disasters. They have all received first aid training, are knowledgeable in manning the radio in the fire house, and in answering the call to duty when ambulance service has been called, by reporting to the fire station to aid in any way needed. They also furnish hot coffee and sandwiches at times of disaster."

Through the 1970s-90s, the Auxiliary made first aid kits for firemen's cars, stocked the firehouse kitchen and "disaster pantry," operated the radio during fire emergencies, bought a large percolator for the station, catered periodic dinner meetings for fire wardens, and held receptions, parties, and dances for socialization and fundraising. Parties were a big part of FVFD life. In 1975 the Auxiliary hosted a "Halloween Freaky Frolic" costume party and a "Spring Fling" dance. Betty Jones served as president in the mid-1980s. Following that, for many years Linda Abbott and Karen St. Cyr led the team. Like the long terms of service by the male leaders of the FVFD, this continuity of leadership has been a key to the sustained and robust support provided by the Auxiliary. Linda Abbott retired from the Auxiliary in 2020 after more than 40 years of service.

During the 1980s, the Auxiliary began selling food and drink at Town Meeting. Other Auxiliary services were added in the following decades including selling smoke detectors and fire extinguishers, compiling the town phone directory, donating first aid mannequins for Rescue Squad training, sponsoring Girl Scouts, hosting FES students at the firehouse, participating in the annual FVFD Open House for National Fire Prevention Week, and contributing to events like the Christmas Giving Tree and the Welcome Basket project. Following the national disaster of September 11, 2001, the Auxiliary started twice-yearly blood drives which continue to the present. The team provides an annual reception for veterans at Town Hall on Veterans' Day. Over the years, the Auxiliary estimates that it has donated $18,000 to the FVFD. The FVFD correspondent in *The Francestown News*, Jenny Fritz, shared this testimonial, "In 2001, the FVFD and eight other departments battled a large brush fire on Woodward Hill Road. The Auxiliary provided three full meals a day for two days for 60 firefighters and rescue workers on virtually no notice. I was approached by numerous members of other towns who were in awe of the quantity and quality of the food." After another fire event, a firefighter celebrated the work of the Auxiliary, "They are the unsung heroes of the night … thank you, thank you, thank you for providing hot drink, hot food, and comfort on a cold night during a fire fight."

The Foote Farm Fire of 1995

A very memorable event in the FVFD's history of firefighting after 1970 took place on a blisteringly hot weekend in July 1995 -- the immolation of the Foote Barn on New Boston Road. About noon on July 13, with the temperature in the high 90s, and a 20-25 mph wind blowing to the southeast, hay in the barn on New Boston Road combusted. In less than an hour the structure was consumed, leaving only the foundation.

The structure destroyed that day was not just any barn. Built in 1899 by the Whitings, it was known as the largest attached barn in the State of New Hampshire, perhaps in the eastern United States. It was 150' long, almost 50' broad, and had three levels. Much of the top two stories of the barn were filled with hay. The Foote family purchased the farm in the 1930s and milked dairy cows until Ernest Foote sold the farm in 1977. The owner in 1995, called it Dandelion Hill Farm, and stabled retired thoroughbreds. The house to which the barn was attached burned as well, leaving two families homeless. The FVFD responded quickly, but the size and intensity of the conflagration meant that the structure could not be saved. Two horses were rescued but seven died.

Severe drought conditions that summer intensified the danger the fire posed to neighbors and adjacent forests and meadows. Chief Donny Abbott focused his men on preventing the fire from spreading to structures on neighboring properties, evacuating residents down wind, and fighting many brush fires set by burning fragments carried for miles in the strong wind. Chief Abbott's task that day was enormous with twenty-two neighboring departments responding and more than 1000 personnel deployed. For two days FVFD poured water into the footprint of the huge barn and put down brush fires. Getting enough water to the fire was a challenge. Both Scobie Pond and the Soapstone Quarry were used, but both were inconvenient. In the following days, members of FVFD enthusiastically sang Chief Abbott's praises as a calm and decisive leader. The Fire Auxiliary mustered and made sure the firefighters were kept hydrated and fed. Photos of the fire taken by Mary Lindstrom were on the front page of the *Manchester Union Leader*. Many Francestown residents better remember the Foote Barn fire than they do another major news event of that week, the O.J. Simpson trial in Los Angeles.

Over the last two decades several homes in town have burned. The owner of a house on New Boston Road died when her house burned in 1999. Fifty firefighters from seven departments responded. In 2001 Isabella Hill's home on Pleasant Pond Road burned and several pets were killed. The St. John house on Avery Road, empty at the time, burned in 2006, followed shortly by the Paquin home on Dodge Hill Road, and Warren Kiblin's house on King Hill Road. In 2017 the Brecca family lost all their possessions when their home on Campbell Hill Road was destroyed. Another major fire was the 2001 brush fire off Woodward Hill Road that involved sixty firefighters. A story from the Paquin fire conveys the conscientious and neighborly nature of the volunteer fire company. During the "overhaul," the crew found plastic totes full of soggy family photos in the water-logged cellar. Six firefighters rescued the tubs and took them to the station where through the night and early hours of the morning, they carefully laid the photos out to dry on every available surface. The dried photos were returned to the family.

Passing the Baton

After 32 years in the FVFD, over twenty as chief, Donny Abbott retired from the FVFD in December 2007. Abbott was celebrated for his humility and dedication. The FVFD elected Larry Kullgren as chief. Not yet 40 years old, Kullgren had grown up in the FVFD. Both the election of Abbott in 1987 and the election of Kullgren twenty years later represented a passing of the leadership baton from one generation to the next. Kullgren's generation was even more deeply committed to "professionalization" than its predecessor and was more technology savvy in a world where technology is increasingly necessary. After each election there was a natural attrition of members who found a change in leadership to be an opportune time to move on. However, membership rebounded.

Chief Kullgren was a 17-year veteran of the FVFD. His twin brother David was a captain in the FVFD and works for the state in fire control and took on the role of forest fire warden. The new chief was a Level II State Certified Firefighter. He had been fire ward and deputy fire warden for the town and a special deputy warden for the state, as well as a certified fire inspector, and EMT. Through the 2000s, there was an increase in the number of volunteers in the FVFD whose day jobs are professional firefighting in other jurisdictions. This includes Deputy Chief Brian Delahanty and Rescue Squad Captain and Emergency Management Director Kevin Holdredge.

Beginning in the late 1990s, several local firefighters joined the NH state team that responds to forest fires in fire prone areas in western parts of the country. Examples include, in 1998 Larry Kullgren and Mark Couturier went to Minnesota, and in 2016 and 2017 David and Larry Kullgren fought major wildfires in the mountains of Washington and Idaho. Brian Delahanty has also been part of NH's out-of-state teams.

Following the Ice Storm of December 2008, the FVFD provided exceptional service to the town. FVFD personnel went door to door doing well-being checks and making sure that people isolated by blocked roads were contacted and rescued if necessary. The FVFD saw that downed power lines were inspected and fallen trees were cleared from roads. The governor of New Hampshire honored the FVFD in a ceremony in Concord with the "Spirit of New Hampshire Award." The award celebrates outstanding contributions to volunteerism throughout the state. After Francestown was up and running again, Chief Kullgren called for a review of emergency preparedness. He advised the Select Board to require all town departments to demonstrate their ability to meet FEMA's certification requirements.

The Rescue Squad

From its inception in the late 1970s, the Rescue Squad grew into a very busy and skilled companion to the firefighting team. By the early 1990s, the number of rescue calls rose by 25% and became half of the FVFD's activity. Rescue calls rose with the population, but FVFD leaders believed that another factor increased rescue calls -- new residents had a lower threshold for the sort of emergencies they thought required an ambulance. Also, more people in need of hospitalization preferred transport to Manchester or Concord, rather than Peterborough. FVFD leaders, Donny Abbott, and Alan Thulander, were particularly supportive of the development of the Rescue Squad. Thulander made sure that the squad had up-to-date medical equipment. The original Army surplus ambulance was replaced by a true rescue vehicle in 1984. Each year through the 1980s-1990s more firefighters gained EMS certification. FVFD by-laws were changed to allow members to serve on the Rescue Squad without being firefighters.

Bev Abbott, a registered nurse and an experienced emergency responder, became the Rescue Squad captain for a couple of years. In the early 2000s, professional firefighter and EMT, Kevin Holdredge, was elected Rescue Captain and the capability of the Rescue Squad was upgraded further, "We are excited to announce that ... our department will begin providing Advanced Life Support services to the town. This will greatly benefit everyone, but especially patients with cardiac, respiratory problems or sever traumatic injuries." In 2016 the department acquired a new rescue vehicle that was dedicated to the memory of Cole Wohle, a young, greatly admired firefighter who passed away that year.

Several members of the Rescue Squad have been women, beginning with Bev Abbott and Elizabeth Hill in 1978. Abbott served 20 years. Judi Miller was the third woman to join the department, followed by Betsy Hardwick, who also served at least twenty years. Around the turn of the millennium several women joined, including Celeste Lunetta, Jenny Fritz, Amy St. Cyr, and Jennifer

Hardwick. In 2000 Celeste Lunetta was recognized as Firefighter of the Year by her colleagues. Subsequently she was chosen as rescue captain, and in 2015 she was elected as a fire ward, the first woman in Francestown to serve in that capacity. For a decade, Jenny Fritz wrote monthly reports for *The Francestown News* informing the town's residents about the various activities of the department. In the mid-1990s, Chief Abbott thought it would be useful to have official documentation of the activities of the department and asked Fritz to serve as FVFD photographer. Later, she qualified for service on the Rescue Squad, assumed clerk duties following Pitman's service, and continued to document FVFD events.

FVFD as a Social Organization

Fire suppression and rescue are serious business requiring a sober focus on the emergency tasks at hand, but for many years FVFD also served as a social organization. While much of the socialization took place during the training and maintenance activities, formal celebratory events were held to facilitate camaraderie as well. Among the events on the FVFD social calendar were the Hillsborough County Fire Dinner and the FVFD Spouse Appreciation Dinner where both serious and funny honors were awarded. Celebrations of milestones include the banquet for Norman Stewart's retirement in 1972 and the department's 50th Anniversary fete which also marked the end of Clifton Foote's service as chief. That event included a parade and fireworks. The social function of the department included many ad hoc contributions to town events, especially when a tall ladder was needed. When the FIHS Christmas tree on the Common needed lights hung or repaired, a fire truck often appeared. When FIHS bought American flags for the power and telephone poles in the village center, fire personnel installed them. From time to time the department has sponsored an Explorer Scout post for local teens interested in service as first responders. The FVFD was responsible for erecting the structure of the town's Heritage Museum.

Future Needs

Due to the physical demands, fire service is a younger person's activity. However, several members of the FVFD have served into their seventies. Two men had especially long and remarkable careers in service to the town as first responders. Dick Leavitt and Al Van Cleave both passed away in 2017. At that time Leavitt had served the department for 55 years and Van Cleave for 43. Their dedication and experience were inspirational for younger members.

As noted above, having enough volunteers has been a challenge for the FVFD for the past three decades. Local firehouses will probably survive because of the nature of fires -- the speed with which they destroy property and threaten lives. Even so, the day when a town the size of Francestown can provide first response solely through its local volunteers may be numbered. Some paid, full-time staff may be in the offing. Regionalization and professionalization are likely the future of emergency medical services and rescue squads. Small steps toward a degree of professionalization have been taken, beginning in 2007 when Town Meeting voted a stipend for the fire chief. The 2019 Town Meeting approved stipends for officers of the FVFD. In 2020, Town Meeting voted for stipends for FVFD members to cover expenses for uniforms and personalized equipment. The expense to the town is modest, about $20,000 per year. In 2020 the number of active members of the FVFD is around fifteen. The department continues to cushion the town as much as possible from the expense of a full-service fire department. In 2018, the FVFD proposed to the Budget Committee to reduce apparatus replacement by one vehicle which means a potential savings over $600,000 -- the cost of a new pumper. When the Budget Committee proposed a Warrant Article to buy new SCBA units and a filler device, FVFD was able to obtain a large grant from FEMA for part of the expense.

THE COMMUNITY CHURCH OF FRANCESTOWN

The Community Church of Francestown (CCF) was founded in 1959. According to John Schott's history, in the late 1950s, three church groups existed in town: 1) The Unitarians who possessed title to the Old Meeting House (1801), known as the White Church, 2) the Congregationalists, whose home was the Brown Church (1883) on Main Street (named after the trim, not the cream-colored clapboards), and 3) a faction known as the Community Group who had no physical location. It was this latter group that aspired to form a single, unified, non-denominational church – the Community Church of Francestown.

The Congregationalists and the Community Group agreed to merge into a single congregation. The Unitarians, "few in number though they were ... demurred." The two factions in agreement formed a single, denominationally unaffiliated congregation in the Brown Church on Main Street. About 35 families and a dozen individuals were on the original membership roll. By the 1990s the CCF was loosely associated with the United Church of Christ (UCC), a major mainstream national Protestant denomination. For example, when CCF needed a "supply minister," which happened frequently, the UCC helped to provide one.

The CCF was dissolved as an organization in 2020 after 62 years of service to its members, the town, and the larger world. The challenge in telling the story of the CCF is not to let the eventuality of this closure characterize the entire life of the congregation; this is not a story of failure. The essential story of the CCF from 1970-2020 is not that it fell short of its own aspirations, but that it was able, for so long, against substantial challenges, to serve its members and its parish.

Declining church membership

The CCF faced four main challenges. Francestown is in New England in the United States of America, not a promising location or a fortuitous era in U.S. history for a small church in a tiny town. Church membership declined in U.S. in the 1960s and the years following, and it declined particularly in New England. Older generations of Christians in the United States were raised to join a church, support it with regular donations, attend services and events regularly, and accept that the message from the pulpit might not always seem relevant to their life experiences. Even so, they were "Christians" and Christians joined a church. Loyalty to a congregation was a traditional value. By the 1990s the mentality of younger Christians, many of them move-ins to town, changed. Combine this trend with the population of Francestown – tiny -- and you have the first challenge.

Second, the founders of the CCF recognized that a denominational church with an exclusive creed in a tiny town was likely to fail. The alternative was for the church to try to be broadly inclusive, avoiding the embrace of a set of beliefs, teachings, and expectations that would exclude potential members whether Presbyterian, Methodist, Lutheran, Baptist, Episcopalian, Catholic, or Unitarian. The path of inclusiveness presented risk. This was the warning of one of the temporary pastors who served the CCF in the 1980s. Pastor Lynda Tolton encouraged the church to adopt a creed with specific beliefs and expectations. She admonished the congregation that if they "tried to be all things to all people" they would fall short of providing members the spiritual nurture they were seeking. The CCF responded by adopting a statement of beliefs. The statement was broad and inclusive, designed to fit the diversity of a congregation that was a melting pot of Christian denominational backgrounds and expectations.

While the CCF chose to be as inclusive as possible, churches in the United States were generally moving to a more exclusive approach. The largest mainstream denominations were shrinking or fracturing. Entrepreneurial churches were drawing members away. Increasingly, many Christians were choosing to worship in a church where everyone embraces a disciplined, consistent, narrowly defined set of beliefs. By the 1990s, some new residents tried out the CCF and found it welcoming and broad-minded. Others found it wishy-washy and too liberal. At times some who sought more theological discipline tried to change the congregation's approach. More often, folks for whom the "all things to all people" approach was unsatisfying found a denominational congregation in one of the surrounding communities. In the view of one long-time leader of the CCF "the core of 'progressive liberals' – those who wanted to be all things to all people -- hurt the church's effort to expand or at the very least, to continue." "More conservative Christians were 'not getting enough feeding …' their dissatisfaction was palpable."

Membership plateaued in the 1990s and then steadily declined through the 2000s.

In the second decade of the 2000s, the future of the CCF was increasingly in doubt and the congregation wrestled over whether to officially affiliate with the United Church of Christ (UCC). The CCF had a long association with the UCC but had never become an official member. This debate placed stress on the unity of the diminishing membership. Eventually the CCF chose not to affiliate but to reaffirm its general identity as a "welcoming and affirming community."

The third challenge was instability in ministerial leadership. Often between 1970-2020 the CCF did not have a resident pastor. This was a structural problem primarily rooted in the size of the congregation, the limit of its ability to compensate a pastor, and its non-denominational status. Churches compete to attract ministers. The CCF was able to attract three young, ambitious, and inspiring pastors in the 1970s-80s, but each of those leaders soon moved on to a larger congregation. For the next thirty years the church found it difficult to find a pastor with charisma or who was "a good fit." Three pastors served in these decades, two for only short periods. Said one congregant, "each time there was a change it generated criticism during the selection process as well as the 'divorce' process; each minister left unhappy and left unhappiness. We were a hard congregation to satisfy. We criticized the minister who snuffled too much, the one whose wife was not social, the one who wouldn't visit the sick and old, and the one with purple hair. There were too many awkward fits for a small-town, mixed congregation."

The fourth challenge is familiar to anyone who has ever owned an historic home; it is a money pit. CCF never had an endowment or sufficient savings to meet the demands of the building, and no one with abundant resources came forward to indemnify the congregation against the burden of its sanctuary. Many congregants loved worshipping in the Brown Church, but the massive, steep roof leaked and there were many other chronic facility issues.

The fact that the CCF endured and at times thrived from 1970-2020 is a success story. Given these challenges a lesser assemblage of Christians may well have given up far sooner.

Church Legacies

Two positive legacies of the CCF were described by veteran congregants. One was the "mission" activity of the church. The other was a specific "witness" the CCF provided during the Ice Storm of December of 2008. Though revenue rarely exceeded expenses, the church was steadfast in its commitment to spend a substantial amount of the money it raised each year for support of or service to those in need outside the church. The congregation contributed to causes and projects overseas, nationally, regionally, and within Francestown. Even as insolvency approached, the membership increased its generosity measured as a percentage of the budget.

The congregation's outreach expanded substantially in the 1980s-1990s. The church supported seminary students in Maine and the chaplain at the Crotched Mountain Rehabilitation Center. Donations were made to support refugee children, a medical clinic in India, a domestic violence shelter, and a soup kitchen and homeless shelter in Manchester. The church bought clothing for Native Americans in need, gave to the UCC's One Great Hour of Sharing, and annually participated in the Church World Service CROP Walk. In the 1990s the church added donations to Heifer Project and Habitat for Humanity. The scope of the church's outreach became a grievance for some church members and potential donors. Some members wanted more of CCF's outreach to target residents of Francestown. The church created the "Helping Hands" project to provide a local mission – food and clothing for those in need, as well as care for elderly and handicapped town residents. Helping Hands received the Oak Hill Grange's "Citizen of the Year" award in 1989. Other locally targeted activities were Christmas season donations to needy families, and a Tree of Warmth with mittens, scarves, and hats. But CCF continued to send the lion's share of its mission funds out of town. In 1998, members approved a partnership with a congregation in Zimbabwe in need of assistance to build a sanctuary.

In the 2000s, CCF strove to keep benevolence a priority. The list of organizations receiving donations remained very much the same as in earlier years, though a pregnancy care center and the River Center in Peterborough were added. The food pantry for Francestown grew in collaboration with the town's Public Assistance Coordinator Phyllis Naegeli. CCF member Lori Hardwick took over a tradition started by her extended family of providing "Welcome Baskets" for residents new to town. Beginning in 2009, CCF began supporting her efforts and continued to do so for several years. Girl Scouts met in the Vestry. Representing the church, Cher Barker served in Louisiana following Hurricane Katrina and Jim Barker visited the Ukama congregation, CCF's partner in Zimbabwe. The church's dedication to generous mission donations persisted. In 2019, even while facing closure, CCF chose to donate $6,566 to its set of targeted causes.

A high point in the church's story between 1970 and 2020, was its service to the town during the Ice Storm of December 2008. CCF members mobilized to provide meals, warmth, and respite for individuals and families who lost power, had no heat, or could not get to their homes. Following twenty-four hours of freezing rain on December 11, 2008, most residents of town were without power for many days. For the next week the church fed townspeople in need. Led by Cher Barker and Mike Petrovick, with help from many members of the church and a squad of teenage volunteers, CCF made sure hot meals were available morning and night. Residents and the Village Store donated the fixings. The Select Board opened the Town Office as an emergency shelter and the FVFD provided a generator that powered the church as well as the Town Office. With shelter available and warm meals at the church "it really helped keep people's spirits up," said Select Board and church member Betsy Hardwick. A leader of the CCF proudly testified that "our mission to provide Christian service to our community truly came to pass during the Ice Storm."

Church Activities

In some respects, a church is a club. As such it provides activities to nurture its members. Sunday worship services and Sunday School for children were the core activities of the CCF. Over the years, youth groups came and went, depending on whether there were enough teens and an eager leader. When attendance was sufficient, a summertime Vacation Bible School, or Peace Camp, was offered. In 2012 Peace Camp was declared "a roaring success," perhaps in part because the children climbed "Mt. Sinai" (Crotched Mountain) and were met by "Moses" (Gordon Sherman who asked "Aaron, is that you?"). When enough children were available the Christmas Eve service included a pageant.

The annual CCF calendar included special celebrations. The church's Fall Festival and Christmas Fair were long-running standards. The Fall Festival had the feel of a mini-Labor Day, and the Christmas Fair was both a celebration of the season and a fund-raiser selling various home-made craft items and food. Both events involved the Women's Guild. For many years the church offered Saturday community breakfasts and luncheons for senior citizens. In the 2000s, the church hosted community suppers curated by Chef Petrovick (e.g., "Paellas of Valencia") and celebrations of lives well-lived like Joan Hanchett's memorial service and Sonny and Dot Hardwick's 50th anniversary. In 2019, the congregation celebrated the 60th anniversary of the founding of the church.

Church Membership

Active membership peaked toward the end of 1980s at around eighty. At Annual Meetings attendance was consistently about 25-30; the 30 core leaders were much the same each year. Sunday attendance usually averaged in the forties. Of the 118 members (active and inactive) on the roll in 1987, 35 had been members in the 1960s, 27 joined in the 1970s, and 56 were new to the church in the 1980s. In 1989 there were 52 children on the Sunday School roll, though attendance was lower. These numbers offered promise. Typically, most churches' attendance is much larger for Easter and Christmas services. Such was the case for CCF. In 1989 Easter drew 100 and 150 came for Christmas Eve. Attendance plateaued in the 1990s, even as the population of the town grew. There were between 60-70 active members. Average attendance was in the low 40s from 1991 to 2012. Easter and Christmas Eve were still big draws. Sunday School and Vacation Bible School attendance was erratic. By 2012 average attendance at the Sunday service declined to 30 and fell to 22 by 2019.

Only about a dozen members were involved in the final decision-making meetings.

To the membership's credit, over the years they were less dependent on the leadership of a minister than are many congregations. It was a very democratic body. Not being blessed with long-term, highly inspirational ministers gave the core group of lay leaders a great deal of authority and responsibility. During the 1970s and 1980s, leadership of the church overlapped significantly with participation on town boards, commissions, and committees. For many years the moderator of the church was Phil Ireland, who also was town moderator. In 1998 the presidents of both FIHS and OMH, Gordon Sherman (FIHS) and Derald Radtke (OMH), were members of CCF. But, by the 2000s, leaders in town governance were less likely to be CCF members. In the 1970s-1980s church officers' surnames were Jones, Hardwick, Foote, Place, Cutter, Radtke, Baptiste, Usinger, Brien, Leavitt, Mace, McNeill, Pettee, Hoyt, Hubbell, Sweeney, Davis, Prest, Benedict, Holbrook, Hanchett, Barr, Leavitt, and Lord. Many of these family names "aged out" of leadership in the 1990s.

A changing of the guard began in the late 1980s. New to town, Jim and Cheryl Barker, flush with enthusiasm for the little church, dove into leadership. Both Barkers held multiple front line leadership roles for the next thirty years. For the years between 1986 and 2020, either Jim or Cher served as CCF moderator, and they each chaired a committee. Jim often chaired the Board of Trustees, and Cher took on different committees as needed. Cher also was elected president of the Monadnock Council of Churches during the 1990s. Another couple joined the church in the mid-1990s and were stalwarts in leadership and hard work for the next 25 years, Mark and Shirley Pitman. Mark chaired the deacons or trustees for sixteen years in the last two decades. Since 1995 the list of members who served on committees for several years include Demetria McKaig, Heidi Dawidoff, Denice Glover, Dorothy Hardwick, Lori Hardwick-Way, Betsy Hardwick, Ed Gienty, Dick Cilley, Brian Mosher, Jeff Tarr, Stacy Borden, Lisa Gargano, Carol Ireland, Daryl Hazel, Janet Hazel, Shirlee Ferrara, Randall Ferrara, Mark Marony, Shirley Pitman, David Connard, Ron Reimer, Carol Lunan, Nancy Lundgren, Derald Radtke, Barbara Radtke, Kim Dalley, Pat Place, Dariel Peterson, Linda Compton, Jill Rolph, Mike Petrovick, Brad Howell, Bridget Howell, Bonnie Arpin, Susan Cooke, Ray James and Beth Wallace.

Ministers

After a succession of short-term ministers in the 1960s, CCF had a popular leader from 1969-1973, Paul Martz. As a result, membership grew to over 80 and there were about two dozen registered Sunday School children. Martz received a call from a larger church and moved on. CCF went almost four years without a permanent minister. Emily Lord, the CCF's historian in this period, observed that "there were few highlights" during the time of the interim ministers. The hiring of John Maes in the late 1970s made a big difference. CCF went from fewer than a dozen persons in attendance on a Sunday, to an average attendance near 50. In two years, Maes brought in twenty new members. Pastor Maes was replaced by Gary Alger, a third popular and inspirational preacher who also stayed only a few years. Martz, Maes, and Alger were the only CCF ministers with truly powerful charisma. Reverend Keta Jones served eleven years as the CCF pastor, from 1990 to 2001. This was unprecedented. While Jones provided CCF with stability it did not result in membership growth. In 2000, Jones took a medical leave of absence. Ed and Shirley Jones filled in for some of her duties through their "Ministry of Visitation." Guest preachers included CCF stalwart Dorothy Hardwick. Shortly after Jones returned from leave, she resigned due to disagreements and misunderstandings with lay leaders. For eight of the next nineteen years there was no resident pastor. In these years, the CCF patched together preaching with interim ministers and members who volunteered. Notable among the volunteers was Randy Ferrara, a retired minister who had settled in Francestown. Two pastors were called by the congregation. However, they proved to be awkward fits and did not help grow the membership.

Church Finances

A focus on the CCF's problematic finances may underrepresent the spiritual nourishment and camaraderie members generated and received. Reverend Jones observed, "Numbers and statistics are not an indication of success in a church. Faithfulness is the only goal and its only measure." That said, the CCF often faced the uncomfortable reality of "numbers and statistics," as recorded in their Annual Reports. Finances were challenging even in the 1970s. The decade ended with a tight budget. Even as CCF experienced growth in the 1980s, revenue from pledges fell short of covering expenses each year. The books were balanced by taking money from the Investment Fund which was the CCF's savings. Jim Barker, Board of Trustees chair in 1989, presciently warned that "[t]he church's members and friends need to realize that their current level of financial support is not adequate to meet current and future needs." That message was repeated often over the next three decades.

Church records are an accounting of continual maintenance and repair of the aging building. In the 1990s the trustees reported that major projects "are piling up." Dramatic revenue growth was needed to cover the cost of a new roof and exterior painting. Either the existing members had to increase their pledges, or membership had to grow. Pledge amounts increased modestly, but membership did not grow, and the gap widened. The CCF was able to hold its own for much of the 1990s due to a large memorial donation, a couple of modest capital campaigns, and increasing revenue from events like the Fall Festival and the Christmas Fair. For the first capital campaign, over six hundred letters sent to community residents yielded only 37 contributions. By 2002 the minutes note that "the trustees had drained all undesignated endowment funds."

The town's Master Plan of 1995 bluntly captured the CCF's plight, "The CCF faces chronic financing challenges for its annual budgets. The viability of the congregation in its current facility has been a serious question for several years. Were the church to close, the community would have a strong interest in the preservation of the building within the planning expectation that 'preserving the rural and colonial character of the community' is a priority." Stalwart congregant Dariel Peterson made the case for community support of the CCF, "We provide many services other than the usual church activities to the community, such as a community food pantry, meeting space for the Scouts and other youth organizations, [and] monthly luncheons for seniors." But salvation by the community was not forthcoming.

Still the congregation's optimism endured. Grants were obtained to upgrade CCF's kitchen enabling the church to maintain its singular role in providing a commercial kitchen to the community. Another grant enabled an improvement to the nursery area of the Vestry. Leaders focused on strategizing for the CCF's survival. In 2014, they identified a set of options including relocating to a space less expensive to operate, seeking grants for building repairs, and building a better relationship with town residents so they might embrace the survival of the church. Though leaders agreed that "we are a church, not a building" there was a deep attachment to the building even as it was draining the congregation's resources. CCF sold the parsonage, but not the sanctuary. Expenses continued to exceed revenue for too many years. In 2017, the trustees changed their estimation of "stress on the membership" when they observed that given current and projected deficits "viability" would be gone in 1-2 years. With deficits of $20-35,000 per year, and the church building's needs increasing, the endgame was on the horizon. In 2018 the projected loss per month was estimated at $3,300. Quarterly meetings were held to update members on the CCF's status and to make critical decisions. Legal counsel was retained.

Eulogies

Sixty-one years after its founding, the CCF closed its doors -- as much as was possible since the front door would no longer lock. The building was sold in 2021. Three members of the CCF from 1959 were still members in 2020 -- Dorothy Hardwick and Ed and Shirley Jones. The families on the membership roll in the 1970s-1980s were largely absent in 2019. In a town where hundreds of thousands of dollars were raised to rehabilitate the Old Meeting House, the Town Hall, the Beehive, the Long Store, and even the horse sheds, no individual or group chose to endow the congregation. No campaign was mounted to keep the church building in something approximating public hands.

The last moderator of the CCF, Mark Pitman, placed this statement into the last Annual Report of the church, "As Moderator I feel responsible for the dwindling Sunday service attendance and the poor financial support we receive. The wonderful old building we call our church is in need of major repairs. In

November the ceiling of the Pastor's Office collapsed due to the leaking roof. I worry how we are going to pay to have a new roof installed and then fix the damage the leaks have caused. I worry when only 4 people attend a Sunday worship service. I worry if the walkways are going to be slippery when it snows. Don't even mention the front door that will not shut and lock. I worry that I am not spiritually capable of leading our church community in a Christian direction. So, I put my head down and pray for strength and hope. Then I walk up the steps on Sunday morning and enter the building that I love, and a weight starts being lifted off my shoulders .... I walk out of church smiling and looking forward to next Sunday ... We are struggling, but hope remains strong."

A non-church-going resident, Ron Cheney, spelled out what the CCF had meant to the community in a Letter to the Editor of the *Monadnock Ledger-Transcript* in 2020,

"Main Street in the Village in Francestown is different now. The Community Church closed several weeks ago. Put its building on the market. Sold immediately. And now rumored to become a residence. Gone is the Rainbow Flag and the All-Are-Welcome banner imparting a beneficent spirit generous and uplifting to passersby. Its kitchen no longer serving community dinners once a month to anyone hungry who came to its doors. And also, the special dinners to raise money, white tablecloths, BYO amidst candlelight, bringing a good number of us together. No one can forget the Ice Storm of 2008 – five days without electricity town wide. Where did the food come from every night to feed us all? Loaves and fishes?

Teenagers serving and cleaning up and getting together with each other and across generations. Good Samaritans all. We gathered in from cold houses to be warmed by our comradery sharing and supporting each other in our adversity. A small group of believers they were. How proud when the congregation filled a container of contributed things shipped to its sister church in Zimbabwe .... It was a band of believers struggling with finances while serving our community and the world afar. Their presence, the spirit that emanated from their place of worship, influenced us in ways we were not aware of. They reminded us of the better angels of our nature, that we are not enemies, but friends, with our next-door neighbors and folks far, far away."

THE WOMEN'S GUILD

When the CCF was formed in 1959, the Women's Guild was inherited from the Congregational Church. It was founded in 1884 as the Ladies Benevolent Society. It was a women's club that met weekly primarily as a social and fund-raising group. Its religious aspect was understated. Some of the members of the Guild were not members of the CCF. The CCF bulletin stated that "Any women in the community who would like to join the group would be most welcome," although at times the organization did have a more exclusive aspect. The Guild met at lunch time, so working women employed outside their home found it inconvenient to participate. The Guild was an adjunct of the church contributing to its budget through money earned by fairs, food sales, wedding receptions, suppers, and the sale of quilts. Donations were made to other organizations and causes deemed worthy. The Guild sent cards to ill townspeople and delivered Thanksgiving baskets to shut ins. In the early 1970s, the Guild had as many as 40 members. The biggest event of the Guild's year was the Christmas Fair. This event involved the sale of crafts and baked goods. In the 1970s-1980s, home-made chocolate candies were a big draw. In the 1980s membership declined. Members were aging and new families moving to town were not joining a "women's club." In the mid-1990s the church bulletin reported the Guild's self-assessment: "our group is getting smaller, and older."

The Guild was replaced by the "Thursday Fellowship" organized by Dariel Peterson. Meetings were held at a more convenient time for most women. The Fellowship continued to be a source of crafts, but it also took on preparing the monthly CCF mailing, as well as its traditional activities of hosting receptions, and the Christmas Fair and Fall Festival. In 2008, the Thursday Fellowship's Fall Festival was able to provide nearly $5,000 to the CCF. As with other traditional organizations, like the Grange and Masons, the Thursday Fellowship faded away when its long-time leader became disabled. At that time there were only five regular attendees.

For about five years between 2002 and 2007, another church operated in Francestown. Pastor Andrew Dean organized the Village Chapel Baptist Church. For much of its existence it met at Francestown Elementary School. By 2008 the church was no longer meeting. A denominational congregation in Francestown was less likely to survive than was the CCF.

The "other church" in town, until 1987, was the long-standing Unitarian congregation, descendants of the original church in Francestown. As early as the 1950s, the denominational church was dying; that is, its membership was small, new residents were not joining, and the congregation could not care for their building (the Old Meeting House). Members continued to worship in the "White Church" through the mid-1980s, though without a pastor. The Unitarians hosted public musical performances, in particular concerts by Monadnock Music. This tradition was continued by OMH, Inc. The congregation was dissolved in 1987 when they sold their sanctuary to Old Meeting House, Inc. The last deacon of the Unitarian congregation was Harry Varnum. Dick Edwards and Matilda "Mit" Boyle represented the Unitarians in their negotiations with FIHS that led to the sale of the building for a dollar.

THE FRANCESTOWN IMPROVEMENT AND HISTORICAL SOCIETY

In keeping with a tradition followed throughout New England, a private organization – the Improvement and Historical Society – played a quasi-governmental role in the life of the town from 1970-2020. The Village Improvement Society was founded in 1911. The Historical Society was born in 1923. The two organizations merged in 1961, though they did not get around to officially incorporating and registering the new organization's name with the state, "F.I.H.S.," until 1971. Even into the 1980s some residents referred to FIHS as the Village Improvement Society.

As its name suggests, FIHS has multiple missions. The *historical* society function of the organization calls for preservation, and sometimes restoration, of historically valued materials such as documents, artifacts, and ephemera, as well as vehicles and structures. Additionally, the founders tasked the society to look for ways that private initiative could *improve* the lives of town residents through recreation, beautification, cultural enrichment, and support of public services. Although not officially stated, an over-arching mission for FIHS has been to build community. The annual Labor Day celebration, for which FIHS is solely responsible, is a major manifestation of this aspiration.

On occasion, FIHS' identity has been an issue. At the Annual Meeting in 1986 members discussed whether the Society was "elitist." The President at that time evinced concern about an "elitist reputation in the eyes of new people in town." John Schott's history of Francestown (1972) described the Society's leadership as "long prominently associated [with]... summer people" who "earnestly sought and on occasion received the active support of the native element (165)." That elitist characterization appears to correspond to the socio-economic status of the organization's leadership in the 1960s-70s of which John Schott was an exemplar. Over the years since that era, an effort has been made to involve town residents from all walks of life in the leadership and activities of FIHS. However, any organization that serves as a fundraiser and grantor of money for expensive projects -- which has been a central role of FIHS during the last fifty years -- is bound to be closely associated with the status of its most substantial donors. Yet elitism in fundraising does not necessarily translate into elitist outcomes. FIHS' identity is best judged through the story of its actual contributions to the quality of life in town over many years. That contribution has been substantial.

During the last fifty years FIHS has been a partner in many town initiatives. Some projects have been solely the province of the Society. The following story of FIHS' role in town over the fifty years since 1970 explores both its function as an historical society and as a town improvement committee. The success of FIHS in both of its roles, historical society and boosterism, has led to "spin offs."

FIHS was the progenitor of recreation programs in Francestown. The town Recreation Commission was the first offspring of FIHS, which later begat a long-term lease of property to the town including the baseball field, tennis courts, and other recreational spaces. FIHS' "Historical Rooms," hosted on the second floor of the town library, eventually lead to the creation of a separate Historical Museum known by the nickname for the building in which it is housed – the Beehive. FIHS paid for the restoration of the town's Concord Coach, two 18th century hearses, and a Hand Tub pumper for firefighting. They then collaborated with the Fire Department and booster Alan Thulander to establish the Heritage Museum in the Thulander Building on FIHS property. The Heritage Museum is the repository of the restored vehicles and many other pieces of historically interesting equipment. In the 1980s as FIHS considered how to best address the condition of the horse sheds on the Common, the Society commissioned a study that made recommendations for preserving all the historical structures in town. This led to the founding of the Old Meeting House, Inc. by men and women within the ranks of FIHS' leadership. The study also addressed the condition of the Francestown Academy building, known as the Town Hall. By the time the Town Hall's deterioration forced its future to be resolved, the scope of town governance had broadened to the point where the Select Board, through a Heritage Commission, relieved FIHS of the responsibility for saving another edifice. But in a real sense, the town's renovation of the Town Hall was a spin-off from the path established by FIHS. In 2017, the Long Store building on Main Street where the Village Store was located, was re-possessed by a bank. A private foundation bought the structure from the bank and donated it to FIHS. The Society renovated the building and initiated a new iteration of the Village Store. In short, FIHS has given birth to several important institutions in Francestown through its activities over the years. Each case led to the town's "improvement." FIHS has certainly fulfilled its mission many times over.

Labor Day Celebration

The tradition of Francestown's Labor Day celebration began in 1918 to raise money for the Red Cross as World War One continued in Europe. It is a tradition for the residents of Francestown and the region. Each Labor Day, several thousand people participate in a variety of activities, culminating in the Grand Parade on Main Street. A typical Labor Day since the 1990s begins on the weekend days with tennis and mud-volleyball tournaments, a competitive road race, and a golf scramble. Often on Friday or Saturday evening there is a dance. Sunday evening's Vespers in the Old Meeting House is the official kick-off to Labor Day. By 1970, religious features of the event had been replaced by secular entertainment. The prior year's births and deaths are acknowledged, music is played and sung, memories and stories are celebrated, and on occasion there has been professional entertainment. For the last two decades Ethel MacStubbs has been the producer and curator of the Vespers service. It is a beloved tradition for many residents.

Labor Day itself features sales of juried arts and crafts, White Elephant items, used clothing, plants, and several options for food. Usually games for children, or adults – such as a dunk tank -- are held on the Common. Other children's entertainment may include a clown, a magician, or a juggler. Live music or storytelling may be provided, inside or on the lawn of the Old Meeting House. "Tags" have been sold since 1918. The parade kicks-off in early afternoon featuring floats of varying sizes and sophistication pulled by trucks or tractors. Walkers -- skaters, dancers, family groups or clubs with banners --

and horses, vintage cars, tractors, fire trucks, and a clown, stilt walker, or musicians are interspersed between the floats. Various bands have played in the parade over the years; the Temple Band has been the featured ensemble over the last twenty-five years. For many celebrations the day has culminated with a supper hosted by the volunteer fire department during which names are pulled for a big raffle.

The entire Labor Day event is a fundraiser for FIHS. The money raised is distributed in the coming year for improvement projects conducted by the town, by other organizations, or by FIHS itself. Chairing FIHS' Labor Day is an esteemed position. In the last fifty years leaders including John Taylor, Don Prince, John Schott, Pat Place, Lawrie Barr, John Arnold, Gordon Sherman, BJ and Scott Carbee, Mark and Holly Stanley, and Charlie Pyle have taken on this role for a few, or many, years. Gabby Paige stepped into the role in 2019, only to see the event cancelled in 2020 due to the COVID emergency. A key part of the leader's duty is to recruit dozens of volunteers to chair and populate committees responsible for each of the activities. As many as a third of town residents have worked Labor Day events over the years.

There is a perception that the Labor Day celebration has not been as "big" in the 2000s as it was in the 1980s-1990s, but photographs of the crowds from those periods don't support that conclusion. Parade floats were more numerous and elaborate in the past. However, when the number of activities and earnings are compared it is clear the celebration is still robust. For decades, the most dependable source of elaborate floats has been the Hardwick family. Matriarch Dorothy has been the mastermind of float design. Her float for "Snow White and the Seven Dwarfs" won both most artistic and the grand prize. At times the Hardwicks teamed with the Kiblins or the Wheelers. Special creations have been a sugar house with real smoke, trains with a golden spike, and a blacksmith shop with a live pony.

Here are a few highlights, and a lowlight, from the many Labor Days celebrations:

- For several years in the 1970s renowned artists living in Francestown, Peter Milton and Ozzie Sweet, designed the Labor Day posters; in 1976 the pair sold balloons to children on the Common.
- In 1975, the recently restored Concord Coach was introduced to the town in the Grand Parade. In 1976, twenty-eight men, mostly town year-round residents, competed in the tennis tournament.
- In reading reports from forty-nine Labor Days, a common refrain after the event was that it was "the best Labor Day ever!" The 1987 event was celebrated as such; it featured numerous floats, multiple bands, record attendance and revenue. The chairs were Lawrie Barr and John Arnold. Yet, by 1990 the FIHS Executive Committee was discussing "re-thinking Labor Day" because of the difficulty of finding volunteers and a decline in interest in some of the traditional activities.

- The Juried Arts and Crafts show and sale, was introduced in 1990. This was controversial. There was concern about whether private individuals should sell things for their own profit. The activity commenced and became a three-decade staple of Labor Day. Pam Dewitt was the first Juried Arts impresario, but soon after Carol Prest Barr stepped in as chair and the program has thrived.
- In 1995, two memorable events took place. A raucous staple of the last 25 years was introduced, a mud-volleyball tournament. By 2003 it had become a big enough event that it was moved to the Recreation Fields where a special bog was created for the event.
- Also in 1995, five thousand people lined the parade route and were thrilled by Sibby Kunhardt's grand prize float addressing the 75th anniversary of women's right to vote with the message "We don't do windows!" The parade theme was "Windows on the World."
- In the late 1990s, the Francestown Five Road Race was introduced along with a softball tournament.
- In the 2000s, the Garden Club contributed a plant sale, and an OMH ice cream social was added.
- A key contributor to the Labor Day celebration in the 2000s was Warren Kiblin. He devoted hundreds of hours to creating signs and setting up and taking down structures for the various events.
- In 2017, FIHS produced the 100th Anniversary Labor Day Celebration. A robust parade, a long fireworks display, and other crowd-pleasing festivities showcased the historic village's long tradition of the celebration. The newly restored Historical Museum was finished just in time for the celebration due to the efforts of a dedicated crew of volunteers and the hard work of Bub Rokes and Bill McNeill.
- A "low-light" came in 1993. A golf cart being used by organizers was in the horse sheds parking area. It was momentarily unsupervised, and a young child accidentally released the parking brake. Six people were hospitalized.

Labor Day is Francestown's celebration of "community." It does so, as Carolyn Lord expressed in 1952, by "bringing together both summer and winter people until the difference between the two is less and less observed." Similarly, for the 100th celebration in 2017, the roster of volunteers spanned the full range of social groups in town.

The Historical Society

FIHS is the town's historical society. Many small towns in southwestern New Hampshire have an historical society or some group that functions in that capacity. Many towns have an historical museum, often a tiny structure housing an eclectic collection of ephemera. In Francestown, for many years the George Holmes Bixby Memorial Library (GHBML) was home to the historical society's collection. In 1923 George Holmes Bixby's granddaughter, Alison Bixby Hill, purchased and then donated the Titus Brown House to serve as the new home of the town's library. Her bequest included a mandate that space be provided for collection and display "of anything of historical interest and importance relating to the town." By the 1960s the fulfillment of that directive was the storage and display of the Society's collection of material in the Historical Rooms on the second floor and attic of the GHBML.

Curators

FIHS appointed a curator for the historical collection in the library. Connie Dodge (1964-1977), Eleanor Kiblin (1978-1989), Lillian Harrigan (1990-1991), Ellen Neilley (1992-2002), and Veda O'Neill (2002-2008) served in that role during the years the collection was housed in the library. The curators were responsible for the preservation and display of the collection. Connie Dodge arranged for the second-floor rooms to be open to visitors on scheduled occasions in the 1970s. Access was facilitated by two dozen volunteer hostesses. The number of volunteers declined in the 1980s limiting access to the collection. Donations to the Society's holdings were continuous. Particularly valuable contributions came from descendants of longtime families when their patriarchs and matriarchs died. An extensive collection of soapstone artifacts was donated in 1979. During the 1980s, there were periodic initiatives for volunteers to improve labeling and cataloging of materials in the collection and to protect the materials. Toward that end, on several occasions, professional curators and conservators from other museums were invited to visit the historical rooms to provide advice, direction, and training.

For many years the executive board of FIHS tilted toward the "improvement" role of the Society's mission, especially support of recreation. However, when Lawrence Barr became FIHS president in 1988, he explicitly asserted his aspiration that the historical function of FIHS be given more attention. He partnered with newly involved move-in Lillian Harrigan to advocate for upgrading cataloging and increasing preservation activity. Harrigan and a few other members of the society attended curatorship classes in Concord to receive training from museum professionals. Barr appointed an Historical Committee within FIHS for the purpose of closer supervision of the Historical Rooms and the activities of the curator. This reflected Barr's dissatisfaction with the current curator, Eleanor Kiblin. Kiblin had served as a conscientious conservator for many years and consulted professional advisors when necessary. Kiblin's assessment was that "Barr decided I wasn't 'good enough.'" She saw Barr's dissatisfaction as elitism, favoring educational degrees above lived experience. Kiblin resigned both as the curator and as the town's appointed historian. Lillian Harrigan, chair of the Historical Committee of FIHS, stepped in as curator. In her brief stint -- the family moved out of town in 1992 -- Harrigan recruited a new set of volunteers to help with care of the Historical Rooms.

Ellen Neilley is credited with establishing a higher order of archival practice. She discovered the missing Boston Post Cane and reinitiated the tradition of the cane being awarded to the oldest living resident of the town. In consultation with experts, like Bessann Triplett, and museum professionals, she and her assistants attended to labeling, cataloging, and protecting the integrity of the collection. They began digital record-keeping. In 2000, a professional curator from Shaker Village held a workshop for several volunteers. Also in 2000, Neilley, Veda O'Neill, Kris Holmes, Priscilla Putnam Martin, and Carol Brock researched and created a "Walking Tour of Main Street." The booklet was published in 2002 with FIHS and grant funding. It was updated in 2005. Veda O'Neill's service included moving the collection from the library to the Town Hall Annex, she and Ellen Neilley reorganized the collection following the move. Curators following O'Neill included Michael O'Neill, Marie Rechkemmer, and Charlie and Sarah Pyle.

Moving to the "Beehive"
In 2000 the Town Offices moved from the Town Hall Annex to the former Red School on Main Street. This made space available in the Annex for the FIHS' historical collection. The library's second floor had been condemned by the Fire Marshal and the library trustees wanted to use the second floor for its circulating book collection when the space was allowed to re-open. FIHS leased most of the Annex from the town and moved the Historical Rooms there in 2001. The next move of the Society's historical material came in 2017 when the collection was transferred to its current home, the "Beehive."

In the 19th century, the Beehive building had served as a dormitory for students and teachers at the adjacent Francestown Academy. The Academy closed in 1921, and the Beehive became a private residence. In 2003-2004, B.J. Carbee, FIHS president, and Charlie Pyle, FIHS treasurer, facilitated the organization's purchase of the "Butterfield Block" of land, including the "Beehive" building. The process of renovating the aging structure took 14 years. Two committees, the Beehive Development Committee, and a Beehive Restoration Committee, researched the physical and social history of the building and what needed to be done to return it to its 19th century condition. A campaign was launched to raise money for restoration. Charlie and Sarah Pyle raised $165,000 and obtained a $90,000 LCHIP grant. Sarah Pyle was the project manager of the renovation, as well as the LCHIP grant coordinator. Phase One of the restoration addressed the foundation, basement, sills, and drainage issues. Phase Two was the interior renovation. The final push to ready the Historical Museum for the 100th anniversary of FIHS' Labor Day began in 2016. Bub Rokes and Bill McNeill did the work with architectural guidance from Mike Petrovick. Landscaping was provided by Rick and Steve Miller. In 2017 a moving committee – Jan Hicks, Robin Haubrich, Eli Rokes, and the Pyles – brought the collection from the Annex to the Beehive and prepared the displays. Sarah Pyle designed the exhibits. After many years in cramped quarters the full collection of the Society's artifacts and ephemera was displayed. The Beehive also serves as the headquarters of FIHS.

Research and Presentations

In 1989 Greg Thulander, Francestown resident, son of Alan Thulander, and master's degree candidate in historical preservation, presented a project to the FIHS membership at their annual meeting. He planned to compile the architectural history of every structure, past and present, in town. To do this he needed current owners to complete a survey about their properties. He asked for help in cultivating the cooperation of town property owners and for funding. FIHS paid for the project's expenses. Thulander produced a comprehensive assessment of the structural history of the town. His thesis and accompanying documentation are part of FIHS' collection in the Beehive.

In the early 2000s, another architectural survey was completed. This one focused solely on barns. The Barn Survey, which is also in the collection of the Historical Museum, was produced by a team of local historians: Frank Hanchett, Kris and Len Holmes, and Frank Jones. Greg Thulander's photographs of barns were used in the final document. The project culminated in 2003 with a public presentation of their findings. Periodically from the 1980s-2000s, FIHS sponsored lectures and presentations on historical topics. For example, a gift from the Whittemore family led to a series of historical lectures. This series included presentations on Colonial New Hampshire, the Sheep Boom of the mid-1800s, and the story of Poor Farms and Poor Houses.

FIHS supported oral history projects. In the mid-1980s Lois MacAdam and other volunteers recorded interviews with several dozen older residents. FIHS provided a cassette tape recorder for this project; the tapes have been converted to CDs and are in the library. Another round of oral history was initiated in the 2000s. Elementary and middle school students led by Hillary Graham, Nancy Gagnon, Diana Place, and Kendall Bush interviewed older residents about "Memories of the Homefront" during World War II for a Hilary Graham documentary. This 2008 film received recognition from NH Public Television and Ken Burns, director and producer of the PBS series, "The War." The students who contributed to the documentary were Kelsa Danforth, Jakob Rupp, Elizabeth Taft, Jimmy Gombas, Austin Hoffman, Mathew Foote, Emily Peters, Joel Barwood, and Ben Westcott. The project was funded by FIHS and the NH Council on the Arts. In 2009, some of the same organizers led a group of middle school students through another project. The students created video recordings of the memories of older native residents. They also collected photographs of daily life in town in the early to mid-20th century. The project – "Francestown NH First-Person Histories" -- took three years to complete and was also funded by FIHS and the NH Council on the Arts.

Preserving Historic Vehicles and Structures

A bridge between the two missions of FIHS – celebrating and preserving the history of the town, and actions to improve life in town – is the preservation and restoration of historically significant artifacts and buildings. Beginning in the 1970s, FIHS became an active participant in the preservation of town treasures. The town owned a Concord Coach, two 19th century hearses, and a Hand Tub pumper for firefighting. FIHS paid to have each of those vehicles restored in the 1960s-1970s. In 1971, the gilded eagle atop Town Hall was also restored by FIHS. Logical concerns followed the restoration of these antiques. Where to store them so they receive proper protection from the elements, and how should they be displayed or used? These concerns were not resolved until 2013.

For many years the coach and hearses were stored in the bays of the horse sheds, which protected them from the direct impact of rain and snow but not the indirect effects of humidity, vermin, heat, and cold. The idea for a "vehicular museum" was first broached in the 1970s when FIHS paid to rehabilitate the coach and hearses. A fund was started at the inspiration of the Norman Stewart, Clifton Foote, Lawrence Kullgren, and Alan Thulander. The project was restarted by Thulander in 1985. He proposed building a second set of carriage sheds on the land immediately to the east of the Meeting House. In 1991 Town Meeting voted in favor of such a plan and FIHS pledged support. But the Old Meeting House, Inc. objected to building anything in their side yard. The OMH group saw such a structure as incompatible with the beauty of OMH.

In 2000, following the closure of the Red School and its renovation as the Town Offices, Town Meeting rescinded its 1991 vote, and approved a new site for the museum -- behind the Town Offices. When Alan Thulander stepped down from the Select Board, establishing a vehicular museum became his driving ambition. By 2005, Thulander and the Mt. Crotchet Firefighters Association (MCFA) proposed the town lease from FIHS the land between the Beehive and the Town Hall as a museum site. It made sense to locate the vehicular museum adjacent to the Beehive and to create a "museum complex." The vehicular museum concept had grown beyond housing the coach and hearses. It now included a large collection of farm and business implements including a sleigh, a hay rack wagon, and a 1937 John Deere tractor. The MCFA made a commitment to erect an appropriate structure on that site. FIHS, under the leadership of Priscilla Putnam Martin, agreed to lease the land to the town.

Thulander located a timber frame barn structure in Weare and negotiated the purchase. The one-hundred-year-old barn was taken apart and brought to Francestown by members of the Francestown Fire Department. Predictably, Francestown Sand & Gravel and D.H. Hardwick and Sons donated their services to prepare the site. Other local contributors were the Robblee Tree Service and Gary Webber Foundations. Siding for the exterior was milled from trees cut in the town forest by Jeff Tarr. Those logs were hauled to a mill and set into the frame by Tom Paige. David and Deborah Stewart Adams provided lighting design. The chief of the works for the erection of the building was Fire Chief Larry Kullgren. FVFD members completed the reassembly of the barn in 2010. Funds for the project came from several sources including the MCFA and FIHS, as well as private donors. An article by Thulander in *The Francestown News* in August 2011 recounted the history of the project.

The museum's grand opening coincided with the 75th anniversary of the Francestown Fire Department in 2012. It was dedicated as the "Heritage Museum in the Alan Thulander Building" in August 2013 a few months before Thulander died. He personally donated several objects to the museum. The largest was a 1920 Ford Model A that had been a fire truck in Francestown.

The town owns the building and the collection in the museum. The Select Board appointed a committee, with members from FIHS, FVFD, the Heritage Commission, and the Select Board, to supervise and determine governance. The committee chose former Select Board members Bill McAuley and Bobby Abbott to serve as caretakers of the museum. Both shared an interest in vintage equipment and tools. McAuley wrote a monthly column about the museum in *The Francestown News* for a couple of years prior to creating a standalone monthly newsletter that explains to readers how items in the museum's collection were used and how they fit into town history. Subsequently, Jennifer Vadney joined McAuley and Abbott as a curator and host. In 2018, as the museum's collection expanded, a floor was poured in the building's basement so that all the apparatus owned by the museum could be displayed appropriately. Again, volunteers from the Fire Department and Francestown Sand & Gravel prepared the space.

Preserving Historic Structures

"Think big!" In the early 1980s, inspired by the town's first ever Master Plan, Jack Arnold threw that challenge to the FIHS' members at their annual meeting. Arnold recommended that FIHS undertake a "big project" to "galvanize enthusiasm for town improvement." Arnold had some specific projects in mind: an inflatable "bubble" structure that would house tennis courts and a swimming pool, and the acquisition and restoration of the soapstone mill. In response to Arnold's challenge, a committee was formed to work on a visionary plan. The committee took a different tack than Arnold imagined. They envisioned FIHS acting as the primary advocate for the restoration and preservation of historical structures in town. A prioritized list was made with the horse sheds, including storage for the historic vehicles, at the top. The sheds appeared to be in danger of collapse. The Meeting House was second, Town Hall third, cemeteries next, followed in order by the Soapstone Mill in Mill Village, the trees on Main Street, and what they saw as the post office "eyesore."

Bill Hansen investigated what it would take for the top three structures to qualify for national-level historic designation and to facilitate grant acquisition for their renovation and upkeep. FIHS Board member Johanna Staub supported this direction stating "preserving ... historic beauty and significance" ought to be the primary role of FIHS. Several board members wanted to give the Annex a "colonial facelift," as well. Hansen invited architectural historian, John Merkle, to join the project and develop recommendations for how best to preserve the structures on FIHS' list. Merkle studied the designated buildings and presented his report at a public meeting in 1983. The report became the blueprint for future renovation of the Old Meeting House.

In 1985 based on the Merkle Report and the prioritized list, FIHS President Derald Radtke recommended that OMH be the next target for improvement by FIHS. There were obstacles. The status of the Unitarian congregation that owned OMH wasn't clear, and the legal ownership and responsibility for the building's upkeep was murky. Further research was undertaken. *The founding of OMH, Inc., an organization independent of FIHS, will be explained in a separate section later in this chapter.*

From the mid-1960s onward, the horse sheds on the Common have been repaired frequently. This structure was built in the 1800s as a companion for the Francestown Academy building. Although the town owns this property it depended on the Village Improvement Society, and its descendent FIHS, to organize and finance its upkeep. Preserving the integrity of the structure gained importance when town-owned antique vehicles were restored and housed in the sheds. A case could be made for FIHS to take responsibility for the structure given that FIHS used the horse sheds for its Labor Day carnival, and stored dozens of tables and sawhorses in the sheds. In 1971 FIHS installed canvas awnings on the sheds. Every few years FIHS arranged for repair, painting, or roofing of the sheds. In the mid-1980s, following Merkle's report, a Warrant Article proposed that FIHS and the town share the costs of horse shed maintenance. It passed. For the first time, the town government would assume some responsibility for the sheds, but Thulander still viewed FIHS as the primary caretaker. In 2000, Kris Stewart dealt with FIHS, not the Board of Selectmen, when he made a deal to trade work on the sheds for FIHS funding of skateboard facilities in the recreation area.

Jack Arnold's interest in preserving the Soapstone Mill was shared by other leaders of FIHS. In the late 1960s, attempts were made by members to stop the deterioration of the mill through negotiation with the owner. When the owner did not show interest in preserving the structure, FIHS posted "Danger!" signs around the perimeter of the quarry and mill; the signs were removed when the owner protested that they encouraged peoples' curiosity. In the 1980s, Society leaders authorized a member of the executive board to knock on the door of the Colorado home of the unresponsive non-resident property owner, without result. In 1991, President Bill Hansen encouraged the Select Board to take ownership of the property and then sell it to FIHS. The board declined. New Hampshire towns are loath to invoke eminent domain. In 2008, the mill collapsed.

In 2011, Francestown's chapter of Masons, known as the Pacific Lodge, merged with the Masons of Milford. They donated the building on Main Street to FIHS. The structure was built in 1868 to be a Masonic Lodge. FIHS was able to use the Lodge as a place to hold its meetings and as a location for the Labor Day book sale. It also made the space available for special events, like the Arts Fair held for a few years in the 2000-teens. By 2020, FIHS owned the Beehive, the Lodge, the Colburn Store Park, the recreation fields and courts, and the Three Sisters Building that houses the Village Store.

Following work on the horse sheds and the spin-off of Old Meeting House, Inc., FIHS leaders intended to address the needs of Town Hall. They never moved beyond preliminary conversations. In 1996, the Select Board appointed a Buildings Study Committee chaired by David Jonas which was charged to study the future of the Red School and the maintenance needs of the Town Hall. The committee focused on the Red School which required immediate action. Nothing was done by the town or FIHS to address the condition of the Town Hall in the 1990s. By the early 2000s, without making a formal decision, FIHS narrowed the scope of its sense of responsibility for town structures. By the time the building's steady deterioration forced it onto the town's agenda, restoration of the Town Hall had been ceded to the Select Board. As described in Chapter 5, the appointment of a Heritage Commission in 2005 was the key step in the town's assumption of responsibility for the future of Town Hall. Another area where FIHS ceded preservation activities to the town was cemeteries. In the 1980s, FIHS funds were allocated to support repair of broken gravestones by Dick Leavitt. However, by the 2000s the Cemetery Commission took on improvement activities entirely independent of FIHS.

The Improvement Society

The traditional scope of government in small New Hampshire towns was limited to road maintenance, police, and fire service, assessing property for taxation, and burning rubbish. Due to this tradition of limited governance, many towns had an organization like FIHS. A key function of such groups was to organize public services that Town Meeting did not see fit to authorize, but which the residents valued. This was the "improvement" function of FIHS. Prior to the founding of Francestown's Recreation Commission, the Society was the town's recreation department. Even after the RecCom was inaugurated FIHS continued to support recreation activities particularly regarding tennis, baseball, and the beach.

Recreation

The Labor Day tennis tournament was a key annual event for many years. The presence on FIHS' executive board of influential summer folk from a tennis culture background probably accounts for the Society's founding of a public tennis facility in what was after all a small, rural New Hampshire village. FIHS paid for the construction of the first tennis court in 1964 on property it owned on Old County Road South near that road's intersection with Greenfield Road (Rt. 136). By 1970, many people in town from all walks of life had become enthusiastic aficionados. A lot of native residents took up tennis. While summer people saw the Labor Day tournament as the seminal tennis event in Francestown each year, natives and their sons and daughters competed in weekly round-robins and frequent pick-up games throughout the year. In 1976, for example, the men's tennis cohort was busy from June through August. The Peterborough paper reported that in the winter of 1976, thirty-two residents of Francestown played round-robin matches at the Amoskeag Tennis Club in Manchester. Mr. and Mrs. Dick Leavitt won the doubles tournament. That Labor Day, twenty men entered the tournament; most were town natives. At Town Meeting 1973 voters authorized the town to lease the original tennis court and adjacent land owned by FIHS on Old County Road South, and to help fund the building of the second court. Ultimately fund-raising from private sources was so successful that no contribution from the town government was needed. FIHS facilitated the proliferation of tennis in town. It supported summer tennis lessons for kids taught by mothers and sisters using both town and private courts. Lois MacAdam saw to it that the young instructors were paid. Even after the creation of the Recreation Commission, summer tennis lessons were arranged and funded by FIHS for several years.

Due to the town's embrace of tennis, care of the courts became a preoccupation for FIHS. Not a year went by when maintenance, repair, or replacement of the tennis courts was not discussed at the Society's meetings. By 1978, the FIHS' Tennis Committee concluded that court number one should be replaced. Because of arguments about jurisdiction between the town and FIHS it took a full decade to address the situation. In 1987, Gary Schnackenberg, chair of the Tennis Committee, recommended that the town and FIHS jointly solve the problem. Through a Warrant Article at Town Meeting 1988, residents approved the replacement of court number one with contributions from both taxation and FIHS. Volunteer labor and materials donated by Francestown Sand & Gravel reduced the price. Once again, private fundraising was successful, and the court was replaced without any need for town funds.

In 1987, as a memorial to Taylor family patriarch John, a long-time leader of FIHS in the 1960s and early 1970s, the forest area adjacent to the tennis courts was designated the John H. Taylor Memorial Woodland.

Care for the town baseball field and support for the youth baseball teams was an FIHS role from the 1960s through the 1980s. In 1981, FIHS transferred governance of the program and care of the field to the Recreation Commission, but FIHS continued to provide funds. FIHS owned the field, though they leased it to the town. Ed Farhm, Joe Ludwig, and Dr. Paul Jane coached the youth baseball program for years. Rita Farhm organized fund-raising for uniforms and equipment. FIHS paid Ralph Rokes and Rob Ames to build benches that served as dugouts. In addition to their other activities toward beautification of the village, the Underhills, neighbors of the ballpark, regularly organized clean up "bees" for the field and the abutting area. Due to his dedicated maintenance of the facility and support for youth baseball overall, the field was dedicated to Jack Underhill in 1980. When Underhill died in 1987, FIHS installed a sign to memorialize "Underhill Field." In the late 1980s, to honor Lefty Abbott, long-time coach of the youth baseball program in the 1950s-1960s, a memorial fund was raised to pay for baseball uniforms. Eventually, the RecCom took full responsibility for the recreation area.

By the late 1960s, the town held a lease on the beach at the east end of Scobie Pond on Dodge Hill Road. Even with the advent of the Recreation Commission, FIHS leaders exercised authority over the beach. The Society provided the swim and dive raft at the beach. At one point FIHS' Beach Committee chair removed the raft temporarily because it was "a source of mischief" for unsupervised teens. Several town meetings resisted donation of the raft to the town, but eventually it was accepted. Well into the 1980s, FIHS members maintained the raft and arranged for its winter storage, organized "clean up 'bees,'" bought a life-saving ring, and arranged for Red Cross swim lessons.

For almost thirty years with support from FIHS as well as the RecCom, Mary Jane Marsden organized weekly summer contra dances and lessons in Town Hall. As many as a dozen dances were held each summer on Friday evenings. Prior to 1970, carpools of local youth made regular pilgrimages to dances in Peterborough. The town's dances took on greater importance for youth and young adults in Francestown when Peterborough stopped sponsoring dances. The long-standing dance program in Francestown certainly prepared the town's youth for the big Labor Day dance. On a typical summer weekend in the 1970s-80s, three to four dozen residents participated. By the mid-1980s, the town's Recreation Commission took on responsibility for the contra dances and Morris dances.

FIHS supported winter ice skating, but it was not always able to arrange a location. For several years in the late 1960s and early 1970s, FIHS erected a skating rink on the Colburn Store lot, empty since the store burned in 1964. However, due to liability concerns the lot's owners did not always approve. An alternative location was the Bixby Creamery Pond, but once the town accepted FIHS' donation of the pond and dam it too was not always made available.

Beautification

Beautification of the town was always a core "improvement" responsibility embraced by the Village Improvement Society (VIS) from its inception. FIHS had a Beautification Committee in the 1970s to "spiff up Main Street and the Common." The Underhills were the backbone of the Beautification Committee. They cared for the Oak Hill triangle as well as plantings around Town Hall, the Fairbanks scale, and the water trough. Yet, as they expanded their beautification efforts, they provoked issues of jurisdiction and style. When the Beautification Committee landscaped the Red School there was pushback from the school district. In the 1980s, there was a dispute over whether town buildings were appropriately landscaped according to traditional New England landscaping standards. Some folks in town asserted that New England tradition eschewed the planting of bushes and flowers around the foundations of the public buildings. Other residents wanted to follow the landscaping style popularized in the suburbs with shrubs and flowers planted along the foundation. A second-generation version of the Beautification Committee embraced the traditional approach and removed plantings at Town Hall and the Red School that violated the 19th century pattern even though those plantings had been done by an earlier version of the FIHS Beautification Committee. New England style landscaping "purists" have held sway up through the Town Hall renovation project of 2017.

Through the 1980s, Johanna Staub led FIHS' beautification efforts which involved an annual planting of bulbs. Thousands of bulbs were planted in the village over the years. During this period, a tradition of hanging seasonal wreaths on the public buildings was embraced by FIHS leaders. Lina de Tarnowski (Lina Lane's namesake) led an FIHS effort to buy park benches for several locations around the Common. In the 1990s, FIHS landscaped Underhill Field and the recreation area. The Society also supported Ann Stewart's initiative to plant elms along Main Street. She bought disease-resistant elm stock. The young trees were nursed in the backyards of several residents though without long-term success. In 1977, FIHS purchased the Colburn Store lot so that it could serve as a Main Street "park." It was leveled and planted by Kris Stewart but has remained largely unimproved. In 2013, Misty Paige Kiblin, Priscilla Putnam Martin, and Scott Carbee, led an army of volunteers in addressing over-grown bushes and trees.

It's not clear when FIHS became responsible for the large evergreen on the Common that serves as the town's Christmas tree, but a tree was present and decorated by 1970. Doctor Wiederhold informally assumed responsibility for the lighting of the tree in the 1970s. In 1973, during the first national "energy crisis," the tree was not lighted. From time to time the tree would "age out" and a new one was planted and nurtured to succeed the old one. To avoid burdening the FVFD, for several years Larry Laber was able to provide a lift for stringing the lights on the tree. The Town Report for 1995 notes that "the tree on the Common was restored to its former glory" through the efforts of Wiederhold, Laber, the Kullgrens, and several teens from the Explorers' post. FIHS beautification stewards in the 1980s also began the tradition of putting candles in the windows of the structures on the Common during the holiday season. Alan Thulander and Mit Boyle were leaders in this effort; they encouraged Main Street residents to "candle up." On a weekend in early December each year, FIHS held a kick-off celebration of the holiday season.

The American flags that appear on utility poles in the Village area of the town also have an FIHS origin. Though conversation about municipal flag display preceded the September 11, 2001, national tragedy, that event broke loose prior resistance. Shortly following 9/11, Charlie and Sarah Pyle and Kris and Lisa Stewart sought and acquired permission to put up close to three dozen flags on the utility poles along four of the five roads that converge at the Town Common. Charlie Pyle negotiated with Public Service New Hampshire, the power company, and AT&T, the phone company for permission to place flags on their poles, which is not something that is easily granted. Francestown may have been one of the first, if not *the* first, town to gain flag display permission from the utilities. It was a propitious time for such a request. In keeping with their notion of limited town governance, the Select Board did not want to take on the responsibility for the logistics of periodic display of a large set of flags. Once again, FIHS assumed the duty. The Pyle-Stewart foursome put up the brackets and the first set of flags. Over the years, the flag display has become a valued routine for Memorial Day and Veterans' Day. Josh Stewart, Larry Laber, Tom Anderson, and Blair Morin have been the flag raisers.

Support of Public Services and Community-Building

FIHS has been the first stop for donations for many project initiators who seek to improve the community. For many years it funded some routine public services. FIHS donated the original land for the dump, gave the Bixby-Creamery dam and pond to the town, and provided support for some Fire Department projects in the 1970s-1980s including firehouse cosmetics and signage. It regularly supported the library through donations to purchase books, to paint and decorate, and to offer special programming. For over a decade in the 1970s-1980s, the Little Red Wagon puppet theatre was hosted by the GHBML and FIHS paid the bill. For many years, local youth were sent to summer conservation camps. Gerry Miller, Sylvia Leavitt, Ricky Miller, and Kris Stewart were sent to the Bear Brook State Park Conservation Camp in the 1960s-1970s. In the 1970s-1980s FIHS paid for the FES 6th grade class to attend Camp Union's conservation camp. At various times over fifty years, FIHS supported Scouting through donations or sponsorships. At the request of the elementary principal, FIHS paid for historical presentations or materials such as a Ben Franklin reenactor and a set of NH history photo slides. The Society also sponsored school field trips; FIHS paid for a bus to take students to the Boston Museum of Science. On several occasions the Community

Church received funds from FIHS, particularly to care for the building. FIHS leaders viewed the church building as a community asset and encouraged donations for its upkeep. Over the years, FIHS made donations to many other projects. Prominent examples are the Tri-Town Kindergarten, the Community Pre-School, the construction of a public bulletin board, chairs for the Paul Bradley Room in the fire station, a piano for Town Hall, refurbishing the elementary school playground, and outdoor lighting for the Meeting House and the Town Hall. In the late 1980s-early 1990s, FIHS published a newsletter for town residents. The Society commissioned Francestown Christmas cards featuring images from local artists and photographers. On several occasions from the 1980s into the 2000s FIHS organized town wide cookouts as a kickoff to summer. A specialty of FIHS over the years has been organizing events that bring town residents together in unity and pride.

Village Store in the 2000s

In 2003, Jason and Jennifer Martel bought the Long Store building and the Village Store business it housed hoping that the re-opening of a ski area on Crotched Mountain would provide enough additional patronage from passing motorists to make the business viable. They stocked an abundance of craft beers at a time when most stores primarily sold mass marketed brands. After several years, they began to produce frozen dinner entrees. They installed large freezers in the south end of the building from which they distributed their products to other stores. The food production side of the business prospered under the brand name "Francestown Village Foods."

In 2013 the Martels put the store and building on the market so they could focus on expanding their frozen entrée business. A family from Nevada with relatives in New Hampshire bought the store and building. Rob and Christina Wohle took on the business with great enthusiasm and optimism, but there were several obstacles to its viability. The purchase price and the resulting mortgage were formidable. Carrying an abundance of craft beer was no longer a unique marketing niche. Ski traffic was disappointing, as was residents' patronage. In 2015, the store owners were told by the town that they were not zoned for customer seating. The Wohles instituted several marketing initiatives and worked hard to increase sales. Critically in 2016, the store lost about 30% of its revenue stream when its gas pumps were closed. The gas pump issue dated back more than a decade. When underground gasoline storage tanks from the 1920s had been removed, soil samples showed that a significant amount of gasoline had leaked from the old tanks. Monitoring wells were installed, and some remediation steps were taken and paid for by the NH Petroleum Reimbursement Fund. In 2012 and 2016 additional wells were drilled to monitor the level and movement of the leaked gasoline. More aggressive state regulation of underground gasoline tanks came into effect in 2016. Installing the equipment required by the state to license the pumps was not affordable. Pumps at other small stores across New Hampshire were shut down at this time. Also in 2016, the family experienced a tragedy when their 18-year-old son, William "Cole" Wohle, died suddenly. He was widely respected as "a kind and mature young man with a great sense of humor and a guy who was always there for you." Cole was an enthusiastic and valued member of the Francestown Fire Department. An escort of State Troopers and firefighters from throughout the region, accompanied his body back to Francestown. Hundreds of residents came to a memorial service at the Meeting House. This tragedy added weight to the burden on the family posed by the store's shaky finances. Later in 2016, the bank holding the mortgage on the store building required the Wohles to place the store on the market for sale. A buyer did not materialize, and the store was closed in June 2017. Hard feelings accompanied the financial demise of the store. There was sentiment that town residents had failed to sufficiently support the store. It was viewed by some as a town institution, like the library, the community church, or the fire department.

Village Store, Closed and Re-Opened

FIHS had the agility to respond when serendipity called. In 2017 when the owners had to close the Village Store, the building was auctioned and the bank holding the mortgage bought it. It was then that William Smith of Boulder City, Nevada, read about the store's demise in the *Wall Street Journal* and contacted the Town Office. Remarkably, he bought the building from the bank, paid off the back taxes, and donated it to the Society.

FIHS took on the task of re-starting the store. In late 2017, it began assessing the viability of a store and investigating alternative business models. A public forum was held to gather residents' input on what they wanted in a store. Many participants recommended that the building be renovated so it was more up to date physically. FIHS created a "Store Committee" of volunteers to research business plans of other general stores in small towns, identify and solicit sources of funding for renovation, solicit prospective store operators, organize clean-up and renovation of the building, and hold events to create community support for the effort to "bring back the store." More than a dozen people served on the Store Committee over the next three years. Many events were held to raise renovation funds. Sarah and Charlie Pyle were the backbone of the effort to re-start the store. Eventually more than $200,000 was raised to renovate and outfit the building. FIHS received a prestigious New Hampshire Preservation Alliance 2021 Preservation Achievement Award for the "Rescue and Revival of the Long Store Building."

A "Thank You, Mr. Smith" event was held in the spring of 2018. Smith and his three daughters visited Francestown to see the store and meet the community. The renovated structure was renamed the Three Sisters Building after Smith's daughters. Renovation and fund-raising continued through 2019. Bub Rokes was the primary renovator; structural consultation was provided by ubiquitous local architect Mike Petrovick. The search for a store operator was long and frustrating. Various business plans were proposed. It is not clear that a general store, without a niche side-enterprise can be a viable business in a town of 1,500 residents where full-size markets are only a half-hour away. However, a willing operator, the Richard Lawrence family, stepped forward and the Village Store re-opened in July 2020.

FIHS Leadership

Presidents of FIHS over the years have included: John Taylor, Don Pettee, Ernest Poor, Robert Parker, Charles Onasch, Elizabeth Oppenheimer, Brooks Rice, Derald Radtke, Lawrence Barr, Pat Place, Bill Hansen, Gordon Sherman, BJ Carbee, Priscilla Martin, and Charles Pyle. Priscilla Putnam Martin was encouraged to join the leadership group of FIHS in the 1990s. Putnam Martin developed a special interest in Sylvester Roper, a resident of Francestown in the 1800s, who is credited with inventing the motorcycle. She carefully documented and publicized Roper's legacy. Putnam Martin served as town historian in the last half decade before 2020. Charlie Pyle was treasurer of FIHS from 1996-2006. He then served as president from 2007 to 2020 (and counting) and for most of that time he was also the chair of the Labor Day event. This tenure and double duty were unprecedented. His leadership and service of FIHS is unmatched.

Long-serving secretaries were Mary Jane Marsden, Johanna Staub, Kay Severance, and BJ Carbee. Most secretaries served only a few years. Labor Day chairs have included John Taylor, Donough Prince, John Oppenheimer, Pat Place, Robert Parker, Charles Onasch, John Arnold, Lawrence Barr, James von Rosenvinge, Gordon Sherman, BJ and Scott Carbee, Mark & Holly Stanley, Charlie Pyle, and Gabby Paige. BJ and Scott Carbee served as Labor Day chairs for several years.

For decades the Francestown Improvement and Historical Society has been the organization that says "yes, we can!" when there is a need or proposal to improve life and build community in town. The Society continues to "think big!" and yet to provide the small touch, as well. The influence of FIHS has been and continues to be wide-ranging, imaginative, and pervasive. It is hard to imagine how life in this town would have evolved without FIHS.

OLD MEETING HOUSE INC.

In the 1880s, two congregations held services in the Meeting House on the Common which later became known as the "Old" Meeting House (OMH). The groups were divided, but both used the term "congregational" in the name of their organization. The split was not amicable and led to a legal battle over ownership of the building. The New Hampshire Supreme Court subsequently named the Congregational "Society" as the owners of the Meeting House, also known as the White Church. The Society leaned toward Unitarianism. The other, larger, group leaned toward Calvinism/Presbyterianism and kept the title of Congregational "Church." They built the New Church, or Brown Church, on Main Street and eventually became the Community Church of Francestown following a reorganization in 1959. By the mid-twentieth century, the small Unitarian congregation was not able to maintain the Old Meeting House building. In 1953, donations were solicited for extensive renovation. In 1961, townspeople again raised funds for necessary maintenance. Relations between the town and the Unitarians were sometimes rocky. The Unitarians believed that when the town and the congregation reached an agreement over use of the steeple clock in the 1800s, that the town also assumed responsibility for upkeep of the exterior of the building. Subsequent Select Boards did not agree. In 1970 and 1976 the building needed exterior painting, but the Select Board refused to pay. FIHS paid for painting.

Until the mid-1980s, the Unitarian congregation continued to worship, albeit irregularly, in the Meeting House. In 1987, the Unitarians sold the building to a private organization known as The Old Meeting House of Francestown, Inc. The independent OMH organization was created following a study by the Meeting House Restoration Committee which had been commissioned by FIHS in 1985. The committee was composed of members representing the town, the Board of Selectmen, the Unitarian congregation, the Community Church, a technical advisor on historic restoration, a fund-raising expert, and legal counsel. The chairman of the committee was Derald Radtke, the president of FIHS from 1985-1987. The committee recommended the formation of a not-for-profit corporation to own and manage the building. The stated purpose of OMH Inc. was to restore and preserve the building's architectural integrity and to manage its use going forward. When OMH, Inc. was officially chartered in 1987 Derald Radtke became chairman of its board of directors. He was joined on the founding board by John P. Arnold, Peter Bixby, Mit Boyle, Judy Danforth, Bob Edwards, Lou Gallop, Louise Greene, and Eldon Munson. OMH was an official "spin off" of FIHS.

OMH and FIHS Merger

From 1987 until 1993, there was an umbilical cord connecting FIHS and OMH. To a degree, OMH operated as a subsidiary of FIHS. In 1990 the FIHS executive committee discussed "the confusion in town about the relationship between FIHS and OMH." In 1991, FIHS ceded its Christmas card fundraising to OMH, and over the next couple of years FIHS donated funds for OMH landscaping. That relationship formally, and somewhat dramatically, ended in October 1993. In early 1993 a "Merger Committee" was formed by FIHS and OMH to study the possible benefits of formally merging the two organizations. FIHS was tentatively committed to pursue the restoration and preservation of all historic structures in town. It had a healthy source of revenue and a strong base for fund-raising. OMH was a key historic structure, as well as host to an array of programs for the community, but OMH needed regular infusions of funds to achieve its restoration goals. The committee, chaired by Bill Swan, included B.J. Carbee, Kay Fincher, Mary Jane Marsden, Derald Radtke, and Alan Thulander, recommended merger. Also, separately, the boards of the two organizations preliminarily backed such a move. The track to a merger appeared to be clear.

However, at the fall FIHS annual meeting former president Lawrie Barr stated his opposition to forming one organization, contending that the Historical Society functions of FIHS would be diminished if the OMH building became the organization's primary preoccupation. He was sure that it would, given OMH's restoration plans. Barr swayed enough participants to reject merger. The vote was close, and it was not without a ruckus over whether members new to FIHS at the annual meeting were eligible to vote. Though a meeting to consummate the merger had been scheduled for October 28, 1993, it was derailed and never reconsidered. Both organizations moved on, separately. To some extent, the two organizations compete for the time, energy, and money of town residents. Generally, though, since the decision not to merge, the two organizations have kept separate jurisdictions and behaved fraternally. OMH was listed on the National Register of Historic Places in June of 1999. In 2001, OMH, Inc. celebrated the Bicentennial of the building including placing a time capsule in the wall, to be opened in one hundred years.

In its first fifteen years, OMH raised $275,000 for restoration work. Radtke, and Mit Boyle, were the key members of the fund-raising and management team. A retired Air Force Colonel, Radtke was a man of action and expected full participation from board members. Though the restoration of the building moved forward steadily, board turnover was high; thirty-eight board members were seated in the first ten years. Early trustees were Radtke, Boyle, Bob Abbott, John Arnold, Carol Barr, Betty Behrsing, Herb Benedict, Dick Edwards, Chester Fesmire. OMH leadership tilted toward move-ins, though some old time Francestown families were brought into the organization's leadership. OMH reflected the change in population that was solidifying by the late 1980s and early 1990s.

The first set of renovations brought the building up to the State Fire Marshal's Life Safety Code. This upgrade made it possible for OMH to host public events. Painting and structural work followed. Basic infrastructure was renewed. In the 2000s substantial additional repairs took place including removal, repair, and replacement of the steeple, the clock, and the weathervane. Rotted timbers and sills were also replaced, as was the furnace. Other restoration included remodeling the minister's study, the bride's room, the men's and ladies' bathrooms, the foyer, and leveling of the front steps. A piano platform was built, new stage lighting was installed, and acoustical sound panels were added.

Funding for initial restoration work was supported by the New Hampshire Charitable Trust. Most subsequent funding came from donations by private individuals, sales of memberships, and memorial gifts. In 1995, the Beveridge Foundation provided a substantial matching contribution during one of the fund-raising campaigns. Some restoration work was donated through in-kind labor and materials such as the septic system replacement by the Miller Brothers in 2014. To support restoration of the building creative fund-raising events were held. "Moveable Feasts" were standbys for several years bringing in as much as $5,000 per year. OMH, Inc. committed to full utilization of the Meeting House. Common usages have been entertainment events, cultural programs, public meetings, weddings, funerals, art and craft exhibits, and Vespers on Labor Day-eve. Town organizations have held their annual meetings at OMH.

Derald Radtke stepped down as OMH President in 2003. There was considerable continuity in the organization's operation over the next two decades. Each OMH President who followed Radtke – Len Allen, Bruce Larsen, Merrill Milke Beauchamp, Stephen Griffin, and Marsha Dixon -- was influential by recruiting board members and in setting the tone for the culture of the organization. In particular, Allen encouraged more input from the board in decision-making, Milke Beauchamp was a champion for engaging the community more fully by booking entertainment events with a wide range of appeal, Griffin re-built the board when its membership slipped to three, and Dixon kept OMH relevant during the COVID emergency. OMH board members had specific, hands-on, roles. For example, Greg Cope stood out as a conscientious steward of renovation, repair, and maintenance of the facility for almost a decade. Cope arranged the implementation of a climate control system. He also conducted excellent historic tours of the building.

A key board member role was the assignment for booking entertainment. Mit Boyle, a wedding planner whose career had been in Manhattan, was the event scheduler in OMH's early years. The performers booked through the 1990s and early 2000s generally were classical or traditional folk artists with an occasional jazz, country, or pop-rock musician, such as Jesse Colin Young, Tom Rush, or Aztec Two Step. Classical offerings including Mozart sonatas and the Manchester Choral Society Christmas show. Jocelyn Bolle and Pam Stevens held a Victorian tea with dramatic readings by Dariel Peterson and Sirkka Holm. Actors and authors Joyce Maynard and Richard Lederer performed the play "Love Letters." Events repeated through the 1990s included an ensemble of local musicians known as the Meeting House Minstrels, as well as Labor Day Vespers, and performances by Monadnock Music and the Monadnock Chamber Singers. For many years, a full day of lectures by gardening experts, "Verdant Visions," was held at OMH in the spring; it was the inspiration of Ann Soper, Sarah Pyle, and Meredeth Allen. Verdant Visions was complemented by several years of Home and Garden Tours conducted in conjunction with the Garden Club and the library. OMH held memorial events for distinguished members of the community, and a public service was held following the September 11, 2001, tragedy.

During the late 1990s, board members Soper and Pyle, pushed for entertainment events that would appeal to a broader range of town residents.

In the early 2000s, OMH President Milke Beauchamp embraced the idea that OMH should be more inclusive. Performance scheduler, Lisa Phillips, arranged a series of adventurous bookings from 2005 through 2008: Johnathan Edwards, Livingston Taylor, Roger McGuinn, Al Stewart, John Sebastian, Steve Forbert, Jesse Winchester, Patty Larkin, and Ellis Paul. OMH aggressively promoted these popular performers and drew audiences of 150-250; many came from out of town. Inspite of such ticket sales the events did not earn much since these performers had higher price tags. However, by broadening the appeal of OMH programs, annual fund contributions from Francestown residents increased in these years. Probably Phillip's most memorable and controversial booking was Rusty Deweese, a rustic comedian who presented "The Logger: A Comedy in Two Ax."

OTHER ORGANIZATIONS

The story of associational life in town continues with brief profiles of several other organizations that have given residents opportunities to socialize and serve their community. In the 1970s-1980s, the town entered a period of sustained change mostly due to forces from the larger society. The increasing population of move-ins had little or no connection to social and service organizations that were traditional in rural, small-town settings. As Baby Boomers entered adulthood, they tended not to value the same groups their parents had. These changes in lifestyle created pressure on traditional associational life in town. As a result, some long-standing organizations died, though several traditional organizations remained active for twenty to thirty years.

The Grange

Chapters of the national Grange were organized in rural towns across the United States in the 1870s. The Grange was founded to promote the political, economic, social, and cultural interests of rural Americans, and also to promote education and community ties. Though strongest in the Midwest and Great Plains, Grange chapters in New England were staples in rural towns. By the 1970s, Granges were primarily community-building groups that included educational opportunities for their members. The Francestown chapter was chartered as the Oak Hill Grange (OHG). In 1971, its 43 members met monthly in Town Hall. The OHG had a youth contingent and grew to 50 members by 1990, declined to 34 in 1999, and by 2008 when the local members joined Antrim's Grange, membership had slipped to 15. The chapter's charter was turned over to the Milford Grange in 2010.

Annually, before Town Meeting, the Grange would host a meeting or two, where candidates for town offices could introduce themselves and answer questions about issues. The Select Board presented the proposed Warrant Articles and clarified why they were recommending them. This became known as "Candidates Night." On occasion, the Grange organized meetings to inform residents about important voting issues, for example when the school district asked for approval for a bond or proposed changes to its funding formula. When the OHG folded, *The Francestown News* took over this role. Another community-building tradition of the OHG was to name a "citizen of the year." Over the years those named included: Dr. Wiederhold due to his service to the ConVal schools, Fire Chief Clifton Foote, Lois MacAdam for her charitable work, Community Church historian Emily Lord, Fire Auxiliary leaders, town Historian Connie Dodge, the original Old Meeting House, Inc. board, the 4-H organization, the FVFD Rescue Squad, Greg Thulander due to his historical survey of town structures, Cher Barker, church moderator at the time, Joan Hantchett, librarian, BJ Carbee, FIHS president, and Herman and Dottie Miller upon their retirement as clerk and deputy clerk. Others honored were Virginia Rogers, Kris Stewart, *The Francestown News*, FES' PTO, Denise Glover, Don and Kay Severance, the Cemetery Commissioners (Linda Kelly, Betsy Wiederhold, and Ethel MacStubbs), and, for the last year the honor was bestowed, the Highway Department.

In 2002, the OHG received recognition at the Hillsborough County Fair for their exhibit on "How Much Do You Know About Our Flag?" Also, that year, member Dick Cilley, donated $300 so the OHG could provide a dictionary to every graduating 4th grader at Francestown Elementary School in memory of his mother Gladys Vadney. This tradition continued for several years. Other notable service projects included teddy bears for the Fire Department, hearing aid batteries for elderly residents, and helping to buy flags for the war memorials. A long-standing service of OHG to the town was, inconspicuously, attending to the needs of shut-ins and the elderly.

A typical meeting of the Grange in the 1970-1980s might include a quiz (for example, matching a tool to a task), a reading of a humorous poem, singing of folk songs, and playing bingo. There might be discussion of the paintings and sculpture of Michelangelo led by Dariel Peterson, or an agriculture education program led by the Clarks and Hoyts. Once a year there was a Youth Night, where officer positions for the meeting were held by teenagers like Warren Kiblin, Betsy Hardwick, Peggy Jones, Chloe Kiblin, or Arthur Merrill, Jr. Annual events included picnics and dinners at members' homes. The OHG sponsored the local 4-H chapter for many years. Stalwarts in the Grange leadership through the years were Ramona Jones, Merle Jones, Dorothy Hardwick, Winnie Hoyt, Dariel Peterson, Heather Kiblin, Evelyn Vadney, Nina Abbott, Richard Cilley, Mary Clark, Andrew Clark, Olive Colburn, Clayton Hobbs, and Harry Miller.

Masons

"Freemasons" is a men's fraternal organization focused on developing persons of integrity. Members help one another reach that goal and achieve a sense of purpose. The local chapters also serve their communities through charitable work. Francestown's Pacific Lodge originated in the 19th century and was still active, though with steadily dwindling membership, until the early years of the 2000s. They made donations to various projects in town, such as the Fire Auxiliary. In its waning days notable members were George Whipple, George Sanderson, and Greg Pierce. The Order of the Eastern Star (OES) is, essentially, an auxiliary for the Masons. Men can be members, but usually members are women who have a specified relationship with a Mason. Often an Eastern Star chapter sponsors one or both of two women's sorority-like groups, Job's Daughters, or Rainbow Girls. Like the Masons, the focus of the organization is to nurture good character. The OES also is a service organization. Francestown's Atlantic Chapter No. 28 celebrated its 75th anniversary in 1972. It included members from Greenfield and Antrim. In 2000, it merged with the Milford OES.

4-H

4-H clubs help youth achieve their personal potential by cultivating citizenship, leadership, responsibility, and life skills. They are often associated with agricultural projects through which members take on responsibilities that nurture maturity. The type of learning projects taken on by 4-H members need not be agricultural. Projects can cover a wide range of skills including practical and fine arts, home economics, science, engineering, and technology. The 4-H name refers to the organization's commitment to develop its members "head, heart, hands, and health." In the 1950s-1970s, the 4-H club in Francestown had many participants and was very active. It was supported by the Grange and the Community Church. In their youth, Bobby Abbott and Deb Stewart won trips to the national 4-H convention in Chicago. Adults volunteered as 4-H leaders. Barbara Caskie taught dress making, George Kunhardt sheep raising, Betty Jones photography, and Betty Stewart cooking and other home economics skills.

In the 1970s the 4-H organization was known as the "Faithful Workers 4-H Club" or the "Hill Riders," depending on the predominant activity of its members. The iteration of 4-H in the 2000s has been called "Farming Fun 4-H." From the 1990s on, the local 4-H club's fortunes followed a cycle of dwindling to a handful of members and then rebounding. Much depended on the availability of interested youth, supportive parents, and more than any other factor, an enthusiastic and committed leader. Traditionally, agricultural projects have predominated, but in the 1970s, 4-H members put on winter plays for the town. In 1972, the club presented "A Christmas Carol." That year the club was led by President Robert Rokes; members had the surnames of Kiblin, Foote, and Hardwick. Its adult leaders in the 1970s included Willis Hadley, Betty Behrsing, Eleanor Kiblin, and Barbara Thulander.

The 4-H club of the period from about 2005 to 2020 has had as few as five members and as many as fifteen. Lori Hardwick has been the primary leader of the group, and some members of the club have embraced her personal project of preparing Welcome Baskets for residents new to town. Members have also raised animals – horses, cows, sheep, goats, and poultry -- and showed them at the county fair. Other members have pursued cooking, sewing, crafts, photography, and community service projects.

Welcome Baskets

Baskets prepared and given to new residents in town had two separate but intersecting origins. Winnie Hoyt, and her daughter Dorothy Hoyt Hardwick, prepared baskets of goodies and local craft items for new neighbors in the 1970s-1980s. Later, the Community Church was looking for a way to introduce itself to new residents. Lori Hardwick Way, daughter of Dorothy, connected the two initiatives. She assembled and distributed Welcome Baskets as a church mission, but over time it was disassociated from the church. Contributors make food and craft items, and businesses and organizations donate samples or brochures. Community Church and Fire Auxiliary members help identify new residents and solicit items for the baskets. And, as noted above, 4-H participants have had a role in preparing the baskets. Notable adult helpers have been Pam Prentice, Kay Anderson, Diane Noonan, Jess Marony, and Amy Hardwick.

Scouting

Boy Scout and Girl Scout troops have been a feature of life for youth in town throughout the era from 1970-2020, but as with 4-H, the number of participants has waxed and waned. At times, both organizations have closed for a year or two and then been reborn by a new set of parents and leaders. Town historians noted in their annual reports that a Cub Scout pack was organized, and a Boy Scout troop revitalized at separate times in the 1970s. In the early 1990s the active Cub pack was a combination of boys from Antrim, Bennington, and Francestown. In 1995, Francestown had its own pack with 32 Tigers and Cubs. During the 1990s, Scott and Lorie Jenkins and Brian Delahanty revitalized the local Boy Scouts. Delahanty served as Scout Master for several years. This era also involved Scott and Kathy Sanderson and Al Van Cleave. In 1999, Delahanty took a group of Scouts to the quadrennial Boy Scout Jamboree at Gunstock, where 7,500 Scouts assembled. From the late 1990s into the early 2000s there was a bubble of Scouts and Cubs approaching 40 members. These were banner years for scouting in Francestown. Carol Lape and Beth Wallace were Cub pack leaders in this period. In a poignant testimonial in *The Francestown News,* Bob Hunsaker celebrated the "graduation" of "Nine Lil Guys" who were moving on from Cubs to become Boy Scouts. He describes the joy he felt as an adult watching these boys grow into young men and all the experiences they shared over the years. Large contingents of Boy Scouts attended summer camp during this time. The Sandersons donated a trailer to the troop and Al Van Cleave renovated it to haul their supplies to events. In 2005, Francestown had five Eagle Scouts: Matt Lape, Adam Normile, John Normile, Nate Sanderson, and Liam Delahanty. By 2011-2012

Ben and Monica Harrington were leading a small number of Cubs and Boy Scouts in town.

Girl Scouting was organized with Fire Auxiliary support in the mid-1980s. There was a run of consistency in the 1990s with Girl Scouting's various levels -- Scouts, Cadettes, Juniors, Brownies, and Daisies – totaling 52 girls in 1995. By 1997 the number was 36. Leaders in the 1990s were Cher Barker, Lois Powers, Linda Compton, Nancy Lundgren, Pam DeWitt, Jan O'Donnell, Kim Wheeler, and Shawna Ireland. By 2001, a Girl Scout troop was not functioning. A few years later Sam Coughlin, Maxine Gerbino, Holly Stanley, Ann Cilley, Sarah Morgen, and Jennifer Parker stepped forward to lead.

At times an Explorer Post was formed by volunteers from the Fire Department for young men and women who wanted to learn about firefighting and rescue services. For example, during the 1995 Foote Barn fire five Explorer Scouts participated under the guidance of Randy Wheeler.

Garden Club

Gardening enthusiasts met at Nancy Gagnon's home in 2000 to organize a Garden Club. In the following years, club members produced dozens of articles in *The Francestown News* educating readers about different plants and pests and extolling the joy to be found in gardening. The GC began holding an annual Plant Sale in May 2001 on the Common. The proceeds were used for town beautification projects and to offer a post-high school scholarship to a Francestown resident. In keeping with the tradition established by the Old Meeting House's "Verdant Visions" education series, the Garden Club held meetings with informative speakers. The club's calendar for 2016 is an example of a typical year: four informative and entertaining programs, the May plant sale fund-raiser, awarding a college scholarship, a plant sale at Labor Day, garden tours for club members, maintenance of the triangle garden at Oak Hill Rd and Main Street, and a planting and display at the horse trough.

In 2006 the GC re-landscaped the Oak Hill Triangle and then maintained that garden with annual work "bees." Master Gardener Martha Coutts-Eisenberg designed the plantings so that something would be blooming in every season. The Select Board supported the project and material was donated by Kris and Lisa Stewart as well as shade, cool water, and bathrooms from neighbors Margery Foster, Brooks Place, and Ann Stewart. Hard work was done by Kay Severance, Judy Badot, Dianne Curran, Ben Watson, Len Allen, Susan Avery, David Connard, Janine Cowell, Roon Frost, Jan Griffin, Paula Hunter, Ian and Jacob MacKay, Karen Paul, Shannon Turcott, and Maureen von Rosenvinge. Plants were donated by Mike Petrovick and Bill McAuley among others.

Francestown Food Co-op

A food purchasing cooperative club was established by several families in town in the late 1970s. Mary Jane Marsden was its primary leader for many years. In 2000 the cooperative involved twenty families. The co-op brought in bulk quantities of organic foods and members divided the shipments. By the late 2000-teens it was no longer in operation.

Francestown Friends

A public assistance administrator is elected by the town to provide support for people facing emergency financial challenges. The rules for the town's support of individuals and families in need are generous in some respects and limited in others. To fill gaps in public assistance, Phyllis Naegeli and Dariel Peterson created Francestown Friends in 2008 as a charitable non-profit. The Friends can help with summer camp and after-school program fees, car registration and driver's license fees, dental care, and personal care items. The funds collected are at the disposal of the public assistance administrator. Many individuals, the Fire Auxiliary, and the Community Church contributed to the fund over the years.

Pond associations: PPPA, SPPA

Each of the two "great ponds" in town have had abutters' associations to assert stewardship over the health of the pond. The purpose of the groups is to monitor and protect the pond's environment. The Scobie Pond Preservation Association (SPPA, from the 1990s) and the Pleasant Pond Protection Association (PPPA, from 2004) meet annually. In 2003 invasive Variable Milfoil plants were found in Scobie Pond. For most of the years since that time Town Meeting has supported Milfoil abatement and mitigation efforts. Town funds and grants from the NH Department of Environmental Services (DES) have paid for some abatement activity – hand-pulling, suction harvesting, or herbicide application. The spread of the invasive weed has been controlled, though not eradicated. SPPA members have worked cooperatively with DES personnel to facilitate the mitigation efforts. Through 2020, Pleasant Pond has been invasive-free. A significant reason for this may be the Lake Host program organized by the PPPA in cooperation with the NH Lakes Association. Lake Hosts inspect boats entering Pleasant Pond at the NH Fish and Game boat launch. Several times hosts have identified suspected invasives and the watercraft has been cleaned before being placed in the lake. Town Meeting provides funds to support the Lake Host program.

Francestown Academy

When the private Francestown Academy closed in the 1920s the corporation had remaining assets that became a trust fund generating some yearly income. These funds are overseen by a volunteer board that dispenses them as financial assistance to Francestown students attending a college or trade school. The recipient of aid must have completed one year and be enrolled in a second year. Scholarship awards continue as of 2020.

Pleasant Pond Snowmobile Club

Beginning in the 1970s, the Pleasant Pond Snowmobile Club maintained trails on the northside of Francestown. In the 1990s a spin-off, the Pleasant Pond Trails Association was formed to promote the use of trails by snowmobiles in the winter and horses in the warmer months. It worked cooperatively with the Piscataquog Area Trailways organization. In the 1990s and early 2000s, leadership of the Snowmobile Club was provided by Dick and Jeri Cilley, Tom and Joanne Fairfield, Mike and Joan Stone, and Helle Goodrich, Heather Whittemore, John Chute, Jim King, and Scott Goodrich. By 2010, due to declining membership and reduced winter snow cover, the PPSC dissolved. The Crotched Mountain Ridge Runners Snowmobile Club from Greenfield has continued to maintain trails.

CHAPTER 7

JOYFUL LIVING

The town's story told in Chapters 1-6 is dominated by the politics of how the town has coped with development and growth. Considerable stress and disputation accompanied these changes. However, lost in such a story line is how most people actually experienced life in Francestown on a daily, weekly, monthly basis – the joy of living in this small, rural town set in the beautiful hill country of southwest New Hampshire. Profiling some of the joyful activities and events of the last fifty years captures the spirit of the town at its best. Many of the examples of fun in Francestown are from the last twenty-five years, because a key contribution of *The Francestown News*, founded in 1996, has been to keep "the minutes" of town activities. Many of the fun times are due to the town's organizations and the events they sponsored. These organizations are the superstructure on which residents played, danced, fundraised, laughed, partied, and enjoyed life. But much of the good life is also attributable to spontaneous or extemporaneous events.

THE "FUN" 1990S

The 1990s, and early 2000s, were a generally a happy period in town. There were many children in Francestown from the late 1980s through the early 2000s, peaking in the mid-to-late 1990s. Families attend their kids' activities, socialize with other parents, and are drawn into recreation, school activities, and community events. Stewart and Carol Brock, for example, fondly remember the parties, plays, picnics, and BBQs during these years when they were young parents with young children. Other parents recall the high level of adult participation in putting on the Halloween Haunted House on the second floor of the Town Hall with elaborate costumes and decorations. Still, others remember the tight-knit group of parents who moved together through pre-school and FES, vividly recalling school talent shows and holiday events. As the population of children in town tipped downward after 2005, some of the opportunities for fun tapered off as well.

The expansion and revitalization of the recreation fields in 1994 facilitated greater athletic opportunities for town youth over the following decade. The recreation program expanded with a steady stream of activities for children from the first fishing derby of the spring to the Halloween celebration in October. Young parents are willing volunteers. The building of the new school led to parent mobilization to landscape, improve the playground, and offer after-school activities in the new school's spacious environment.

Entertainment for adults expanded as well. The Old Meeting House's performance schedule was packed, as were their fund-raising events. New activities were added for Labor Day, particularly the mud volleyball tournament and the road race. The Community Theatre performed a play or two annually during this era. At the drop of a hat, for celebration or fund-raising, adults in town would plan a dance using local musicians eager to perform. And there was fun to be had through spontaneous activities such as the Wheeler-Stewart touch football series in the sand pit.

THE FRANCESTOWN NEWS

For some, reading *The Francestown News* (TFN) is fun, but mostly TFN contributed to Francestown fun by publicizing events, and then reporting on them. In its tenth anniversary issue in 2006, TFN celebrated this role. Three women made TFN happen: Ann Soper, Mary Frances Carey, and Sarah Pyle. All three were relatively new residents in town in 1996. Soper took the recommendation of the 1995 Master Plan to heart -- that there was a need in town for a newspaper – and sold the idea to Carey and Pyle. Soper served as the original business manager, Carey solicited advertising and organized circulation, and Pyle was the editor-in-chief. TFN was a non-profit; Charlie Pyle saw to the 501(c)(3) status. FIHS provided a loan of $1000 as "seed money" which was paid back within one year. Soper passed away in 1999 from cancer. Sarah Pyle remembered, "Ann was wonderful at getting people to volunteer ... she made every job so much fun, people loved to join in." In the first 10 years, over 300 people contributed a story or a photograph to the paper. The three founders brought in key volunteers including Cindy St. Jean as layout editor, Abigail Arnold as business manager, and Beth Wallace as a correspondent. Wallace covered all things "school" contributing 112 articles in the first 120 issues. St. Jean and Wallace served more than 20 years on the TFN team.

"From the beginning, almost every organization in town appointed a volunteer writer to keep the community updated about their 'happenings'." Photographs were one of the keys to TFN's success and are visual archive of the town's current history. Photos were contributed by Jenny Fritz, Ray and Beth Wallace, Mary Lindstrom, and others. Another source of joy provided by TFN have been vignettes of history written by a collection of amateur historians including James von Rosenvinge, Elliott Hersey, Dick Cilley, Frank Jones, and Elizabeth Hunter Lavallee. These pieces would be a great read if compiled. Hunter Lavallee, a "move in" from Boston in the 1990s, has contributed well over one hundred profiles of Francestown residents over the years. Her work chronicles the lives of many long-time native residents as well as creative folks and notable volunteers. Other frequent contributors to TFN were Dick Cilley, Joan Dietrich, Martha Eisenberg, Jane Hooper, Parnee Gilman, Kim Wheeler, Jill Delorey, and Tonya Dreher.

In addition to enhancing residents' sense of community by practicing pure "boosterism," *The Francestown News* provided humor, most purely in its annual April Fools issues. Examples include "Hug your Fire Chief Month," bringing back the "HOLLYWOOD"-style "Francestown" sign on Crotched Mountain, and taking advantage of the newly re-opened Crotched Mountain snow-making technology by offering "Schuss into Labor Day." TFN spoofed a plan to expand the potential for tourism by having Mill Village look like the 1700s and Main Street the mid-1800s with no asphalt, concrete, or power lines. This would create something like Old Sturbridge Village in Massachusetts, with old-timey demonstrations of butter churning, candle dipping, etc. The April Fools tradition continued past 2005 with the announcement that the Woodbury-Thulander home would become a tavern, the Town Hall rehabilitation called for the complete demolition of the structure, the town administrator would be provided an apartment in the lower level of the Town Offices, and the transfer station would have Saturday night hours with a bar that served wine, beer, and soft drinks.

In the October 1998 issue of TFN, Pam Nation placed a coupon that asked residents to suggest a slogan that captured "the essence" of Francestown. The winning slogan was from Rob Ames: "Francestown: Centrally located 45 minutes from everywhere." A long list of entries tied for second and third, including: "Life as It Should Be," Maria Regan; "Unchanged Values and Untouched Beauty," Marianne Cyr; "Keep Out!", Rob Ames; "Where the Hysterical and the Historical Meet," Frank Hanchett, who also submitted "Where Strangers Become Friends and Friends Become Strange (or Stranger?)." Cindy St. Jean produced humorous family life sketches with Erma Bombeck touches. Gerri Bernstein shared her survey of the beer preferences of Francestown litter bugs following one Earth Day roadside clean-up. Bud Light dominated. In addition to TFN's journalistic humor, Adam Evans, the Internet and Facebook sensation as Francestown's "hillbilly weatherman," brought smiles to locals' faces when featured on WMUR's NH Chronicle.

COMMUNITY PROJECTS

Community projects frequently led to camaraderie. Clubs and organizations often called for "bees" of volunteer workers. The Fire Auxiliary held blood drives twice a year – helpful, positive, and at times inspirational. The volunteers who erected the Heritage Museum's Thulander building did their work with enthusiasm. The RecCom's expansion of recreation fields in 1994 involved dozens of individuals working as a team. Routinely the RecCom sponsored beach and recreation field clean-ups involving entire families, like the Skate Park facelift in 2009. The landscaping and playground projects both at the Red School and FES brought parents and students together in construction fellowship. In the early 2000s, FES was recognized as a Blue Ribbon School largely based on impressive volunteerism. One hundred and thirty volunteers logged over 1850 hours helping before and after school, assisting in classrooms, preparing teaching materials, baking, chaperoning, presenting special programs, and landscaping and making improvements to the playground. The After School Program included pottery, jujitsu, gymnastics, ASL, drama, and the "Library Adventure." FES participated in Read Across America and celebrated Dr. Suess' birthday. FES Talent Shows with as many as twenty performers were produced by the PTO. Key organizers of FES volunteerism were Beth Wallace, Celeste Lunetta, and Linda Lindgren. Many residents turned out to move the entire library book collection to the Town Hall so that the renovation and expansion could be undertaken. Another large group saw that the books were brought back and shelved in the new space. Many have contributed to the community woodpile, where cord wood for winter heating is collected for those who cannot afford to buy it. Fund-raising efforts, whether to help Kingsbury Hill farm buy a conservation easement, or to renovate the Village Store building, were often as fun as they were productive.

DISASTERS AND TRAGEDIES

Disasters and tragedies often bring out the best in people, and leave positive, even heart-warming, memories. Residents' response to the December 2008 Ice Storm exemplified positive community spirit. For twenty-four hours on December 11, 2008, ice rained down. The town was without power for a week. *The Francestown News* celebrated the town's response: "The real story of the Storm of 2008 is not the darkness or the cold or even the isolation. The real story is the thousands of kindnesses shown and the heroic efforts made by the people of Francestown." Volunteers from FVFD, Highway Department, and private individuals worked to clear downed trees, powerlines, and blocked roadways. Responses were coordinated by the Select Board with the Director of Emergency Management. Various contractors stopped their projects and helped the Highway Department and Fire Department. The FVFD canvassed the town door-to-door to check on residents. The highway crew brought food to isolated residents like Harriet Cope at the end of Poor Farm Road. Ty Holm was rescued from his Campbell Hill home so he could find power for his oxygen equipment. Soup was served at the Community Church on Saturday night and church volunteers made sure hot meals were available at CCF mornings and night for the next week. Residents and the Village Store donated food. The owners of the store, the Martels, though stranded out of town, gave the Selectmen the store's door lock combination and alarm code so they could access food or anything else people needed. Everything taken was recorded and eventually compensation was made. The Select Board opened the Town Offices as an emergency shelter and Emergency Management Director Paul St. Cyr secured water and cots.

Other storms and floods led to similar, if less dramatic, community responses. In April 2007 almost five inches of rain came down in 24 hours.

Thirty town roads were closed, and a dozen motorists had to be rescued from stranded cars. Many residents' memories of that event include positive stories about the response of the town, especially the Highway Department and Fire Department, as well as dozens of individual volunteers. The Town Report for 2008 summarized the town's heroic responses to this series of weather disasters: "The strength of a town is drawn from the involvement of its citizens, particularly in times of trouble. During the past two years Francestown has had its share of 'times of trouble ....' Each calamity presented its own set of problems .... Throughout, there were Francestownians, D.H. Hardwick and Sons, Francestown Sand & Gravel, Steven and Richard Miller, Yankee Pool, Clarence Paige, and George Whipple, uniquely equipped with both machinery and their time, who stepped up to help the town in its time of need. There are too many other individuals who, either as volunteers in the Fire Department or those who cooked meals at the Community Church, to list.... They, and we, know who they are. We sincerely appreciate their service."

Often a severe illness calls forth a compassionate and generous community response. Several examples illustrate this kindness and empathy. When Lieutenant Scott Quilty suffered terrible war wounds in Iraq in 2006, the community responded. Several fund-raisers were held to provide support for his parents, Scott and Janet, as they traveled to Washington, D.C. to be with their son through a series of operations. The Community Church, PTO, and even individual families held events to raise support. In 2006, Mike Petrovick was diagnosed with cancer, a special fund-raising and spiritual support dinner was hosted by the Community Church; the Library board helped with the event. Three years later a young mother active in the community, Karen Couturier, was diagnosed with brain cancer. The Fire Auxiliary and many individuals rallied to help her family pay medical bills – both Karen and her husband Mark were self-employed. Diane Noonan and Bonnie Jean Kuras coordinated assistance to the family. Also in 2009, the Dreher family received a cancer diagnosis and were thankful to the help from many folks in Francestown. Lisa Stewart worked with Kuras and the FVFD and Auxiliary to plan a dance fund-raiser, "Rock the Firehouse." Donations of food and auction items were collected. 150 people came to the dance. Kris Stewart arranged a late-night karaoke event. The PTO also held a fund-raiser. Lisa Stewart stated, "We all love living in Francestown, and its things like this that make that a little bit more true." When Isabella Hill's home on Pleasant Pond Road burned, it was the second fire in three months to leave a Francestown family homeless. The FVFD's Jenny Fritz observed that "In both situations the strong community network has helped with food, clothing, and relocation, a heartwarming gesture for neighbors in need."

Annual Community Events

The Labor Day celebration is the consummate annual event to which the whole community is invited. Other regularly scheduled community-wide events are foundational for community spirit. In 2005, the "patriotic purposes" line item in the town's budget became the Patriotic Purposes Committee. Since that time, the PPC has planned and hosted Veterans' Day and Memorial Day recognitions. The Veterans' Day celebration is particularly poignant when school children mix with aging veterans for a community lunch in the Town Hall. For many years members of the PPC were Scott Carbee, Polly Freese, and Betsy Wiederhold. Following the expansion and renovation of the Recreation fields in 1994, a decade of "Family Recreation Days" were held on Memorial Day weekend. Participants brought picnics, blankets, toys for the sand pile, and plenty of energy to play strenuous and, at times, uproarious games. Attendance varied with the weather, but each annual event featured games where children and adults playfully competed. Jim Nealand, Larry Laber, Kris Stewart, and Lisa Stewart organized the 1999 version of this event. The Community Church (CCF) held a "Fall Festival" in October. In some respects. Over the years the festival involved demonstrations by blacksmiths, yarn spinners, weavers, and artists at work. For children there was a petting zoo, a puppet show, a hay maze, and hay wagon rides. For adults there was a bake sale, a quilt show, arts and crafts for sale, and an auction of antique items and gifts from local businesses. Musicians performed and group sing-a-longs were organized. There was a food booth, and the evening culminated with a turkey supper. The Christmas Fair was also sponsored by the CCF, particularly the Women's Guild and Thursday Fellowship. When they had a full choir, CCF also presented a Christmas concert. In other years, they invited the Monadnock Chamber Singers to perform a Christmas music program. In later years, CCF's event was held on the same weekend as the elementary school PTO's Holiday Fun Fair. That event featured a large silent auction and arts and crafts made by more than a dozen artisans. On occasion, FES would hold a holiday play or choral concert. FIHS' holiday event was on the first weekend in December. The town's Christmas tree was lit, Santa visited the Common, and residents gathered around the tree to sing carols, drink cocoa, and eat sweets. When possible, students from FES performed songs or put on a play on the Town Hall stage. In the years when FES plays were not available FIHS would bring in presenters such as a puppet theatre. In 2000, Celeste Lunetta organized young performers to share poetry, stories, songs, and dance. In 1995, Mark Holding narrated an original Christmas story and Deborah Hancock led carol singing.

The Fire Department held annual Open Houses. As many as 150 people typically attended and viewed demonstrations of equipment and tools by firefighters. The EMS team demonstrated patient care and equipment such as the "jaws of life." Aaron Eder-Linnel introduced his State Police K-9 partner,

Cody, with a demonstration of Cody's skills. The Auxiliary provided refreshments and a slide show of firefighting and rescues. In the 1970s, Pat Place and Sibby Kunhardt members of the Conservation Commission initiated the Earth Day roadside clean-up. Individuals or groups chose a particular stretch of road and bagged the trash that had gathered in the brush on the roadside. This tradition continues. In 2020, there were still plenty of cans and wrappers to be gathered.

Graduation ceremonies take place at four levels – preschool, elementary, middle school, and high school. A particularly notable graduation from ConVal High School was in June of 2008. Francestown students swept the major senior awards: Siobahn Hurley was Valedictorian; she was also president of the Student Council, Honor Society, and the Interact Club, and on the State Champion Math Team. Siobahn was off to Dartmouth. The Faculty Award went to Alex McGrath. The entire school faculty identifies a single graduating senior who embodies the quintessential ConVal student. Alex was celebrated for his humility despite his estimable academic, cocurricular and athletic achievements. Alex was the editor of the ConVal newspaper and the best male high school runner in NH. Other 2008 graduates, many of whom received honors at graduation, were Krystal Bloom, Elyssa Brock, Anastasia French, Michael Gagnon, Jaqueline Hardwick, Rachel McKaig, Laura Parker, and Zachary Wilson, Sara Estes, Kaitlynne Foote, Deanna Fritz, Matthew Joch, Jessica Miller, Alexander Nolet, and Richard Welch.

The FES PTO organized plays and shows when parents, teachers, and available student talent allowed. In 1999 and 2000, for example, the "FES Players" put on Western theme shows: "Tied to the Tracks," and "Wagon Wheels West." Both musicals featured large casts. At times, they also produced a student talent show. In 2008, two dozen children performed. That year included a special dance ensemble, "The Red-Faced Moms" who claimed that at one time they would have been known as "The 'Red Hot Mamas!" In the 2000-teens the ConVal schools held a "Turkey Trot," a play day for kids from the five elementary schools on the north end of the district. The day included a fun run to promote lifetime fitness, and a collection of items donated for needy families. For a couple of years, the PTO, the library, the RecCom, and FIHS organized a Spring Forest Egg Hunt. Eggs were hidden in the town forest off Farrington Road. Scouting, described in Chapter 6, was a source of fun through camaraderie and personal and collective achievement of goals.

SPECIAL CELEBRATIONS AND UNIFYING EVENTS

The town has always been eager to celebrate special events; in many cases these celebrations serve as unifying moments for young and old. In January of 1981, the Meeting House bell rang for nearly an hour, as town residents spontaneously gathered at OMH to celebrate the release of the U.S. hostages held for 444 days by the Iranian Revolutionary Guard. Bicentennial and centennial events connect current residents with the town's past. In 1972, the town celebrated its founding in 1772. In 2001, Old Meeting House, Inc. celebrated the 200th anniversary of the building. The GHBM Library celebrated its 75th anniversary in 1998, and the Fire Department turned 50 in 1988 and 75 in 2013. The latter celebration included the dedication of the Heritage Museum. Occasionally, a new Boston Post Cane holder is honored, often at Vespers. When some residents felt "the town needs this," there was a "community picnic" or "town wide BBQ." Often these events are held on the Common. FIHS has held several BBQs on the Common to encourage neighborliness.

Individuals are honored as well. Events celebrating Donny Abbott's 20-year stint as chief (1987-2007) were held by the FVFD as his retirement drew near. In a tent at the golf course, about 120 friends, family, and department members gathered to honor Donny for his leadership, dedication, and friendship. Officers from surrounding towns and the State Fire Marshall's office attended and spoke admiringly of their years working with Donny. The evening included a slideshow of pictures of Donny through his 32 years of service. Carol Brock served as the director of the Francestown library (GHBML) for fifteen years. In 2019, she retired and was honored with a reception and testimonials at the library. Two unique celebrations of military service took place in 2012 and 2017. First, a special event was held at OMH to celebrate the friendship of two men who opposed each other in battle. During the Kosovo War, in 1999, U.S. Air Force pilot, Lt. Col. Dale Zelko was flying an F-117 Stealth Fighter-Bomber. The plane was hit by a missile fired by a Serbian battery commanded by Col. Zoltan Dani. Zelko ejected and was rescued after seven hours behind enemy lines. In 2009, Zelko and Dani met face to face; Dani invited Zelko to visit his family in his small Serbian hometown. In 2012, Zelko and his family hosted Dani and his family in Francestown. Their visit included a tour of the town, and a public showing of a film made about their relationship. In 2017, Sirkka Holm, a veteran of the U.S. military during World War II participated in an Honor Flight to Washington, D.C. When she returned, a reception was held at the library where an over-flow crowd gathered in her honor.

EATING TOGETHER

Sharing meals has often been a way to encourage neighborliness. The heyday of the community suppers tradition was in the period from 2007-2015 when Mike Petrovick was the town's chief chef, regularly producing themed meals -- Tuscan, Moroccan, French, etc. -- in the Community Church's kitchen. Monthly community suppers independent of the church sponsorship began in 2003. The suppers were part of a four-town cooperative. In 2006, Kay Anderson recruited "sponsoring" groups to prepare the monthly dinners. Over the next thirteen years, many organizations stepped forward including the FES PTO, FIHS, OMH, FLT, library trustees, homeschoolers, Democrats, the Garden Club, and the Fire Auxiliary. Gerri Bernstein celebrated this phenomenon in *The Francestown News* in 2011: "In the age of Facebook, Twitter, LinkedIn, Meetup.com, Plaxo, and ClassMates.com, just to name a few, no web-based social media site can claim to share a real meal and offer an eye-contact-laden conversation with living, breathing people once a month. Such is the case for our Community Supper." In 2011 the role of lead organizers passed from Anderson and Severance to Heather Whipple-Simard and Lori Hardwick Way. Stacy Borden initiated a Gourmet Club in 1993. Periodically a family would host a meal in their home with a specific theme, such as Greek, Japanese, Afghan, or Southern U.S. These meals were still being hosted up to the COVID emergency.

Meals were a favored form of fund-raising. The Old Meeting House, Inc. began the Movable Feast tradition shortly after its founding. It was a fun and lucrative fund-raiser. The feasts were hosted by multiple families with successive courses being offered in different homes. On occasion, the feast didn't move, for example, when Harriet Cope hosted a Hawaiian luau. This model was used by other organizations for fund-raising in the years that followed. The Francestown Elementary School PTO prepared spaghetti dinners and pancake breakfasts to raise funds for necessary or good causes. Francestown's school board representative, Stewart Brock, famously flipped flapjacks at a series of such breakfasts before Town Meeting during his three terms on the board.

Music

Next to eating together, sharing music is a catalyst for good feelings among neighbors. During the 1990s and early 2000s, The Gigantics -- Patrick Hooper, Gary Schnackenberg, Glenn Kelly, Wayne McLeod – were a mainstay for dances or fund-raisers in town. Other bands with local musicians have been popular before and since. In 2018, Carlos Agudelo's blues band entertained at a fundraiser for the renovation of the Three Sisters Building. Matt Savage, jazz piano prodigy, has had a remarkable career. His trio regularly performed in the Meeting House through the 2000s. Matt's trio released more than a dozen albums and played to sold out crowds throughout the Northeast. Savage's 2006 album reached the top 25 on the Jazz Week charts. Matt performed with several jazz notables as well as on *Late Night with Conan O'Brien* and *The David Letterman Show*. His career is still going strong in 2020. Another young local musician of note is Jacob MacKay. He is the Resident Cellist and Education Director at the Newport String Project, and serves on the faculty of Salve Regina University, St. George's School, and the Rhode Island Philharmonic Music. Jacob has performed many times at OMH. Early in his career he performed with his siblings, later with the Apple Hill String Quartet. OMH has been the primary venue for most "concert" music presented in town from the late 1980s through 2020. The annual line-up has featured Irish to folk, rock to classical music, local performers as well as the nationally renowned. Tom Rush, who has a summer home in Deering, performed several times at OMH, as did other once prominent musicians, now working smaller venues. OMH also hosted performers booked by the Electric Earth organization and the Monadnock Folklore Society; both organizations have strong local connections. James Bolle, maestro of Monadnock Music which he founded in the 1960s and conducted until 2009, lived in Francestown with his wife Jocelyn in the 1970s-1980s. Bolle's ensemble performed many times at the Meeting House and the Community Church. Bolle also founded the New Hampshire Symphony Orchestra.

PARTIES AND DANCES

On December 31, 1999, a New Year's Eve ball was held at Tory Pines to usher in the new millennium. *The Francestown News* rhapsodized: "Francestown proved that it is a town that knows how to party at the Black and White Ball on New Year's Eve. The crowd of 270+ looked smashing, with some spectacular hats making an appearance. Who knew there were so many tuxedoes in the back of closets all over town? The dance floor was filled all night, and a large group cheered in the New Year out front with fireworks. This memorable evening would not have occurred without a group of party planners extraordinaire, who began working on the event last March … Ellen Neilley, Lennie and Marie Rechkemmer." The Rechgkemmers collected and stored the fireworks with funds from FIHS. The launch crew included Terry Barnes, Greg Neilley, and Rob Staub. Judy Danforth, Dodie Finlayson, Hannah Proctor, and Barbara Radtke organized decorations. Ellen Neilley, Joan Hanchett, and Connie Varnum managed ticket sales and publicity. Food was arranged by Jo Staub and Susie Barnes; Joan Kullgren made the cakes. The Master of Ceremonies for the evening were the dignified Paul Lawrence and humorous Pam Nation. Jenny Fritz memorialized the event in photos.

Smaller scale party events were notable such as the Brock's Halloween costume dances in 2015 and 2016. The dances were fundraisers for the Town Hall restoration project. The decorations – a Carol Brock specialty – and imaginative costumes worn by more than one hundred residents, created a vibrant party atmosphere. The Bixby Library Trustees and Heritage Commission shared sponsorship. Community wide Halloween parties for kids were a long-standing project for the Recreation Commission. The parties included a haunted house, traditional games, a costume parade, scarecrow contest, and trick or treating on Main Street, or a trunk-or-treat in the horse shed lot. Pam and Mike O'Neill and their eight children organized a Main Street "block party" in 1999 that entertained more than one hundred neighbors. The Fire Auxiliary made a specialty of dinner dances to build unity in the Fire Department while often raising money for a good cause. In 2014 their Spring Fling Dinner Dance and Silent Auction raised funds for OMH steeple replacement.

Dance events were memorable as well. For decades – literally – Mary Jane Marsden organized contra dances, many of which began with lessons for ingénues. A July 1998 contra dance was held to celebrate Dudley Laufman's 50th year as a caller. Many musicians who played for years with Dudley in his Canterbury Country Orchestra came to this event. A 28-piece band shared the dance floor with approximately 100 dancers. Leo and Diane Paquin of Dodge Hill Road were missionaries for clogging. Periodically they held classes and dances in town, and they were a staple in the Labor Day parade for several years. The New Hampshire Dance Institute (NHDI), through Great Brook School, involved Francestown children in choreographing and performing dance routines. Around 2000, NHDI performers from Francestown included Hannah Gilman, Heidi Jones, Amanda Gagnon, Belinda Bodnar, Angela Jones, Abby Compton, Ryan Fotter, Alex Bixby, Quinn Delahanty, Jessica Hunsaker, Andrea Cyr, and Stephanie Barker.

LIBRARY

The George Holmes Bixby Memorial Library (GHBML) was a meeting place for several local organizations and an ad hoc gathering space during its regular hours. Library directors and children's librarians during the period from 1970 to 2020 developed special programs for adults and children. Annual summer reading programs for children had high rates of participation. Each year had a different theme with a goal to encourage and celebrate reading. This was illustrated in 1999, when Nancy Houlihan, a popular children's librarian, led several dozen children in the finale of the Summer Reading Program. The event was held at the Underhill ballfield. Kids and parents played games and listened to a live band of local teens. A raffle and a "reading relay" were part of the celebration. One hundred and forty children participated in the program. Ben and Song Moeller, Village Store owners, served the kids ice cream as a reward for making weekly goals. Don and Mary Sipe donated free movie rentals and pizza for the raffle.

For most of the last 30 years, volunteers have led periodic adult book discussions. Elizabeth Hunter Lavallee has been a primary organizer of these discussions. For many years, Heidi Dawidoff curated a winter movie series combining classic and popular films. Special presentations by authors, artists, musicians, naturalists, performers, and informers are part of the GHBML's annual calendar. Many programs cater to both children and adults, such as the 2006 appearance by author Sy Montgomery of Hancock who read from and signed one of her many books for children.

In 2004, as a fund-raiser for the future library renovation and addition, the library trustees organized the production and sale of a unique calendar. Each month of the year featured a photograph of a group of town residents, for example the Rescue Squad, the staff of *The Francestown News*, a runners' club, and the Select Board, in what was made to appear as a complete state of undress. Known as "the Naked Calendar," it sold well.

Long-time GHBML Director, Joan Hanchett was a beloved legend who dispensed wisdom and compassion as much as information about books. After her passing in 2007, the library trustees, *The Francestown News*, and the board of the Francestown Land Trust collaborated in initiating the Joan Hanchett Nature Series. Twice a year, the series offers a program for families featuring a natural phenomenon – otters, caterpillars and butterflies, salamanders, etc. The first program presented Nancy Cowan of the NH School of Falconry, including two of her collection of birds of prey in person. In 2008 two hundred people attended a presentation by Ben Kilham, who has raised several orphaned bear cubs. He is the author of a book, *Among the Bears,* and is featured in a National Geographic film, "Papa Bear." The series continues as of 2020.

Several documents promoting Francestown's history are in the GHBML collection and available to the public. This includes the various oral history collections and the "Walking Tour of Main Street" described earlier in the discussion of the Historical Society.

GARDENING

Creating and maintaining gardens is a staple of life in Francestown for many residents. The Garden Club encouraged individuals to have fun in their own gardens, sponsored entertaining events where gardening expertise could be shared, and fostered neighborly fellowship. Ben Watson, a local gardening expert with several books to his credit, wrote advice and education articles for *The Francestown News*, the *Monadnock Ledger*, and Yankee publishing. He also presented in several local venues over the years on a variety of gardening topics. OMH hosted "Verdant Visions" gardening seminar for a decade from the mid-1990s.

The Garden Conservancy, a national organization, featured local gardens in its national "Open Days," event in 2010. Twelve New Hampshire gardens were recognized among 300 notable gardens throughout the United States. The Francestown gardens of Len and Meredeth Allen (on Bible Hill Rd Extension) and Paula Hunter and Joe Valentine (on Reid Road) were among those profiled. The Allens came to town in 1998 and built their extensive gardens from scratch. Hunter and Valentine started their English-style gardens around 2000. Later, the Allen's garden was featured in *Country Gardens Magazine* (2013) while the Hunter-Valentine gardens were on the Garden Conservancy's national tour, again, in 2014.

TOWN ARTISTS

Francestown has had a rich supply of residents with professional, or at least notable, artistic talent. These artists, and others, often were able to share their work locally, enriching the culture of the town. Resident musicians include

James and Jocelyn Bolle, Roger Hall, Jacob MacKay, Matt Savage, Candace Wharton, Tom Malouf, and Allan Block (who was also a leatherworker). An abundance of visual and material artists, some with national and international reputations, also made Francestown home including: Peter and Edith Milton, Oscar "Ozzie" Sweet, Nancy, Angell, Wally Tripp, Rosemary Conroy, Jessie Dawes, Allison Erickson, Marcy Bixby Tripp Graham, Isabella Britain Hill, John and Diane Lomas, Peg Lopata, Anne Moeller, Pat Nelson, Jessie Pollack, Bessann Triplett, Michael Truelson, Carol Russell, Beth Wallace, Janet Hicks, Kirsten Barwood, Jenny Fritz, Ruth Behrsing, Ann Behrsing, Scott Jenkins, and Dariel Peterson. Notable authors include Constance Leonard and Ben Watson. On several occasions OMH presented lectures and displays. For a few years beginning in 2013, a set of local musical, visual, and material artists held an "Arts Fest" headquartered at the FIHS Lodge on Main Street; Marcy Bixby Graham and Ethel MacStubbs chaired this effort. The Monadnock Quilters' Guild has a Fall Festival every year. Local quilters -- Jan Hicks, Gail Wilson, Kirsten Barwood -- have hosted the event in town on occasion. In 2015 the town hosted a town-wide quilt show – "Quilts Old and New." The displays were centered at the Old Meeting House with creations displayed on both levels, but also included the Heritage Museum, the FIHS Historical Rooms in the Annex, and the library. Some of the quilts were by local artists. That September OMH hosted presentations and displays by quilting experts.

COMMUNITY THEATRE

In the 1990s and early 2000s, Francestown was lucky to have two theatre troupes offering plays using local talent – the Francestown Community Theatre (FCT), and the Pleasant Pond Players (PPP). Barbara Quinn and the Wheeler family began organizing a theatre troupe in 1989. That autumn Randy Wheeler asked the Select Board for permission for an acting club to use the Town Hall. This company operated for the next fifteen years as the Francestown Community Theatre. In the early years of the FCT the leadership team was Randy and Kim Wheeler, Pam Nation, B.J. Carbee, Al and Joan Van Cleave, Linda Shea, Mary Tempone, and Jane Hooper. According to Town Historian Kris Holmes, the FCT's startup money came from the Fire Auxiliary. Kim Wheeler directed the first productions in 1990 and 1991, "I'll Get My Man," and "Exit the Body." In the fall of 1992, the third play presented in Town Hall was "Down to Earth," with Jane Hooper and Pam Nation directing. The company had over forty participants mostly from Francestown. According to Kris Holmes, "Their goal is to provide entertainment for the group and the community." Accrued profits were pledged to restore the stage in the Town Hall. In 1997 the Town Hall stage was renovated with $4,000 contributed by the FCT.

In 1993, the members decided to enter the New Hampshire Community Theatre Association's (NHCTA) annual competition. FCT presented "The Old

Lady Shows Her Medals," by J.M. Barrie. Their efforts were rewarded with a Best Actor Award for Mark Holding and the Best Stage Management Award. At the NHCTA competition in 1995 the FCT brought their one-act version of "Blithe Spirit," and the company was awarded Best Set owing to Al Van Cleave's creativity and hard work.

The company gained steam as the 1990s unfolded; sold out performances were the rule. From 1994-1999 FCT presented "The Twelve Pound Look," "Blithe Spirit," "Cocktails with Mimi," "The Odd Couple," "The Night is My Enemy," and "Harvey." The "Odd Couple" production was notable because the pair was female. In 1996 the FCT put on a children's Christmas play. There was no production in 2000, but Theo Hardwick Wheeler, the matriarch of the Community Theatre's founding family, appealed for new participants through an article in *The Francestown News*, and in 2001 a revitalized FCT presented "The Foreigner." The final production, "Social Security," was mounted in 2005. By that time the founders and primary participants had moved into different stages of their lives.

Directors through the years were: Kim Wheeler, Randy Wheeler, Sarah Pyle, Jane Hooper, Pam Nation, Hilary Weisman Graham, and Luis Perez. Producers and members of the crew were Ann Soper, Mary Tempone, Theo Wheeler, Anna Stein, Deb Adams, Rich and Carla Pierson, Al and Joan Van Cleave, Linda and Bert Jepsen, Rosemary Gallaher, Carol Ivester, Sheila Farres, Denise Hunsaker, Jane Jackson, Meghan Scott, Parnee Gilman, Betsy Wiederhold, Cherie Scott, Carla Nickerson, Mark Pitman, Jessie Dawes, Bill McNeill, Scott Carbee, Bryant Hardwick, Betsy Hardwick Paige, Nancy Jones, Linda Abbott, Dot Hardwick, Shirley Pitman, Peggy Abbott, Jimmy Knight, Pam Delahanty, Pam Pitchard, Jeff MacQueen, Charlie Pyle, Paul Susca, Hilary Weissman Graham, Luis Perez, and, always, the Wheeler family.

The list of actors who trod the Town Hall boards is long: B.J. Carbee, Heidi Thornblad, Ron Brenner, Andy Paul, Cher Barker, Sandra Whipple, Elizabeth Colby, Kim Dalley, Mark Holding, Denise Hunsaker, Ben Moeller, Melissa O'Neill, Maria Regan, Randy Wheeler, Putnam Ecoline, Pam Nation, Krista Berry, James Fiest, Kate Fitzpatrick, Sandy Whipple, Wayne McLeod, Sheena Floreani, Pierrette Hackett, Carla Nickerson, Richard Pierson, Patti McNeill, Jimmy Knight, Paul Susca, Donna James, Tom Dowling, John Brekka, and Dominick Scott. Deb Stewart Adams and Dave Adams of Adams Lighting of Cambridge, Massachusetts played key roles in lighting the stage in a professional manner.

Around 2000, a new theatre group formed from the seasonal community on the east side of Pleasant Pond. Jeff and Barbara Levis, with deep professional theatre background in Venezuela and Miami, mobilized Michael and Marsha Tennis, Caroline Jacobs, and Bob Keiser to form the Pleasant Pond Players. Over a five-year span, the PPP put on "Lovers and Other Strangers," "Footsteps of Doves," "Love Letters," "Summer Shorts," a set of Neil Simon playlets, and "Falling Shorts." Attendance was high and the company was able to donate proceeds from ticket sales to the town library's renovation fund. The productions involved the Levises, Tennises, Jacobs, Keiser, as well as Kerrah Cutter, Gerri Bernstein, Mark Holding, Ann Stewart, Marcy Tripp, Carolyn Woodbury, David Tripp, Bonnie Kuras, and Ken Paradis. Wally Tripp illustrated the programs.

RECREATION

The most common recreation activity for Francestown residents was walking or hiking through the hills and forests in the town and region. The Conservation Commission, Francestown Land Trust, and Piscataquog Land Conservancy offered guided hikes in all seasons. Organized recreational sports also brought joy to the lives of children and adults through the decades. Much of the friendly competition was organized by the town's Recreation Commission, or FIHS. Some memorable recreation activity was extemporaneous, like the storied touch football wars. For several years, a Randy Wheeler team faced off in the gelid confines of the Stewart's sand pit against a Kris Stewart team in the Thanksgiving "Turkey Bowl." This game was followed in February with Francestown's version of the "Super Bowl." These matchups took place in the late 1990s and early 2000s. The team "owners" and coaches remained the same, though the mascots changed – one year the "Ravens" faced the "Giants," the following year the "Titans" played the "Rams." In December 2000, a special game was played, the "Y2K Bowl" on New Year's Eve. A post-game report in *The Francestown News* from one of the Super Bowls captures the spirit of the event, "After a total of nine games, five Super Bowls, and six years without a win, Kris Stewart, and his team finally experienced the thrill of victory. On Sunday Randy Wheeler brought his team and their undefeated record into Stewart Stadium to face the home team for the bragging rights to Francestown's Superbowl.... The player draft was followed by an inspiring rendition of the Star-Spangled Banner by Parker Wheeler, fireworks, and a bonfire. Referee Mike 'I'd Rather Be Playing' O'Neill...and Assistant Referee Cahal Mowery explained the rules." That year, Bob Hunsaker, Adam Hunsaker, Scott Jenkins, Mark Oles, John Hutchinson, Donnie Hardwick, Jr., and Pete Kazanovicz squared off. Hutchinson was MVP for his field goal. The final score was 9-6. Stewart celebrated: "So this is how it feels to win, this is great, I think we may have a dynasty going here." Randy Wheeler rejoined: "We will be back next season with a renewed determination to add to our 8-1-1 lifetime record and win back that Super Bowl Trophy."

The Old Meeting House began sponsoring a "Tour d' Francestown" in 2013 and has done so each year since. Founding bikers Jennifer Vadney and Carlos Agudelo organized the events which consist of multiple routes along the byways of the region. It is non-competitive but no less intense. As early as 1993, the New England Cycling Club in conjunction with Spokes and Slopes of Peterborough sponsored a bike race starting and finishing at Tory Pines.

On the mountain biking side of things, Jim St. Jean stands out. He has led an initiative to create a dedicated mountain biking trail network in the Fisher Hill area. Working in partnership with FLT, ConCom and private volunteers, the resultant trail network connects conserved lands and town forest lands including the Fisher Hill Town Forest, the Shattuck Pond Town Forest, and Turnpike Trails. He also participated in the Hampshire 100 bike race which came through Francestown for many years. This race is a premier ultra-endurance mountain bike race and an ultra-trail run. That year there were 352 competitors. In 2017, the local winner of the ultra-trail run was Chris St. Jean with Scott LaPlante, Ella Dishong, and Molly Dishong finishing at the top as well. The Dishong sisters competed nationally that summer in "cyclocross" races.

Running, whether by marathoners or grade-school children has been a source of pleasure for many residents. Running the Boston Marathon has been a goal of many runners from Francestown over the years. Unfortunately, a complete list of those who have finished the Patriot's Day race is not available. In 2004, five local runners completed the Marathon – Thomas Peters, Jim Roche, Paula Hunter, Greg Neilley, and Rick Leandri. Bruce Harrington ran the long race in 2007. For twenty-five years Labor Day included the "Francestown Five" road race. The 12th annual edition included over 100 runners. That year, Tiffany Calcutt was the first finisher from Francestown in the 5k, followed by Ed Naegeli, Stewart Brock, Greg Neilley, Sandy Chute, and Shannon Turcott. Local five-mile competitors were Jim Roche and Sorrell MacKay. For several editions, the organizers were Greg Neilley, Linda and Jim Roche, Jane Papageorge, Karen and Paul St. Cyr, and Rick Leandri. Francestown Elementary School and Great Brook School have at times sponsored "Girls on the Run" clubs. Typically, the program calls for ten weeks of training for 3rd through 8th grade girls. In 2014 and 2015 the event culminated in a 5k run in Concord with girls from across the state. Several young men and women have well represented ConVal high school in track racing over the years. Most notably, perhaps, was the state champion 4X800 relay team that featured Nick Jenkins, Ben Jenkins, and Scott McGrath.

In most years, group exercise classes have been available to Francestown residents. Sometimes they have been sponsored by the Recreation Commission, at other times by enthusiastic leaders. In 2012 Amy St. Cyr led Zumba and Peggy Marcellino organized Yoga sessions.

Kingsbury Farm's summer Riding Camp on Dennison Pond Road nurtured three generations of horseback riding. Natalie and Nate Sanderson started the Kingsbury Hill Riding Camp in 1966. Lisa Campbell, daughter of Natalie, lived on the site and directed the camp in the last years before the business closed. The facility provided training in show jumping and had three arenas, a full-size dressage arena, cross country courses, and stalls for up to thirty-five horses, bunkhouses, and cooking and dining facilities. Kingsbury Hill was sanctioned by the United States Eventing Association. Another equestrian facility, Harmony Hill, was developed in the 1980s by Jenny Fritz off New Boston Road near the town line. Also featuring an arena and stables, Harmony Hill boarded horses and provided instruction and training. Many town residents own horses and ride the dirt roads and trails available; some are members of the Piscataquog Area Trailways.

Snow skiing and ice hockey provide great pleasure through the long NH winters. Francestown's claim to fame in the outside world in the 1970s-1980s was its ski hill. Until the area closed in 1989, many residents enjoyed the slopes of Crotched Mountain. When the westside area re-opened in 2003, skiing returned as did the fellowship of lift and lodge workers, ski instructors, ski patrol, and racers. Night skiing, especially, was exciting recreation for youngsters. Several local ski racers have distinguished themselves over the years. Chad Demetry drew New England-wide attention for his racing acumen in the early 2000s. In 2020-2022, Eva Calcutt represented ConVal High School well racing on the Nordic Trails, and the Dishong sisters, Ella and Molly, garnered state-wide honors in Alpine skiing,

Recreational ice skating was standard winter entertainment. For a few years, the RecCom boxed in a portion of the soccer field and created a "pond" for skating. As noted earlier, FIHS sponsored skating on the Creamery Pond and the Colburn Store lot in the 1970s. For several years teams of adult hockey players from Francestown competed in the World Pond Hockey Championships in New Brunswick, Canada. They played teams from a dozen countries. In 2007, the team, humbly if deceptively tagged the "Dull Blades," was composed of Rob Ames, Paul Lawrence, Kip Dalley, and Andy Hungerford. The 2008 edition was Hungerford and Dalley, with John Arnold, Jr., and Alex Schaffer. The ConVal Boys Hockey team were state champions in 2004. That team included Francetown's Nate and Jamie Sanderson, and Adam and John Normile.

The Recreation Commission facilitated an active summer for youth in town. In 2008 Recreation Director Donna Noonan supervised a full calendar. Ketchum's Kickers, a soccer skills training team, were brought in, and youth baseball teams competed in the Crotched Mountain Little League. Supervised swimming and swim lessons were offered at the town beach. Other camps were offered for art, tennis, volleyball, golf, adventure walks, and theatre.

After World War Two, Francestown parents, with support from the Village Improvement Society, made organized baseball available for youth. Chapter 4 described FIHS' involvement in youth baseball. Two stories from *The Francestown News* further illustrate the fun provided by local baseball. "A long drought in championship form by Francestown Little League teams was broken in 1998 when the team became 'second place champions' in the

Crotched Mountain Little League. The team was comprised of Scott Leavitt and David Munson who shared pitching duties, Tim Samuelson, a 'fast and intimidating catcher,' Brian Swenson at third base, Chris Lawes sweeping center field, and Dan Davis in left." Other team members were Chris Kazanovicz, Matt Lape, John Normile, Adam Normile, Sam Paige, Ben Jenkins, Joe Kendall, and Kaleb McEntee. Scott Jenkins and Peter Kazanovicz coached these 11–12-year-olds, supported also by Brian Leavitt. Donny Abbott, of course, was the home plate ump. Field umpires included Chuck Kendall, Jack Normile, Betsy Hardwick, and Sandra Lawes. Lorie Jenkins kept the book. "No Francestown team had ever made it this far in the playoffs…Though they lost the championship game against Bennington, five fire trucks and the police cruiser met the caravan returning across the mountain and escorted them into town with siren's blazing!" Ben and Song Moeller provided the boys with free ice cream at the Village Store. "It was a terrific season."

In the 2000s, the Cal Ripken baseball program operated with 40-60 boys and girls ages 5-12 playing on T-ball, Rookies, Minors, and Majors teams. In 2007, Francestown's Cal Ripkin Minors won their first ever league title by defeating Peterborough. This special group of athletes, coached by Bub Rokes, Chris Sullivan, and Pete Kazanovicz. Players included Harrison Glaude, Eli Rokes, KC Kloeppel, Connor Langlois, Quinn Williams, Jacob Rupp, Justin Dahlquist, Baxter Glaude, Cole Eby, Stephen Kazanovicz, Osiris Terry, Nick Cheaney, Ben Wescott, Chris St. Jean, and Dillon Sullivan. This team's success characterized a run of winning baseball teams in the 2000s. Though several coaches were responsible for leading the boys and girls, Bub Rokes was the long-time leader of the program. Mike Beisang also provided key leadership. In the 2000s, the baseball season kicked-off with a parade up and down Main Street led by fire engines, followed by a cookout at the Rec Fields.

LABOR DAY ATHLETICS

Mud Volleyball is a highlight of Labor Day weekend for many families in town. It began in 1995 and moved to the Recreation Fields a few years later. The Highway Department and Fire Department both provide support in setting up this activity. The Stewart family initiated the event and organized it for many years. Highlights of this unique event include Bub Rokes' teams often playing for the championship, sixty players competing in 2011, and nine Hardwicks playing for the championship in 2012 (Blair, Eddie, Chris, Marilyn, Megan, Jeb, Donnie, Ben, and Sarah). The non-Hardwick ringers were Mike and Robin Beisang, and Jamie Pitchard.

Many years a "scramble" style golf tournament was organized at Tory Pines on Labor Day weekend. One year first place was won by an all-Cilley team" Joe, Al, Dennis, and Jim. Jim was a NH State Amateur Golf Champion. That year second place went to the team of John Suprenant, Gavin Gorton, Jordan Stinson, and Ryan Fallon.

Each Labor Day for the past fifty years tennis champions have been crowned in three doubles brackets: Men's, Women's and Mixed. Labor Day 2009 saw Jim Barker and Stu Clark, Jr. defeat Don Fusco and Todd Kuty in Men's doubles. Kate Taylor and family friend Jill Brewer won the Women's bracket over Tiffany Calcutt and her mother Julie Flik. Todd and Ambra Kuty defeated the Calcutts, Dennis and Tiffany, in Mixed Doubles. That year 22 teams competed. It is hard to find a year between 2000-2019 when a Taylor or a Calcutt was not in the finals of one of the three divisions.

The activities that bring people joy – recreation, entertainment, performance – pull people together despite differences that might otherwise keep them apart. Francestown has provided ample opportunities to play, laugh, revel in another person's talents or silliness. These shared experiences fostered connections that linked residents and encouraged empathy, camaraderie, and generosity.

CHAPTER 8

KEY CITIZENS

Most residents of a town never serve in elective office or volunteer for an appointment to a town board, commission, or committee. Only a few join the governing boards of private organizations. Most folks in town are content to pay their taxes, vote in elections, obey the laws and ordinances, care for their family, attend social, recreational, or cultural events, and try to be good neighbors and good citizens. When a town history is written, most "everyday people" are not named. The residents who held an office or were appointed to a board or committee, or who were the leaders of organizations are the ones who are memorialized. In the preceding chapters many such citizens have been identified.

Individuals do make a difference in the history of a civilization, a nation, a state, an institution, or a small, rural New Hampshire town. Historian Carl Schorske defined written history as "the story of creative responses in the trajectory of time." Often a creative response to a challenging situation affects the direction of history: the initiative of a particular leader to undertake a project, the founding of a particular organization, or a vote to support a Warrant Article at Town Meeting. Specific instances of creative responses abound in Francestown over the last fifty years. These creative responses are often traceable to a single individual, sometimes to a team. Who were the personalities in Francestown in the last fifty years whose creative responses have altered the trajectory of the town's story?

The following is an annotated list of some of the "creative responders" who shaped the story of the town's governance and organizational life. Their special impact is acknowledged. Some of these folks were warm and fuzzy, others blunt and prickly. Some of the creative responses were viewed as positive by most residents, others were controversial. Several dozen people were interviewed for this book. Each was asked to name individuals they judged to be especially consequential; those suggestions, more than my personal judgement, are the primary source for this list.

BACKBONE FAMILY ENTERPRISES

Between 1970 and 2020, the people of Francestown have been well-served by local businesses operated by native families. These businesses have repeatedly embraced the town's needs, in emergency situations or as donations for improvement projects. Tens of thousands of dollars of private profit have been set aside so that the community would benefit from the care and expertise of these native sons. The dedication at the beginning of the 2008 Town Report captures the importance of these home-town businesses to Francestown:

"Someone once observed that the strength of a town is drawn from the involvement of its citizens, particularly in times of trouble. During the past two years Francestown has had its share of "times of troubles." In 2007 we suffered through the worst floods in years. 80% of the town's roads were affected requiring extensive repairs. In 2008 we had the second worst winter on record in terms of snowfall culminating in the ice storm in December. Each calamity presented its own particular set of problems, either in road reconstruction, or removing the vast amount of downed trees to allow the power companies to repair the extensive damage done to the electrical infrastructure. Throughout, there were Francestownians -- D. H. Hardwick and Sons, Francestown Sand & Gravel, Steven and Richard Miller, Yankee Pool, Clarence Paige, and George Whipple -- uniquely equipped with both machinery and their time, who stepped up to help the town in its time of need. There are too many other individuals who, either as volunteers in the Fire Department or those who cooked meals at the Community Church, to list here. They, and we, know who they are. We sincerely appreciate their service."

Often the time, materials, and equipment donated to the town have been for community projects in non-emergency situations. Examples include the development of the recreation fields and courts, work on the building and grounds of the Old Meeting House, and assistance in bringing the two town museums to life. Native families – the Footes, Millers, Hardwicks, Paiges, and Stewarts -- have been, and continue to be, the backbone of Francestown.

THOSE WHO SHOW UP

Everyone knows them because they show up. A small town relies on volunteers to support events, projects, and organizations. These are the people who, if asked, will say "Yes," or more often "Yes!" And, if not asked it is very likely that they will be there anyway. These people come, look for what needs to be done, and do it. They are good neighbors; they check on you, watch your house when you are away, or bring you food when you're ill. They don't expect to be thanked or given credit. They are there to serve others and make things happen. The Fire Department knows them well, as does the Recreation Commission. Most extended families have them. From recent years here are several exemplars who many will recognize: Kim Place Dalley, Mike Tartalis, Jan Hicks, Larry Laber, Jeff Tarr, and Harry Woodbury. The readers of this book will easily be able to add a dozen names off the top of their heads from the organizations in which they are involved, the events they attend, or the projects on which they have worked. These people make it happen.

SUMMER PEOPLE

Another collection of families and individuals who have been especially important to the quality of life in Francestown are "summer people" many of whom have been coming to Francestown for sixty or seventy years. Their loyalty to the town, expressed through an affectionate and positive spirit, by participation in community activities, and through generosity when projects needed financial support, has been of immense value to the town. The Town Hall, the Beehive, the Old Meeting House, the Three Sisters' Building, the library, recreation facilities and programs, and the conservation of land have all been made possible by the devotion of historic summer families, who in some cases, have been coming to town far longer than some who consider themselves natives. This certainly includes the Taylors, the Houstons, and Woodburys, as well as other stalwart "summer" families. They eschew attention, but they should be remembered gratefully.

SIX EXCEPTIONAL CONTRIBUTORS

Odin Alan Thulander. Thulander and his wife Barbara moved to Francestown in 1968. He served six terms as a Selectman, from 1971-1977 and 1992-2002. During the second stint, Thulander was essentially the town administrator. In addition, he chaired the ZBA in the 1980s, and served at various times on the Budget Committee, Cemetery Commission, Highway Safety Committee, and as the Emergency Management Director. Francestown and other adjacent communities elected Thulander to the state legislature four times. A stalwart of the FVFD for over thirty years, he founded the charitable Mount Crotchet Firefighters Association. Thulander kept the books for OMH for several of the organization's early years. After stepping down as Selectman, he was the driving force behind the creation of the Heritage Museum which was housed in the "Alan Thulander Building" on the Common.

Alan and Barbara raised three children in the Woodbury home on the Common. Clifton Foote, Norman Stewart, Jack Arnold, Harry Varnum, Water Dodge, and Don Hoyt were credited by Thulander as his leadership role models. Though traditionally a small-government conservative, Thulander believed that the town's government should protect the town from unbridled private enterprise, "Growth may be a given, but uncontrolled growth is not." Notoriously careful with taxpayer dollars, he was skilled at bringing funds to Francestown. He acquired FEMA money to help rebuild the Bixby Dam and for recovery from ice storm damage. Thulander loved Francestown with unrivaled devotion.

Abigail Arnold. From 1987 into the early 2000s Arnold moved town governance from largely *ad hoc* decision-making to one of businesslike administrative practices and careful long-range planning. Raised as a summer visitor in the Bixby family line, following professional schooling and a career in corporate leadership, she settled in Francestown in the 1980s as a full-time resident. Arnold's father, Jack, a town leader in the 1970s-1980s, had a substantial impact on the modernization of Select Board procedures. He encouraged his daughter to move town governance beyond the homespun traditions that were ill-suited to deal with rapid population growth and the new residents' demand for better municipal services. She led the Planning Board from the late 1980s through the 1990s. Under her leadership, the Planning Board introduced Capital Improvement Plans to the town. Having revised the first Master Plan in 1988, Arnold organized a large team to produce the 1995 Master Plan which shaped the town over the following decades. After stepping away from the Planning Board, Arnold joined the open space preservation movement in rolling out the "2010 by 2010" land conservation campaign and serving on the Francestown Land Trust Board during its most dramatic growth period.

In the first decade of the new century, she served the town by coming to Town Meeting prepared to provide data that supported or undressed Warrant Articles. Many regular attendees of Town Meeting testify to counting on Arnold to provide information that was crucial to understanding the desirability or undesirability of a particular Warrant Article. Said one cotemporary, "I often waited to hear from Abigail before I decided how to vote."

Elected to the Select Board in 2011, she reemphasized capital planning and building appropriate reserves to address town infrastructure needs. A believer in the advantages of professional municipal administration, she advocated for a town administrator who was hired in the first of her three terms. Sometimes uncomfortably blunt, Arnold, like Thulander, had a clear vision of how to maintain Francestown's unique character and she pursued it doggedly.

Harry Varnum. "Salt of the Earth." That is the overwhelming consensus of those who knew and worked with Harry Varnum. He married Francestown's Connie Clark in 1940; they were partners in serving the town. Varnum served as a Trustee of the Trust Funds, and on the Budget Committee, Planning Board, Zoning Board, and CIP committee. A skilled heavy equipment operator, he was an important contributor to road improvement planning and served on several iterations of highway advisory or road improvement committees. Varnum moderated Town Meeting for a dozen years with an easy-going demeanor and timely wit. He was a role model to many for his commitment to civil and informed public conversation; on challenging issues facing the town, he was a welcome voice of reason and a mediator. Varnum took on the challenge of clarifying for Town Meeting 2002 how best to proceed with the highway department garage project. Connie was an enthusiastic environmentalist and generously devoted her time to many causes. Harry and Connie were among the first residents of Francestown to donate a Conservation Easement (1989) in support of the ConCom's purchase of the lands that became the Crotched Mountain Town Forest. Varnum was a gentleman admired for his compassion and patience. He was a mentor to many younger town leaders.

Betsy Hardwick. As a daughter of Sonny and Dorothy Hardwick, Betsy's deep roots gave her knowledge and appreciation of the traditions, history, and values of Francestown's native families. Through the years she developed an understanding and empathy for the concerns of a wide range of residents including the move-ins from the cities and suburbs. Hardwick is an ambassador across what is sometimes a serious divide, a leader who makes decisions in the best interests of the town. During a challenging stretch in the mid-2000s, Hardwick served on the Select Board. Her service to the town encompassed terms on the Planning Board, the Master Plan Committee, and various highway advisory committees. As one of Francestown's preeminent conservationists, she led the Conservation Commission for more than twenty years and worked on the FLT Board for a decade. Hardwick's essential role in the open space preservation campaign of "2010 by 2010" and in explaining the benefits of land preservation through regular communication with town folks was described in Chapter 5.

Charlie and Sarah Pyle. Arriving in town in the early 1990s, eager to serve their adopted community, Charlie and Sarah carved out separate spheres of influence. Charlie led the ZBA and Budget Committee and served for more than two decades as Treasurer and President of FIHS, as well as the long-time chair of Labor Day. He served on the school district's Municipal Budget Committee for the entirety of its existence. Sarah has participated in many, many activities in town. Her main official involvement was two decades on the Planning Board and as a founder of the all-volunteer *Francestown News*. She served 25 years and counting as its editor. But the Pyles' greatest contributions to the town were as a couple – converting the Beehive into the Historical Museum, bringing back the Village Store, and celebrating the town's 100th Labor Day. They have eagerly invited new residents into participation in town leadership, and deftly raised an abundance of funds for numerous projects. Genial Charlie and infectiously enthusiastic Sarah are ever-present when community-building is on the agenda in Francestown.

KEY CITIZENS

Except for the six preceding individuals, the profiles of other important "creative responders" are arranged alphabetically. A table illustrating "years of service to the town" is included as an appendix. The master list of individuals from whom the following roll was winnowed had nearly 150 names. That is almost 10% of the current population of the town and is a tribute to how many residents of this town have been truly consequential in weaving the fabric of its story.

Abbotts. A dedication in the 2007 Town Report celebrated **Don Abbott's** service to Francestown as chief of the Fire Department for twenty years. In addition to his steady leadership of the department during years of rapid growth in Francestown, including his command during the infamous Foote Barn fire of 1995, Donny was celebrated for his well-roundedness, "He is your hometown plumber and your furnace repairman who appears at a moment's notice. He's the animal control officer who goes above and beyond the call to reunite a family with its lost pet or assure that all creatures are cared for properly. He is the guy in the mask calling balls and strikes at the little league games." A "quiet and unassuming man," his story is one of "unselfishness, reliability, and availability to all…" During the period from 1970-2020, Abbott has served the second highest number of years in official positions with the town, a total of 77 years. Donny's wife, **Linda Abbott** built and led the Fire Auxiliary from the 1980s through 2020. The Auxiliary's extensive service to the Fire Department and the town is described in Chapter 6. The Auxiliary's almost two decades of twice-a-year blood drives has been particularly important to the community. **Bob Abbott,** Don's older brother, served the town on many committees over five decades, beginning in the 1970s-1980s with two terms as a Selectman. From its founding, he has been Bill McAuley's partner as a curator of the Heritage Museum.

Jim and Cher Barker. The Barkers came to Francestown in 1983 and devoted themselves to the Community Church for over 35 years, serving as moderators, and as chairs of various committees that provided leadership to the congregation. The CCF may not have survived as long as it did without the energy and dedication of the Barkers. Jim pioneered the relationship of the CCF with a congregation in Zimbabwe, and Cher led an effort to support the people of New Orleans following Hurricane Katrina. Jim also served as president of the Water Company for a decade. Cher led Girl Scout troops. Both were tennis enthusiasts. Cher taught tennis in the summer, and they were fixtures in the Labor Day tournament. Oak Hill Grange named Cher one of their "Citizens of the Year."

Betty Behrsing. Betty was the first woman elected to the Select Board, (1979-1987). Before that she served as Tax Collector. After her time on the Select Board, Behrsing was the board's administrative assistant for several years, serving to some extent as a town administrator long before such a role was created. She remained "on call" and completed the terms of two selectmen when they stepped down early. In her later years, she was a regular observer of the Select Board, usually seated next to Polly Freese. In pioneering the role of "Selectperson," Behrsing undoubtedly had to overcome considerable gender bias; she did so with humility.

Stewart and Carol Brock. Stewart represented Francestown on the ConVal School Board from 2005 to 2014. These were challenging years for the district as enrollment declined and cost-reduction was a persistent theme. Relentlessly positive, Stewart embraced the role of translator, relating the school district's needs to the town, as well as representing the town's and parents' interests to the district's administration and board. At the end of his service, Brock stated, "I am proud of where our district is currently. We have been on quite a journey over the last nine years, two new superintendents, two new assistant superintendents, two new GBS and FES principals, a new gym at the high school, a new teacher contract, full day Kindergarten district-wide, to name a few ...There were some really tough times when passions and tempers were high, and times when we could rally behind a single issue and row in the same direction."

Carol was just reaching her stride as Children's Librarian at the George Holmes Bixby Memorial Library when the director became ill, went on leave, and passed away. Carol assumed leadership of the GHBML, and a few months later coordinated the move of all the library's collection and equipment down Main Street to temporary quarters in Town Hall. It was a long, cold winter in cramped quarters, followed by an equally arduous move back into the renovated library a year later. Carol led the conversion of the library to digital record keeping, an online catalog, and expansion of the children's library area. She served the library longer than anyone else from 1970-2020. She led with humility and a sense of humor.

Scott and Barbara Jean Carbee. The Carbees have been ubiquitous in leadership in Francestown for over four decades and have spoken passionately at every town meeting. "BJ" has logged more service years to the town than any other individual from 1970 to 2020. With a can-do demeanor and a quick-draw wit, she has served in seven different capacities for a total of 88 years. A member of the original Recreation Commission, she chaired the group in the early-to-mid 1980s when finding volunteers was a daunting task. For twenty-two years she was the face of public assistance in town. For nearly as many years, she served on the Conservation Commission and as a Supervisor of the Checklist. BJ served as president of FIHS and before that was the Society's secretary for many years. Not always thrilled with official decision-making or the direction of the town, she has never stopped her efforts to make the town a better place to live.

Scott accumulated 43 years of service in four different capacities including nine years as a selectman. He served alongside Alan Thulander in the 1990s and Abigail Arnold and Betsy Hardwick in the second decade of the 2000s. He teamed with recycling stalwart Robert "Dud" Parker in the late 1980s to lead the dump's transition to being a transfer station. All told, Scott was involved in the Waste Disposal Commission for 19 years, much of that time as the chairman. A Vietnam War veteran, he was instrumental in founding the Patriotic Purposes Committee that has embraced the observances on Memorial Day and Veterans' Day. Several times Scott and BJ chaired FIHS' Labor Day celebration. Scot worked with Warren Kiblin for many years to set up the Labor Day structures on the Common and no one sold more tags than BJ.

Peter Flood. The son of a police chief, Flood served Francestown as its chief from the mid-1970s until the early 2000s. His tenure was distinguished by stability and an even-tempered conscientiousness. He worked well with a variety of Select Boards and adjusted his attention to meet the current challenge, be it ski area traffic or an increase in breaking and entering. When he left the position, his steady leadership was missed.

Francestown Land Trust Leaders. The residents who revived FLT in the 2000s have been highly successful in spreading the gospel of preserving open space. They have succeeded in protecting thousands of acres of vulnerable lands by raising funds to buy properties or teaming with landowners to adopt conservation easements. **Dr. Greg Neilley, Dennis Calcutt, Chris Rogers**, and **Larry Ames** were the chairs of the organization for most of the last twenty years. They built knowledgeable and diligent teams of volunteers including Dr. Barry Wicklow, Ben Haubrich, and Betsy Hardwick. The result though controversial for some residents is a comfort to many -- the preservation of the rural character of Francestown to the benefit of residents, wildlife, and posterity.

After Scot Heath and Betsy Hardwick, it is a challenge to winnow a "Mr./Ms. Conservation" out of the dozens of candidates in Francestown. But **Ben Haubrich** fits the title well. After graduating from UNH, Haubrich served as Park Ranger at Monadnock State Park for two decades, followed by a decade of management positions for the NH Division of Parks and Recreation. He retired in 2004 and made volunteering for conservation organizations a full-time commitment. He has been the Land Manager of the Francestown Land Trust for more than 15 years. Haubrich also serves the Harris Center for Conservation Education, the Piscataquog Land Conservancy, and the Forest Society as a board member, land steward/property monitor, trail builder, or map maker. Many of his trail maps are featured on the ConCom website. He has received awards for his volunteer service from several land preservation organizations. His grant-writing has brought hundreds of thousands of dollars to FLT's projects. Another especially important contributor to the work of FLT was **Dr. Barry Wicklow**. His background as a wildlife biologist, including active research within the watershed, has been critical to FLT's grant applications. Wicklow's enthusiasm and outreach to owners of high value conservation land was a decisive factor in many FLT projects.

Clifton Foote was a humble, clear-thinking, family man dedicated to the Francestown Volunteer Fire Department. He led the FVFD for fifteen years, from the end of Norm Stewart's long service to the beginning of Donny Abbott's. In that time a new fire station was built, a rescue squad was mobilized, and a new generation of recruits was brought in, including the first women. Foote also served on the Highway Safety Commission for many years. With his wife Elizabeth, who served as the town correspondent for the Peterborough *Transcript,* Clifton was a leader in the Community Church. His legacy was the strong relationship between town leaders and the FVFD and an *esprit de corps* among the volunteers.

The Footes of the Highway Department. When the five decades began, **Robert Foote** was the elected road agent. He was a veteran of the SeaBees and was tuned-in to getting the most out of the least. During his tenure the department owned very little of its own equipment. He coordinated use of his personal equipment and those of several local contractors to keep the roads clear in the winter and maintained in the summer. Following an experiment with an out-of-town appointed road agent, **Clayton "Junior" Foote** was hired by the Select Board in 1987. Junior led the road crew through its transition from equipment and facility insufficiency. He worked closely with highway committees to implement road improvement programs. Junior was a knowledgeable and creative road agent; the department ethic still was to do as much as possible while spending as little as possible. His Achilles' heel was aggressive tree cutting, as explained in Chapter 4. **Gary Paige** succeeded Junior and while he appreciated the old ethic, his leadership enabled the department to stay ahead of the maintenance needs of the roads. Paige was assertive with equipment needs, eager to replace decaying culverts with legitimate bridges, and deft in communicating with Select Boards. The Foote tradition in the Highway Department has given the town, in a steady and humble manner, good roads the town could afford.

Joan Hanchett. "Legendary" seems to fit Joan. As the director of the George Holmes Bixby Memorial Library for nearly twenty years, she provided an inviting space for readers as well as those looking for good conversation. Genial, caring, and generous, Hanchett provided no-nonsense advice and an uproarious sense of humor. Library trustees eulogized her. Bessann Triplett said, "Joan was kind to everyone, and made us all feel important, interesting, and appreciated. She was gracious, but also loads of fun." Connie Varnum added, "Underneath her geniality, she set high standards at the library and held everyone accountable. She had a brilliant mind and a flawless memory of dates, places, people, and, of course, books." Hanchett came to the U.S. from Ireland in 1957. Frank and Joan bought the Lord Farm on Bible Hill and moved to Francestown in 1974. Another library patron described her as, "Francestown's 'Welcome Wagon.'… She instantly created that positive first impression of our town … She was truly a joy to know and be around." Hanchett passed away after a rare and debilitating illness in 2007.

Dorothy Hardwick. Also known as "Dot," she is the matriarch of the Hardwick family. Dot was a charter member of the Community Church of

Francestown and was still an active parishioner when the CCF closed its doors in 2020. In the intervening years, she served on CCF committees, hosted dinners in her home for members, and on several occasions preached sermons. Hardwick was also a long-time member of the Grange. Sonny and Dot continued the farming tradition of his father and mother, Harry and Eula Hardwick. Sonny was an instrumental figure at the ski area in Francestown, serving as chief of maintenance for many years. Labor Day float building was a love of Dot's and the extended Hardwick family regularly produced clever, award-winning floats. Ms. Hardwick's most important role has been the nurture and care for the numerically largest family in town.

Don Hardwick. Don, a son of Sonny and Dot, was founder of D.H. Hardwick and Sons, one of the largest logging companies in New Hampshire. The company was also involved in construction. As an entrepreneur he created many local jobs. D. H. Hardwick practiced sustainable logging and owned a considerable amount of forest property in Francestown. With a partner from Bennington, Hardwick bought the land where the original westside ski area had been and facilitated the reopening of the Crotched Mountain Ski resort in 2003. His sympathy for preserving open space and maintaining healthy forests led him to make land available at a reasonable purchase price to both FLT and the town. The Rand Brook Forest preserve was made possible by Hardwick's vision. Like Francestown Sand & Gravel and the Miller Brothers, D.H. Hardwick donated time, equipment, and materials to local projects.

Scot Heath. As described in Chapter 2, Heath became chair of the Conservation Commission in the second half of the 1980s and started the commission on a path to major preservation of open space in town. Beginning in 1987, five consecutive town meetings approved dollars for a Conservation Fund. Because of Heath's advocacy, Francestown became the first town in the state of New Hampshire to have a land conservation fund included in its Capital Improvement Plan budget. These funds, combined with grants, enabled the purchase of large acreages for town forests. The ConCom was also aggressive in encouraging landowners to put acreage into conservation easements, a new concept at the time. Heath also was a founder of the FLT and was relentless in contacting landowners and planting the idea of donating their land, or an easement, to the town or a land trust. Over the next thirty years, many of the pitches Heath made as an idealistic young man bore fruit and were harvested during the "2010 by 2010" campaign. Heath has been a powerful force in preserving the forests and meadows of Francestown from development.

The Jones. If only more people could "keep up with the Jones." **Ed and Shirley Jones** were charter members of the Community Church of

Francestown. They served in leadership capacities for many years. Several times, when the CCF was between ministers, or the minister was not attuned to the importance of visitations, Ed and Shirley practiced a ministry of outreach to the elderly and ill. Multiple CCF members credit the Jones' with embodying the core spirit of the church – positive, loving, and generous.

Frank Jones, Ed's brother, and his wife Elizabeth Hoyt Jones celebrated their 50th anniversary in 2000. Frank is another man who is characterized by those who knew him as "salt of the earth." He operated the last major dairy farm in town, but more than that he was a lover of nature and a supporter of conservation of the natural environment. Ever generous with his time and labor, Frank encouraged his family to serve the town he loved.

Larry Kullgren. As described in Chapters 4 and 6, Larry "Skip" Kullgren became chief of the FVFD in 2008. This represented a generational shift in FVFD leadership to firefighters who readily embraced advanced technology and professionalization. Though the FVFD's "social club" role in town may have waned in the last dozen years, the sophistication of its services has kept pace with the field. Several members of the FVFD are also professional firefighters. Larry and his twin brother David were "born into the department" in the early 1970s, as sons of the long-time deputy chief, Lawrence Kullgren.

Kunhardts. **Sibby Kunhardt's** long leadership of the library board and Conservation Commission extended into the 1970s. She worked to make the library a place where everyone felt welcome and along with Pat Place, Connie Varnum, and Connie Bicknell nudged Francestown down the path of conservation and recycling. A unique presence, Ms. Kunhardt was well-loved by town folks. **Henry Kunhardt**, her son, returned to Francestown in the early 2000s and emerged as a leader through his involvement on the Budget Committee and as a conscientious Trustee of the Trust Funds. He particularly distinguished himself by his willingness to roll up his engineering sleeves to supervise major projects from the turnpike bridge to the Town Hall restoration to the police station renovation. Kunhardt took on the challenge of the geothermal system in the library, as well. He served on the Select Board from 2016 to 2021 as the more parsimonious member of the team with Abigail Arnold and Brad Howell. Kunhardt is a Yankee. Linda Kunhardt, Henry's wife, served sixteen years on the Planning Board, a few years as chair. She had encyclopedic knowledge of ordinances and laws and was committed to doing things the right way.

Paul Lawrence. Judge Lawrence served 26 years as town moderator, more than any other person in the last one hundred years. Most long-time town meeting observers credit Lawrence with *gravitas* – dignity, solemnity, and timely wit. He regularly reminded the meeting that they were the legislative body of the town, and that his role was to enable them to exercise their rightful authority fairly and appropriately. Civility ruled. Lawrence also served 15 years on the Recreation Commission through the period of its expansion of facilities and programming. While Kris Stewart was the animated voice of RecCom ambitions, Lawrence was instrumental behind the scenes mobilizing a full range of concerned citizens. "The Recreation Commission and the town owes Paul a large debt of gratitude; Francestown's recreation facilities are far better because of his work," said commission veteran Nancy Rice.

Dick Leavitt. Leavitt was Don Prince's farm manager, a police officer, an electrician, a respected school bus driver, and a 55-year veteran of the FVFD. He served as forest fire warden for 47 years, through three chiefs. He was also the town native who most deeply embraced tennis. Through the years, Leavitt, a fierce competitor, was an advocate for keeping the tennis facilities in good condition.

Celeste Lunetta. Women joined the ranks of the Fire Department beginning in the 1980s. Lunetta joined the FVFD in 2000 and rose to become captain of the Rescue Squad. She was the first woman elected to the position of fire ward. For many years, she was a leader and key contributor to Parent Teacher Organization (PTO) programming at Francestown Elementary School. During the high tide of PTO involvement in the first decade of the 2000s, Lunetta, along with Beth Wallace, was instrumental in innovative projects at FES. One wing of the school was formally dedicated to Lunetta and Wallace in recognition of their service to FES.

William MacAdam and Tim Gannett. As described in Chapter 1, MacAdam put together the investor group behind the construction of the Francestown ski area in the 1960s. Though MacAdam's group was bought out in 1970, MacAdam's ski area played an important role in the culture of the town for over 25 years. He served as moderator of the Town Meeting for seventeen years ending in 1970. Gannett was a principal in the land-holding group that bought the ski area in 1970. He moved to Francestown, and his family engaged in town life while he kept several iterations of the ski hill business going until the late 1980s. Due to his generosity, the ski area played an important social and recreational role in town during those decades.

Bill McAuley. A two-term Selectman during a tumultuous period, McAuley was also a leader for many years in the Water Company and organized the Old Meeting House's bicentennial celebration. His greatest service to the town began in 2013 when he was chosen to be one of the curators of the Heritage Museum in the Alan Thulander building. This was McAuley's calling – organizing and caring for the displays in the museum and educating the public about the vehicles and other historical apparatus. He created a monthly museum newsletter that provides well-researched and wittily presented historical expositions. In 2020, McAuley arranged to bring back to Francestown an antique *Vis a Vis* carriage once owned by Hob and Knob farm.

Robert Parker. Parker facilitated the conversion of "the dump" into a "transfer station." He saw it through its journey from a burn-pit to a collection point for rubbish to be transported to a landfill, and the incremental steps involved in creating a full-scale recycling center. "Dud" Parker worked relentlessly to make recycling a financial benefit to the town even when the market for recyclables was flooded in the 1980s. Parker also served as the President of FIHS and was on the Budget Committee for almost a decade.

Dariel Peterson. When the Women's Guild of the CCF was waning in membership and energy, Peterson created an egalitarian Thursday Fellowship to involve more women. She was also a stalwart in the Oak Hill Grange's programming in the 1980s-1990s. Peterson has been celebrated for her ability to relate to a range of people from all walks of life. In her professional life, she was a learning disabilities specialist at Crotched Mountain Rehabilitation Center.

Mike Petrovick. Ubiquitous architect and generous chef, Petrovick played key roles in the addition and renovations to the library, the Town Hall, Beehive, and the Long Store building. The lion's share of his work was donated or discounted. Petrovick was also CCF's chef. He was instrumental in launching community suppers; during the Ice Storm of 2008 he and a team of volunteers prepared meals for a week.

Patricia Place. Along with Connie Varnum, Place was an original member of the Piscataquog Watershed Association which eventually became the Piscataquog Land Conservancy. She teamed with Varnum and Sibby Kunhardt to pioneer conservation efforts in the 1970s, especially the observance of Earth Day. Connie Bicknell's initiation of large-scale recycling in Francestown received crucial support from Place. She encouraged women to lead and was the first female president of FIHS.

Derald Radtke. Colonel Radtke, following 33 years in the Air Force, came to Francestown and bought a cape in Mill Village with his wife Barbara. The Radtkes opened Mill Village Antiques in 1982. Radtke became president of FIHS in the mid-1980s and was a leader in the Community Church. In 1987, he focused FIHS on attending to the condition of historical structures in town and became a founder, and then long-time president, of the Old Meeting House, Inc. Radtke built, and rebuilt, teams of OMH board members and volunteers who raised funds to restore the beautiful building. OMH became the center for public entertainment in town. Matilda "Mit" Boyle, a relentless fundraiser, was his right-hand. She was a champion of the arts and booked classy entertainers into OMH for years. Radtke was a force to be reckoned with. His military style of leadership got things done, though it also led to a high rate of turnover on the OMH Board. The salvation of OMH and its role in town is Radtke's legacy.

Robert "Bub" Rokes. Rokes made the town a better place for kids than it was for him when he grew up here. He joined the Recreation Commission in 1999 in response to a call for new blood, and served until 2018, for many years as the chair. For several years during his tenure the RecCom was just Rokes and Donna Noonan. Noonan also served as the Recreation Director for several years. They hustled for volunteers persistently and filled in the numerous gaps when helpers were in short supply. Rokes' love was coaching youth baseball. He and the boys on his teams experienced a lot of success. Bub is a softy with a big heart for kids and for outdoor activities. Even after he retired from RecCom leadership, he still baited hooks at the Tim Samuelson Fishing Derby.

The Stewarts. Norm Stewart was the long-time police and fire chief in town into the early 1970s. As a police officer, he was admired for his eagerness to deescalate situations of conflict, especially with youth. Getting the right outcome to a situation was more important than writing tickets or making arrests. As fire chief, he brought in younger leaders who were ready to move the department to a higher level of safety and effectiveness. After stepping down as chief, he continued to serve on the Highway Commission. **Betty Stewart**, Norm's wife, was a nutritionist and dietician, taught home economics in schools, managed the school district's lunch program and restaurant kitchens, worked as a chef, and catered events. Many young people in Francestown learned to cook from Betty Stewart.

Kris Stewart. Kris is the son of Norman Stewart. Even before he graduated from college, *summa cum laude*, Stewart was organizing a street hockey league on the FIHS tennis courts and hustling funds for an ice hockey team that played late at night in Manchester. He built his excavation business and quickly became a fixture in town projects. When he served as the elected road agent in 1980, Stewart received rave reviews for his leadership and budget management from a tough-to-please Budget Committee. Francestown Sand & Gravel, Stewart's enterprise, has been involved in many road, bridge, and excavation projects in town for over four decades. On many projects in town Stewart discounted his price or donated time, equipment, materials, and labor. He joined the Recreation Commission in 1989 teaming with Paul Lawrence and the Rices to launch the initiative to expand the recreation fields and courts. Town Meeting 1995 celebrated Stewart for his key role in seeing the project to fruition. He was a co-founder of Labor Day mud volleyball and built the volleyball court at the recreation fields. A savvy salesman, Stewart is well-remembered for his presentation at Town Meeting 2013 that began with "I come here today to sell you a bridge." He made the sale, though the Highway Department built the bridge. Even when the cards did not fall his way, Stewart maintained his loyalty and generosity to the town. Three generations of Stewarts donated their time and material to completing the basement expansion of the Heritage Museum.

Kris' sister **Deborah**, and her husband David Adams, own a lighting company in Cambridge, MA, while maintaining the family home on the turnpike. They were involved in the Heritage Museum and Town Hall restoration projects through facilitating the lighting design and fixture acquisition for the buildings. They continue to aid in lighting events in town facilities.

The Wheelers. Though the Francestown Community Theatre that mounted more than a dozen productions during the 1990s was a team effort, the Wheelers were the founding family and were the core of its productions. Theo Hardwick Wheeler, her son Randy, and his wife Kim were involved in almost every FTC production as actors, directors, or producers. The FCT sold out its performances and was able to donate considerable funds to rebuild the stage in Town Hall. A lot of joy was brought to hundreds of residents by the FCT.

Dr. Louis Wiederhold. Wiederhold was a medical doctor. He settled with his wife Betsy in Francestown in the 1950s and opened a practice in Antrim. Dr. Wiederhold served for 24 years as chief of medicine at Monadnock Community Hospital. He was Francestown's representative to the ConVal School Board during its foundational period and was a strong advocate for the construction of Contoocook Valley Regional High School. The FVFD and Crotched Mountain Ski Patrol benefited from his service. For many years he organized the Labor Day parade and cared for the FIHS Christmas tree on the Common. For thirty years, he was a Trustee of the Trust Funds.

Bob Abbott

Don Abbott

Larry Ames

Linda Abbott

Betty Behrsing

Abigail Arnold

Cheryl and Jim Barker

Matilda "Mit" Boyle

1970 - 2020

Stewart Brock

Carol Brock

Dennis Calcutt

Scott and Barbara "BJ" Carbee

Pam and Brian Delahanty

Pam Finnell

Chief Peter Flood

Clayton Foote Junior

Clifton Foote

Joan Hanchett

Betsy Hardwick

Dorothy Hardwick

Don and Sonny Hardwick with Kris Stewart (1976)

1970 - 2020

Ben Haubrich

Scot Heath

Brad Howell

Shirley and Ed Jones

Frank and Ed Jones

David Jonas

Chief Larry "Skip" Kulgren

Priscilla "Sibby" Kunhardt

Paul Lawrence

Henry Kunhardt

Richard "Dick" Leavitt

Celeste Lunetta

Lois and Bill MacAdam

Bill McAuley

Rick Miller

Gary Paige

Steve Miller

Herman "Bing" Miller

Dr. Greg and Ellen Neilley

Chris Rogers

Dariel Peterson

Michael Petrovick

Mark Pitman

Patricia Place

Derald Radtke

1970 - 2020

Sarah and Charlie Pyle

Paul St. Cyr, Betsy Hardwick
Steven Brown

Robert "Bub" Rokes

Cindy and Jim St. Jean

Betty Stewart

Kris Stewart

Deborah and David Stewart Adams

Norman Stewart

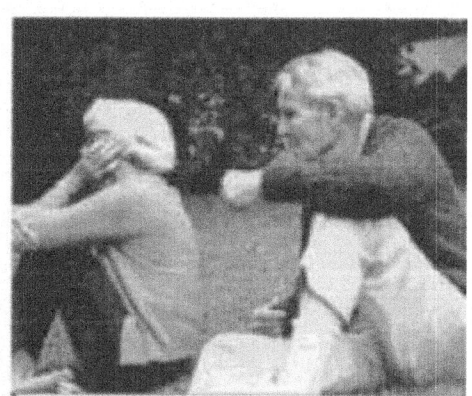
Margaret and John Taylor

1970 - 2020

John, Tim, Margaret, David and Ben Taylor

Dr. Barry Wicklow

Alan Thulander

Harry Varnum

Randy and Kim Wheeler

Dr. Louis Wiederhold

AFTERWARD

"Any work, however conscientious, that partially relies on people's memories (and an often-incomplete historical record) is going to get some things wrong. I believe those instances have been minimized through the help of some amazingly... [helpful] backstops." This thought belongs to the journalist-writer Gene Weingarten. At the risk of pretentiously over-stepping the importance of this story of a small, off-the-beaten-track, hill country New Hampshire town, I agree that anything accurate in this book is due to helpful sources, and any mistakes are due to *my* faulty reading between the lines of the records, misattributing credit or blame, or finding intent when actually things happened serendipitously. Historians, even small-town ones, are loathe to see cause and effect as accidental.

Before this book was printed, a dozen people read the manuscript and offered corrections, suggestions, and edits. Those volunteer editors represent a range of knowledge about the town and the people and events discussed. The book is better because of their contributions, but I hope none of them will feel responsible for my errors of fact or tone, or resentful if they see that their advice was not taken. I am deeply appreciative for their kindness, candor, and generosity of time. Cindy St. Jean, a veteran of decades of laying out *The Francestown News*, did me the enormous favor of preparing the manuscript for publication.

This book's version of Francestown's story from 1970-2020 is based on the records published by the town and the minutes of various organizations including but not limited to the Select Board, Planning Board, the Improvement and Historical Society, and the Community Church. Local newspapers, the *Monadnock Ledger, Peterborough Transcript*, and the combined *Ledger-Transcript* have provided information. *The Francestown News* founded in 1996 has been an important source. For almost twenty-five years (1991-2015) Kris Holmes, the town's appointed historian, kept clipping files that have been invaluable. Holmes' notebooks are in the Historical Museum (Beehive), along with many other files that provided information on various phenomena in town. The town has had three Master Plans – 1980, 1995, and 2015. These Master Plans include a lot of history and a wealth of data. Almost fifty residents, many ranging from natives to long-tenured move-ins, agreed to be interviewed for this book. Many of these interviews lasted for hours and produced dozens of pages of notes which were vital to fleshing out complex episodes and understanding the nuances of personalities and circumstances. The text of this book is full of quotations. Most are attributed, but some are not; generally, those unattributed quotations came from these private, personal interviews. Thanks are due to Jenny Fritz and *The Francestown News* for most of the photos in the book. Others were solicited from the individuals themselves or from their families. I have not provided footnotes – this is a story, it is not an academic history. A writer wisely said, "I know there are mistakes in this book; I just don't know what they are." My thought exactly.

The last history of Francestown was written by John Schott in 1972, *Frances' Town*. Schott was a well-off, well-educated, intellectual who found a peaceful life for his young family in 1960s' Francestown. His history was mainly derived from the town history written by Cochrane and Wood in the 1890s and town reports from the 20th century. It also contained Schott's personal judgments about town residents, their organizations, and their homes. He was fascinated by, though snobbish about, architecture. His writing style was wonderfully grandiose. Several times in this book, I cite, mostly for entertainment value, observations and predictions made by Schott. Schott served as the chair of the 1972 Bicentennial Celebration and as a selectman in the 1970s. He exemplifies those in town who wanted the town to modernize but not to change.

My primary bias has been to write the town's story as the account of the twenty percent of residents who were involved in organizations, on boards, committees, or commissions, or who were credited as volunteers in town records or *The Francestown News*. The reasoning, arguments, actions, and decisions of those whose names appear in the records of the town and its many organizations form the lion's share of the story in this book. Most of the 1,600 residents of this town are never named in the front pages of the annual town report or in *The Francestown News*. Most people in town drive to work elsewhere, but lay their head on a pillow in town, eat with their family, privately enjoy their house and land, are good neighbors, take care of their business quietly, pay their taxes, and vote, at least in more consequential elections. But they do not involve themselves in town government or in the more prominent private social and cultural organizations in town. Most people are unaffiliated. They are good citizens, but in a different way than those who take the initiative to involve themselves in making decisions.

Another bias has been my interest in politics. Politics need not be about political parties. Politics is action taken to create influence on outcomes. Whether viewed as an art, or a science, it is practiced whenever even a few individuals get together to plan, advocate, or decide. Politics, even in a small town where governance is non-partisan, produces controversy and drama.

One of the greatest challenges in writing this story is that many of the readers have lived in Francestown through this period or much of it. They are alive. The advantage of writing the history of a period well-interred in the past is that the witnesses cannot object to the story-teller's choices and interpretations. The author won't run into the protagonists of the story at the transfer station. In the case of "current history" disputation is inevitable. I considered that and attempted to acknowledge both sides when a controversial event or trend was being described. If I didn't achieve the level of fairness I intended, I am sorry.

When my wife and I were contemplating retirement, we visited many little towns in southwestern New Hampshire. When we pulled up to the home in which we currently live, I got out of the car and said, "This is it; this is what I have been looking for." What we could see was a house tucked away in the woods on a pretty pond with an abundance of space for hosting visiting children, grandchildren, and friends. What we did not imagine was the richer life that awaited us. We did not anticipate that Francestown would introduce us to an array of interesting friends and acquaintances and opportunities to learn, belong, and serve. The community of Francestown has been a great gift and we are grateful.

Kevin Pobst, 2022

Author

Kevin Pobst and his wife have lived in Francestown for eight years. During that time, he has served in elective and volunteer offices and been active in several organizations. He has undergraduate and graduate degrees in history. Before retiring, he spent over two decades teaching high school history courses and many years as a school administrator.

APPENDIX 1: BIRTHS, POPULATION, BUILDING PERMITS BY YEAR

Year	Population	Births	Dwelling Lots	Building Permits (dwellings)
1960	495	6		
67		7		
68		5		
69		3		
1970	589	3		5
71		9	12	9
72		6		11
73		5	10	4
74		5	8	2
75		12	11	20
76		2	12	20
77		6	15	20
78		9	12	22
79		12	11	17
70-79	+236	60	91	130
1980	825	17	15	15
81		6	14	8
82		7	14	12
83		7	13	10
84		7	14	25
85		18	38	23
86		23	33	37
87		17	17	22
88		16	12	11
89		16	7	7
80-89	+392	138	158*	170
			*Sixty-seven subdivisions yielded 158 dwelling lots	
1990	1217	21	4	4
91		19	1	2
92		24	1	4
93		16	1	7
94		20	2	5
95		12	3	6
96		15	2	4
97		12	1	9
98		13	1	5
99		10	0	19
90-99	+263	162	16	65
2000	1480	11	3	17
01		16	2	14
02		10	2	8
03		13	3	12
04		17	6	8
05		18	3	5
06		8	4	6
07		21	2	5
08		6	4	0
09		6	2	2
00-09	+82	126	31	79
2010	1562	12	2	2
11		13	1	3
12		7	0	2
13		14	0	2
14		9	0	4
15		4	0	0
16		5	3	2
17		6	0	4
18		12	0	0
19		5	0	5
2020	1610	3	3	8
2010-2020	+48	90	9	32

Appendix 2: Political Party Presidential Voting, Registration

Year	Republicans	Democrats	Undeclared	Presidential Vote in November
1972				Nixon, R 274; McGovern, D 97
1976				Ford, R 263; Carter, D 145
1980				Reagan, R 300; Carter, D 122
1984				Reagan, R 342; Mondale, D 207
1988				Bush, R, 428; Dukakis, D 255
1992	425	265	226	Clinton, D 320; Bush, R 284; Perot, 184
1994	373	195	351	
1996				Clinton, D 372; Dole, R 352; Perot, 59
1998	377	191	384	
2000	391	198	473	Gore, D 415; Bush, R 396; Nader, 51
2004				Bush, R 532; Kerry, D 510
2005	385	244	547	
2008				Obama, D 574; McCain, R 479
2010	372	265	542	
2012	389	270	509	Obama, D 538; Romney, R 449; Libertarian 48
2016	399	279	437	Clinton, D 471; Trump, R 444
2018	374	300	478	
2020	447	365	500	Biden, D 592; Trump, R 534

APPENDIX 3: BOARD OF SELECTMEN, MODERATOR, 1970-2020

Yr	BOS	BOS	BOS	Historic Races	Moderator
65	Mace ('61)	Eggert ('63)	Hoyt		McAdam, W ('53)
66	Mace	Ireland	Hoyt		McAdam, W
67	Mace	Ireland	Hoyt		McAdam, W
68	Mace	Ireland	Hoyt		McAdam, W
69	Mace	Dodge	Hoyt		McAdam, W
70	Mace, Frank	Dodge, Walter	Hoyt, Donald		McAdam, W
71	Mace	Dodge	Thulander, Alan O		McAdam, W
72	Mace	Dodge	Thulander		Varnum, H
73	Mace	Dodge	Thulander		Varnum, H
74	Mace	Dodge	Thulander		Varnum, H
75	Mace	Schott, John	Thulander		Varnum, H
76	Arnold, John	Schott	Thulander	Arnold v Mace	Varnum, H
77	Arnold	Schott	Abbott, Robert	Abbott v Thulander	Varnum, H
78	Arnold	Cutter	Abbott		Varnum, H
79	Behrsing, Elizabeth	Cutter, Robert	Abbott		Varnum, H
80	Behrsing	Cutter	Abbott		Varnum, H
81	Behrsing	Arnold	Abbott	Arnold v Cutter	Varnum, H
82	Behrsing	Arnold	Abbott		Varnum, H
83	Behrsing	Arnold	Fluhr, Willis		Varnum, H
84	Behrsing	Carr, Brownell	Fluhr		Varnum, H
85	Behrsing	Carr	Fluhr		P Ireland
86	Behrsing	Carr	Jenkins, John		P Ireland
87	Behrsing	McClary, Bert	Jenkins		P Ireland
88	Harrigan, Fred	McClary	Jenkins		P Ireland
89	Harrigan	McClary	Jenkins		P Ireland
90	Harrigan	McClary	Jenkins		P Ireland
91	Harrigan*/Thulander	McClary	Jenkins		P Ireland
92	Thulander	McClary	Jenkins		P Ireland
93	Thulander	McClary	Jenkins		P Ireland
94	Thulander	McClary	Jenkins		P Lawrence
95	Thulander	McClary	Jenkins		P Lawrence
96	Thulander	Carbee, Scott	Jenkins	Carbee v McClary	P Lawrence
97	Thulander	Carbee	Jenkins		P Lawrence
98	Thulander	Carbee	St. Cyr, Paul		P Lawrence
99	Thulander	Jonas, David	St. Cyr		P Lawrence
0	Thulander	Jonas	St. Cyr		P Lawrence
1	Thulander	Jonas	St. Cyr		P Lawrence
2	Thulander*/Behrsing	Brown, Steven	St. Cyr	Brown v Jonas	P Lawrence
3	Griffin, Stephen	Brown	St. Cyr		P Lawrence
4	Griffin	Brown*/Behrsing	St. Cyr		P Lawrence
5	Griffin	McAuley, William	St. Cyr		P Lawrence
6	Griffin	McAuley	St. Cyr*/Anderson	Griffin v Anderson	P Lawrence
7	Griffin	McAuley	Anderson, Thomas		P Lawrence
8	Griffin*/Hardwick, Betsy	McAuley	Anderson		P Lawrence
9	Hardwick	McAuley	Anderson		P Lawrence
10	Hardwick	McAuley	Carbee	Carbee v Anderson	P Lawrence
11	Hardwick	Arnold, Abigail	Carbee		P Lawrence
12	Hardwick	Arnold	Carbee		P Lawrence
13	Hardwick	Arnold	Carbee	Carbee v McAuley	P Lawrence
14	Hardwick	Arnold	Carbee	Arnold v Lisa Stewart	P Lawrence
15	Howell, Brad	Arnold	Carbee		P Lawrence
16	Howell	Arnold	Kunhardt, Henry	Kunhardt v Carbee	P Lawrence
17	Howell	Arnold	Kunhardt		P Lawrence
18	Howell	Arnold	Kunhardt		P Lawrence
19	Howell	Arnold	Kunhardt		K Pobst
20	Howell	Dixon, Marsha	Kunhardt	Dixon v Shattuck	K Pobst
21	Ravalico, George	Dixon	Kunhardt		P Lawrence
22	Ravalico	Dixon	Heath, Scot		P Lawrence

APPENDIX 4: BUDGET BY YEAR

Year	Operating Budget Warrant Article	Additional Warrant Articles
2000	$844,000	$835,000
01	927,000	718,000
02	1,000,000	174,000
03	1,200,000	568,000
04	1,200,000	457,000
05	1,200,000	1,900,000
06	1,300,000	568,000
07	1,400,000	896,000
08	1,400,000	981,000
09	1,400,000	1,600,000
2010	1,400,000	1,000,000
11	1,500,000	605,000
12	1,500,000	1,900,000
13	1,600,000	2,300,000
14	1,600,000	1,200,000
15	1,600,000	620,000
16	1,700,000	2,900,000
17	1,700,000	1,900,000
18	1,800,000	821,000
19	1,800,000	925,000
2020	1,800,000	1,200,000

Year	Operating Budget Warrant Article	Additional Warrant Articles
1970	$53,000	$2,000
71	74,000	9,000
72	69,000	6,000
73	90,000	16,000
74	96,000	32,000
75	114,000	15,000
76	125,000	27,000
77	159,000	40,000
78	228,000	43,000
79	241,000	42,000
1980	234,000	151,000
81	280,000	45,000
82	302,000	27,000
83	324,000	71,000
84	404,000	112,000
85	424,000	70,000
86	462,000	82,000
87	515,000	107,000
88	574,000	384,000
89	705,000	126,000
1990	742,000	115,000
91	747,000	115,000
92	741,000	122,000
93	752,000	282,000
94	770,000	190,000
95	806,000	314,000
96	846,000	268,000
97	851,000	387,000
98	838,000	394,000
99	819,000	328,000

1970 - 2020

APPENDIX 5: BUDGETS BY DEPARTMENT BY DECADE

Year	Admin Executive Finance	Clerk Elections	Insurance & Employee Benefits	Legal	Planning	Debt Service	Police	Fire	Facility Maint	Highway all funds	Waste	Library	Recreation	ConComm
1970	$4,000	$180	$3,335	$300	$125	$8,576	$1,000 $300	$1,684	$1,290	$26,090	$675	$3,112	$0	$0
1980	$16,200 $1,450 *most Town Clerk expenses in Admin	*$1000	$19,000	$4,500	$2,600 $1,350	$4,000	$18,510 $1,650	$10,790 $4,000	$5,000	$127,510 $3,100	$14,100	$13,370	$2,000	$150
1990	$54,700 $900 *most Town Clerk expenses in Admin	*$2400 $1,700	$93,100	$15,000	$12,700	$49,000	$43,000 $15,000	$27,100 $22,000	$17,000 $5,000	$267,000 $25,000	$55,000	$31,000	$9,500	$1,000 $10,000
2000	$51,574	$23,097	$75,247	$7,500	$23,129	$2,500	$65,588 $28,000	$29,886 $75,700	$25,450 $157,000	$365,754 $268,000	$83,357	$49 $30,000	$22,625	$650 $20,000
2010	$88,000	$41,667	$163,693	$12,000	$8,182	$89,328	$136,420	$53,109 $242,000	$39,721 $41,000	$467,075 $200,000	$118,907	$70,514	$26,990	$1,375 $30,000
2020	$127,151	$72,552	$193,701	$22,000	$4,700	$105,166	$220,087	$87,210 $10,000	$62,581 $65,000	$522,500 $385,000	$130,525	$98,595	$36,100	$1,440

APPENDIX 6: VALUE OF TOWN PROPERTY BY DECADE

Year	Town Owned Acres	Dollar Value ($) Land & Buildings	Notes
1970		$139,000	Town Hall, Library, Fire Station, Highway Garage, Dump
1980		$806,000	add furniture & equipment
1990	765	$3,071,700	add in cemeteries and town-owned conservation lands
1995	778	$2,620,000	Includes buildings, furniture & equipment, all town-owned land
2000	1,176	$3,753,000	"
2005	1,573	$6,310,000	"
2010	2,171	$7,238,000	"
2015	2,180	$5,864,000	Does not include equipment valued at $2.75m
2020	1,985	$5,896,000	Does not include equipment valued at $2.66m

APPENDIX 7: CONSERVATION FUND AND LAND ACQUISITION

Year	Con Fund Voted at Town Meeting	Con Fund Balance $ 000s	Town Forest Acres	Other Town-Owned Con Acres	Town-Held Easements Acres	Notes
1987	$10,000		28	9.6	59.4	Town Mtg creates Conservation Fund
88	$10,000		459		217.6	
89	$15,000		659.3		228.4	
1990	$10,000		718.5		238.4	
91	$5,000		718.5		238.4	easement land in Francestown (Town, FLT, SPNHF, NEFF, PWA) = 1,314.6
92	$2,500		718.5		238.4	
93	$100		718.5		238.4	
94	$2,500		718.5		238.4	
1995	$5,000		718.5		238.4	
96	$10,000		718.5		238.4	
97	$10,000		718.5		238.4	
98	$10,000	$47,000	718.5		238.4	
99	$20,000	$68,000	718.5		238.4	
2000	$20,000	$79,000	735.2		238.4	
01	$40,000	$144,000	735.2		238.4	
02	$40,000	$182,000	752	1.4	238.4	
03	$70,000	$64,000	753.4	257.9	238.4	
04	$40,000	$117,000	1036.3		238.4	
2005	*	$64,000	1086.3	94.1	307.4	*Bond, $1,000,000; TM. Yes 264, No 44
06		$131,000	1087.4	395.2	414.2	
07		$50,000	1482.6	256	414.2	
08	$40,000	$87,000	1485.4	256	434.3	
09	$40,000	$112,000	1485.4	256	519.6	
2010	$30,000	$41,000	1485.4	392	550.5	
11		$50,000	1485.4	648.7	556.5	
12		$55,000	1485.4	648.7	615.5	
13		$40,000	1485.4	624.6	664.8	
14		$15,000	1485.4	634.6	814.3	
2015		$20,000	1485.4	634.6	814.3	
16		$29,000	1485.4	636.3	814.3	
17		$35,000	1485.4	636.3	913.9	
18		$50,000	1492.2	636.3	913.1	
19		$57,000	1492.2	636.3	926.9	
2020		$49,000	1492.2	636.3	946.8	

APPENDIX 8: YEARS OF GOVERNANCE SERVICE TO THE TOWN 1970 – 2020*

Years	Name	Positions
88	Barbara Jean Carbee	RecCom, 12; Plan Bd, 7; Public Asst, 22; ConCom, 19; Highway, 4; Checklist, 17; Heritage, 5
77	Donald Abbott	FVFD Chief, 20; Fire Ward, 20; Animal Control, 37
58	O. Alan Thulander	BoS, 17; ZBA, 9; Cemetery, 10; Emerg Mngmt, 13
57	Dr. Louis Wiederhold	School Bd, 10; Trust Fnd, 29; Health, 11; Highway, 7
56	Richard Leavitt	Fire Ward, 45; Cemetery, 11
52	Paul Lawrence	Moderator, 26; RecCom, 15; ZBA, 5; Library, 6
45	Charlie Pyle	ZBA, 21; Budget, 21; Treasurer, 4
44	Betsy Hardwick	ConCom, 22; BoS, 7; PB, 4; Highway, 6; Heritage, 4
43	Clifton Foote	FVFD Chief, 15; Fire Ward, 18; ZBA, 8; Highway, 3
43	Scott Carbee	BoS, 9; Waste, 19; Patriotic, 10; Highway, 5
43	Robert Lindgren	ConCom, 22; PB, 21
35	Harry Varnum	Moderator, 13; Budget, 3; ZBA, 13; Highway, 6
31	Silas Little	ZBA, 15; Heritage, 5; Trust Fnd, 11
30	Polly Freese	Patriotic, 12; Cemetery, 13; ConCom, 2; ZBA, 3
30	Richard Mikula	ZBA, 15; Highway, 10; PB, 5
29	Herman Miller	Clerk, 23; Treasurer, 6
29	Larry Kullgren	FVFD Chief, 13; Fire Ward, 16
25	Brian Delanhanty	Fire Ward, 25
25	Donald Hoyt	Highway, 24; BoS, 1
24	Robert Parker	Waste, 15; Budget, 9
24	Charles Onasch	ZBA, 8; Budget, 11; PB, 5
24	Henry Kunhardt	BoS, 5; Trust Fnd, 11; Budget, 8
22	Becky Moul	Budget, 7; Waste, 15
21	Abigail Arnold	BoS, 9; PB, 12
21	Sarah Pyle	PB, 21
21	Elizabeth Behrsing	BoS, 11; Tax Coll, 4; Checklist, 6
21	Elaine McClary	Clerk-Tax Coll, 21
21	Philip Ireland	PB, 12; Moderator, 9
20	Scot Heath	ConCom, 18; PB, 2
20	Kris Stewart	RecCom, 16; Road Agent, 1; Cemetery 3
20	Clayton Foote	Road Agent, 20

* "Service years" include election or appointment to an official position in town governance – a board, commission, or standing committee. Years served before 1970, or after 2020, are not included. This list does not include "ex officio," "alternate," or "deputy" status. Nor are hired, paid employees listed, such as police, highway, or transfer station employees. The list includes the fire chief and fire wards, but not general fire service. The FVFD was not confident of the completeness of their records. By not including years of fire service there is absolutely no implication that serving on a town committee or board is more important than fire and rescue service where men and women risk their lives to save the life and property of others.

INDEX OF NAMES

Abbott, Beverly (Bev), 29, 130, 137
Abbott, Donald (Don, Donny), 24, 68-69, 101, 132, 135-137, 138, 184, 194, 206
Abbott, Lefty, 161
Abbott, Linda, 134, 190, 202
Abbott, Nina, 171
Abbott, Peggy, 190
Abbott, Robert (Bob, Bobby), 12, 13, 18, 41, 127, 157, 168, 172, 202
Adams, David, 190, 211
Adams, Deborah [see Stewart Adams, Deborah]
Agudelo, Carlos, 185, 191
Alger, Gary, 145
Allen, Meredeth, 169, 198
Allen, R. Leonard, 169, 174, 188
Allen, Sara, 34
Ames, Larry, 97, 123, 204
Ames, Robert (Rob), 28, 160, 179, 193
Anderson, Kay, 77, 81, 106, 173, 184-185
Anderson, Tom, 76, 77, 78, 80, 81, 93, 163
Angell, Nancy, 29, 189
Armstrong, Marvin, 34
Arnold, Abigail, iv, 32, 42, 43, 45, 46, 50, 66, 70, 78, 79, 86, 88, 90, 92, 93, 95, 97, 98, 116, 117, 123, 178, 199-200, 203, 207
Arnold, Ellen, 34, 39, 40
Arnold, Frances, iv
Arnold, John (Jack), 12, 13, 17, 19, 41, 157, 198, 199
Arnold, John P., 151, 166, 167, 168, 193
Arpin, Bonnie, 144
Avery, Susan, 174
Ayers, Heather, 82
Badot, Judy, 174
Baer, Adam, iv
Baptiste, Ron, 19, 144
Baptiste, Maureen, 144
Barker, Cheryl (Cher), 142, 144, 171, 173, 190, 202
Barker, James (Jim), 142, 144, 145, 195, 202
Barker, Stephanie, 187
Barnes, Susie, 186
Barnes, Terry, 186
Barr, Lawrence (Lawrie), 144, 153, 165, 166, 168

Barr, Carol Prest, 26, 57, 152, 157, 144, 152, 168
Barwood, Forrest, 116
Barwood, Joel, iv, 116, 155
Barwood, Kristen, 189
Beauchamp, Merrill Milke, 170
Behrsing, Anne, 189
Behrsing, Elizabeth (Betty), 11, 39, 41, 48, 76-77, 95, 168, 172, 202
Behrsing, Joel, 131
Behrsing, Ruth, 130, 189
Beisang, Mike, 57, 101, 194
Beisang, Robin, 194
Bell, Steve, 80, 94
Benedict, Herb, 17, 18, 19, 41, 144, 168
Bernstein, Gerri, 97, 179, 183, 191
Berry, Krista, 190
Bewley, Bob, 25
Bicknell, Connie, 24, 25, 73, 207, 209
Bicknell, Leighton, 25
Birchard, Suzanne, 34
Bixby, Alex, 187
Bixby Dam (Bixby-Creamery Dam), 11, 25, 50, 51, 55, 161, 163, 199
Bixby Library (George Holmes Bixby Memorial Library), i, 12, 79, 82, 83, 84, 101, 124, 152, 187, 203, 205
Bixby, Peter, 28, 55, 57, 127, 167, 186
Bixby, Marcy [see Graham, Marcy Tripp]
Bixby, Ted, 7, 8
Block, Allan, 189
Bloom, Krystal, 183
Bodnar, Belinda, 187
Bolle, James, 4, 186, 189
Bolle, Jocelyn, 144, 185
Borden, Stacy, 144, 185
Bourbeau, Lisa, 95, 97
Bournival, Thomas, 28
Bower, Tim, 42, 43
Boyle, Matilda (Mit), iv, 148, 163, 167, 168, 169, 210
Bradbury, Paul, 132
Branley, Mike, 89, 90, 93, 102
Brecca family, 136
Brekka, John, 190
Brenner, Ron, 190
Brewer, Jill, 195
Brien, Charles, 131, 144

Brock, Carol, 84, 101, 129, 154, 177, 184, 186, 202
Brock, Elyssa, 183
Brock, Stewart, 65, 97, 104, 105, 129, 177, 185, 186, 192, 202
Bromberg, Herb, 123
Brown, Steven, 28, 76, 77
Browne, Phil, 19
Bush, Kendall, iv, 155
Buzzell, Arthur, 29
Calcutt, Dennis, 123, 195, 204
Calcutt, Eva, 193
Calcutt, Tiffany, 192, 195
Camirand, Henry, 29, 97
Campbell, Ken, 66
Campbell, Lisa, 192
Campbell, Steve, 94
Carbee, Barbara (BJ), iv, 43, 57, 81, 101, 154, 166, 167, 171, 189, 203
Carbee, Scott, iv, 29, 48, 52, 58, 76, 78, 79, 80, 81, 92, 93, 95, 151, 162, 166, 182, 203
Carey, Mary Frances, 66, 67, 83, 178
Caskie, Barbara, 172
Caskie, Robert, 18
Cheaney, Nick, 194
Cheney, Ron, 147
Chute, John, 176
Chute, Sandy, 192
Cilley, Ann, 173
Cilley, Dick, iv, 144, 171, 174, 175, 178
Cilley, George, 58, 82
Cilley, Jim (and family golf team0, 194
Clark, Andrew, 171
Clark, Mary, 171
Clark, Stewart, iv
Clark, Stu, Jr., 195
Clark, Thomas, 29
Cleaves, Royal, 131
Cloutier, Robert, 8
Colburn, Olive, 171
Colby, Elizabeth, 190
Compton, Abby, 187
Compton, Linda, 144, 173
Connard, David, 144, 174
Conroy, Rosemary, 189
Cooke, Susan, 144

Cope, Greg, 169
Cope, Harriet, 180, 185
Coughlin, Sam, 174
Coutts-Eisenberg, Martha, 174, 178
Couturier, Karen, 181
Couturier, Mark, 29, 136
Cowell, Janine, 134
Creighton, Jay, 28
Curran, Charlie, 127
Curran, Diane, 127, 174
Curren, Jack, i
Curren, Tom, 117
Cutter, Bob, 131
Cyr, Andrea, 187
Cyr, Dan, 86
Cyr, Marianne, 179
Dahlquist, Justin, 194
Dalley, Kim, 29, 144, 190, 198
Dalley, Kip, 29, 193
Danforth, Chris, 86, 91
Danforth, Judy, 167, 186
Danforth, Kelsa, iv, 155
Dani, Zoltan, 184
Davis, Dan, 194
Dawes, Jessie, 189, 190
Dawidoff, Heidi, 84, 85, 144, 187
de Tarnowski, Lina, 162
DeAngelis, Patricia, 34
Delahanty, Brian, 136, 137, 178
Delahanty, Liam, 173
Delahanty, Pam, 57, 190
Delahanty, Quinn, 187
Delorey, Jill, 178
Dennis, Bruce, 29
Dewitt, Pam, 152, 173
Dietrich, Joan, 178
Dishong, Ella, 192, 193
Dishong, Molly, 192, 193
Dixon, Marsha, 95, 169
Dodge, Constance (Connie), 10, 134, 153, 170
Dodge, Glenn, 127, 128
Dodge, Walter, 10, 14, 199
Douglas, Fred, 94

Dowd, Mike, 94
Dowling, Tom, 190
Dreher, Tonya, 178, 181
Eby, Cole, 116, 194
Ecoline, Putnam, 190
Eder-Linnel, Aaron, 182
Edwards, Dick, 148, 168
Edwards, Bob, 167
Eggert, Charles, Sr., 40, 41, 43
Ellis, Paul, 52
Ellis, Sandy, 66
Ennis, Cailin, iv
Ennis, Katie, iv
Erickson, Allison, 189
Estes, Sara, 183
Evans, Adam, 179
Fairfield, Tom and Joanne, 175
Fallon, Ryan, 195
Farhm, Ed, 161
Farhm, Rita, 160
Farrell, Mary, 84, 85, 101
Farres, Sheila, 190
Fellows, Ted, 127, 128
Ferrara, Randy, 144, 145
Ferrara, Shirlee, 144
Fesmire, Chester, 168
Fiest, James, 190
Fincher, Kay, 167
Finlayson, Dodie, 60, 112, 186
Finnell, Pam Foote, 73, 96, 106
Fish, Fred, 39, 41, 42, 45
Fitzgerald, Karen, 97
Fitzpatrick, Kate, 190
Flik, Julie, 195
Flood, Kay, 16
Flood, Peter, 16, 23, 79, 204
Floreani, Sheena, 190
Foote family, 8, 21, 73, 85, 87, 135, 186, 144, 172, 174, 198, 205
Foote, Clayton (Junior), iv, 21, 25, 53, 85, 86, 87, 205
Foote, Clifton, 23, 41, 132, 133, 134, 138, 156, 170, 199, 204
Foote, Elizabeth, 134
Foote, Ernest, 135
Foote, Kaitlynne, 183

Foote, Mathew, iv, 155
Foote, Robert (Bob), 21, 90, 205
Foster, Margery, 31, 174
Fotter, Ryan, 187
Freese, Polly, 44, 103, 182, 202
French, Anastasia, 183
Fritz, Deanna, 183
Fritz, Jennifer (Jenny), 115, 135, 137, 138, 178, 181, 186, 193
Frost, Roon, 127, 174
Fusco, Don, 195
Gagnon, Amanda, 187
Gagnon, Ed, 51
Gagnon, Michael, 183
Gagnon, Nancy, iv, 155, 174
Gallaher, Rosemary, 190
Gallop, Lou, 25, 29, 167
Gann, James, 95
Gannett, Tim, 8, 37, 38, 208
Gargano, Lisa, 144
Garvin, James, 129
Gerbino, Maxine, 174
Gibbons, James, 28
Gienty, Ed, 144
Gilman, Hannah, 178
Gilman, Parnee, 178, 190
Glaude, Baxter, 194
Glaude, Harrison, 194
Glover, Denise, 65, 144, 171
Gombas, Cathy, 64
Gombas, Jimmy, iv, 155
Goodrich, Colby, iv
Goodrich, David, 34
Goodrich, Helle, 176
Goodrich, Scott, 176
Gorton, Gavin, 195
Gorton, Jeff, 58, 59, 80
Grant, Andrew, 29
Graham, Marcy (Marcy Bixby Tripp), 189, 191
Greene, Louise, 167
Grenier, Eric, 28
Griffin, Jan, 127, 174
Griffin, Stephen, 76, 77, 78, 86, 126, 169
Hackett, Pierette, 190

Hadley, Willis, 172
Hall, Roger, 189
Hanchett, Frank, 34, 144, 155, 179
Hanchett, Joan, 82, 84, 124, 143, 144, 186, 188, 205
Hansen, Bill, 13, 17, 18, 19, 40, 41, 158, 159, 165
Hardwick family, 194
Hardwick, Bart, iv
Hardwick, Betsy, 36, 59, 60, 72, 78, 79, 86, 89, 93, 94, 95, 112, 116, 117, 137, 143, 144, 171, 190, 194, 200-201, 204
Hardwick, Blair, 28, 194
Hardwick, Bryant, 190
Hardwick, Carl (Sonny), 60, 143, 200, 206
Hardwick, D. H. Hardwick and Sons, 68, 114, 156, 181, 206
Hardwick, Donald (Donny), 114, 206
Hardwick, Dorothy (Dot), 143, 200, 206
Hardwick, Harry and Eula, 206
Hardwick, Jaqueline, 183
Hardwick, Jennifer, 137
Hardwick, Lori (Lori Hardwick-Way), 142, 144, 172, 173, 185
Harrigan, Fred, 35
Harrigan, Lillian, 35, 153
Harrington, Ben and Monica, 174
Harrington, Bruce, 29, 192
Haubrich, Ben, 123, 204
Haubrich, Robin, 154
Hazel, Daryl and Janet, 144
Heath, Scot, 32, 33, 34, 35, 43, 46, 115, 122, 204, 206
Hersey, Elliott, 178
Hicks, Jan, 154, 189, 198
Hill family, 25, 83-84
Hill, Alison Bixby, 152
Hill, Edward Burlingame, 4
Hill, Esther, 83-84
Hill, Elizabeth, 137
Hill, Ellen, 35
Hill, Isabella Britain, 136, 181, 189
Hobbs, Clayton, 171
Hoffman, Austin, iv, 155
Holding, Mark, 182, 190
Holdredge, Kevin, 102, 137, 186
Holm, Sirkka, 34, 74-75, 169, 184
Holm, Taisto, 34, 59, 180
Holmes, Kris, 154, 155, 189, 212

Holmes, Len, 155
Hooper, Jane Gallagher, 65, 178, 189, 190
Hooper, Patrick, 185
Houlihan, Nancy, 187
Houston family, 199
Houston, Andrew, 128, 130
Howell, Brad, 79, 95, 144, 207
Howell, Bridget, 144
Hoyt, Donald, 10, 28, 132, 144, 199
Hoyt, Winnie, 144, 171, 172
Hungerford, Andy, 198
Hunsaker, Adam, 191
Hunsaker, Bob, 173, 191
Hunsaker, Denise, 190
Hunsaker, Jessica, 187
Hunter, Paula, 69, 174, 188, 192
Hunter-Lavallee, Elizabeth, 85, 117, 178, 187
Hurley, Siobahn, 183
Hutchinson, John, 191
Ireland, Carol, 144
Ireland, Phil, 15, 25, 48, 51, 144
Ireland, Shawna, 173
Irwin, Jay, 131
Ivester, Carol, 190
Jackson, Jane, 190
Jacobs, Caroline, 190, 191
James, Donna, 190
James, Ray 144
Jane, Paul, 161
Jenkins, Ben, 192, 194
Jenkins, John, 47, 48
Jenkins, Lorie, 194
Jenkins, Nick, 57, 173, 192
Jenkins, Scott, 57, 189, 191, 194
Jepsen, Linda and Bert, 190
Joch, Matthew, 183
Jonas, David, 17, 18, 46, 48, 51, 52, 53, 54, 76, 88, 159
Jonas, Susannah, 53
Jones family, 144, 206
Jones, Angela, 187
Jones, Ed, 48, 145, 146, 206
Jones, Elizabeth (Betty), 134, 172, 206
Jones, Frank, iv, 48, 68, 155, 178, 206

Jones, Heidi, 187
Jones, Keta, 145
Jones, Merle, 171
Jones, Nancy, 190
Jones, Peggy, 171
Jones, Ramona, 171
Jones, Shirley, 145, 146, 206
Kazanovicz, Chris, 194
Kazanovicz, Michelle, 57
Kazanovicz, Peter, 57, 191, 194
Kazanovicz, Stephen, 194
Keiser, Bob, 190, 191
Kelly, Glenn, 185
Kelly, Linda, 103
Kendall, Chuck, 194
Kendall, Joe, 194
Kendall, John, 100
Kerouac, Jerry, 29
Kiblin family, 151, 172
Kiblin, Chloe, 171
Kiblin, Eleanor, 153, 172
Kiblin, Heather, 171
Kiblin, Misty Paige, 162
Kiblin, Warren, 136, 152, 171, 203
King, John (Governor), 35
King, Jim, 176
Kirlin, Dawn and Tom, 57, 101
Kloeppel, KC, 194
Knight, Jimmy, 190
Knight, Paul, 28
Kokul, Andrej and Stephanie, 57
Kraus, Barbara, 34
Kullgren, David, 131, 136, 207
Kullgren, Joan, 134, 186
Kullgren, Lawrence (Skip), 28, 72, 96, 131, 133, 136, 137, 156, 207
Kullgren, Lawrence, Sr., 131, 132, 156, 207
Kullgren, Ronald, 56, 131
Kunhardt, George, 68, 95, 172
Kunhardt, Henry, 69, 79, 92, 93, 95, 128, 207
Kunhardt, Linda, 97, 98, 207
Kunhardt, Priscilla (Sibby), 10, 24, 68, 72, 152, 183, 207, 209
Kuras, Bonnie, 181, 191
Kuty, Ambra, 195

Kuty, Todd, 195
Laber, Larry, 57, 163, 182, 198
Langlois, Connor, 194
Lanoie family, 55
Lape, Carol, 173
Lape, Matt, 173, 194
LaPlante, Scott, 192
LaRoche brothers, 8
Larsen, Bruce, 169
Lawes, Chris, 194
Lawes, Sandra, 194
Lawrence, Jane, 55, 62, 64
Lawrence, Paul, 41, 42, 48, 55, 57, 186, 193, 207-208, 210
Lawrence, Richard and family, 166
Leandri, Richard, 192
Leandri, Stephanie, iv
Leavitt family, 144
Leavitt, Brian, 194
Leavitt, Lois, 160
Leavitt, Richard (Dick), 25, 28, 132, 138, 159, 160, 208
Leavitt, Scott, 194
Leavitt, Sylvia, 163
LeClair, Wayne, 68, 69
LeJaq, Robert Jean, 30
Leonard, Constance, 189
Levis, Jeff and Barbara, 190, 191
Lindgren, Linda, 180
Lindgren, Bob, 97
Lindstrom, Mary, 29, 34, 127, 135, 178
Little, Silas, 127
Lizotte, Bonnie, 29
Lomas, John and Diane, 189
Lopata, Peg, 189
Lord, Arthur, 3, 131
Lord, Caroline, iii, 152
Lord, Emily, 144, 170
Ludwig, Joe, Sr. and Joe, Jr., 127, 161
Lunan, Carol, 144
Lundgren, Nancy, 173
Lunetta, Celeste, 65, 137, 138, 180, 182, 208
MacAdam, Lois, 103, 155, 160, 170, 208
MacAdam, William, 7, 8, 37, 208
Mace, Frank, 10, 13, 14, 144

MacKay, Ian, 174
MacKay, Jacob, 174, 185, 189
MacKay, Marybeth, iv
MacKay, Sorrell, 192
MacStubbs, Ethel, 171
Maes, John, 144, 145
Marcellino, Peggy, 192
Marks, Kenneth, 34
Marony, Jess, 173
Marony, Mark, 144
Marsden, Donald, 18
Marsden, Mary Jane, 57, 126, 161, 166, 167, 174, 187
Martel, Jason, 80, 164, 180
Martel, Jennifer, 164, 180
Martin, Priscilla Putnam, 154, 156, 162, 166
Martz, Paul, 144, 145
Mason, James (Jumbo), 58
Maybee, Harry, 29
McAuley, William (Bill), 76, 77, 78, 79, 86, 157, 174, 202, 208-209
McClary, Bert, 47, 48
McClary, Elaine, 96
McDonnell, Tom, 117
McEntee, Kaleb, 194
McGrath, Alex, 188
McGrath, Paul, 57
McGrath, Scott, 192
McKaig, Demetria, 144
McKaig, Rachel, 183
McLeod, Wayne, 185, 190
McNeill, Patti, 190
McNeill, William (Bill), 28, 97, 144, 152, 154, 190
Merkle, John, 158
Merrill family, 35, 59
Merrill, Arthur, 171
Mikula, Dick, 41
Mikula, Elsie, 29
Miller family, 28, 55, 56, 124, 198, 206
Miller, Dorothy, 10
Miller, Gerry, 163
Miller, Harry, 171
Miller, Herman (Bing), 10, 11, 40, 171
Miller, Jessica, 183
Miller, Judi, 29, 137

Miller, Rick, 28, 51, 91, 132, 154, 163, 169, 181, 198, 206
Miller, Steve, 28, 51, 91, 132, 154, 169, 181, 198, 206
Milton, Edith, 189
Milton, Peter, 151, 189
Moeller, Anne, 189
Moeller, Ben and Song, 29, 187, 190, 194
Montgomery, Sy, 187
Morgan, George, Sr., 82
Morgan, Sarah, 174
Mosher, Brian, 144
Mottard, Dean, 42, 43
Moul, Rebecca (Becky), 80, 81, 82
Mowery, Cahal, 191
Munson, David, 194
Munson, Eldon, 167
Munson, Janet, 18
Naegeli, Ed, 192
Naegeli, Phyllis, 101, 102, 142, 175
Nation, Pam, 186, 189, 190
Nealand, James, 57, 152
Neilley, Dr. Greg, 122, 123, 186, 192, 204
Neilley, Ellen, 153, 154, 186
Nelson, Pat, 189
Nickerson, Carla, 190
Nolet, Alexander, 183
Noonan, Diane, 173, 181
Noonan, Donna, 57, 101, 193, 210
Noonan, Jennifer, 28
Normile, Adam, 173, 193, 194
Normile, Jack, 194
Normile, John, 173, 193, 194
O'Donnell, Jan, 173
O'Grady, Dan and Terry, 45
Oles, Mark, 191
Onasch, Charles, 165, 166
O'Neill, Charles, 186
O'Neill, Melissa, 190
O'Neill, Michael, 154, 191
O'Neill, Mike and Pam, 186
O'Neill, Veda, 153, 154
Oppenheimer, Elizabeth, 165
Oppenheimer, John, 166
Orsi, Dennis, 94, 95

Paige family, 21, 55, 198
Paige, Clarence, 181, 198
Paige, Gabriella, 151, 166
Paige, Gary, 73, 87, 90, 92, 93, 96, 205
Paige, John, 21, 22, 131
Paige, Misty, 162
Paige, Sam, 194
Paige, Tom, 156
Papageorge, Jane, 192
Paquin family, 136,
Paquin, Leo and Diane, 187
Paradis, Ken, 191
Parker, Brenda, 17, 33
Parker, Jennifer, 174
Parker, Laura, 183
Parker, Robert (Dud), 25, 58, 165, 166, 203, 209
Paul, Andy, 65, 104, 190
Paul, Karen, 174
Perez, Luis, 190
Peters, Emily, iv, 155
Peters, Thomas, 192
Peterson, Dariel, iv, 144, 146, 148, 169, 171, 175, 189
Peterson, Governor Walter, 12
Petrovick, Michael, 53, 84, 127, 128, 129, 142, 143, 144, 154, 165, 174, 181, 184, 209
Phillips, Lisa, 170
Pierce, Greg, 172
Pierson, Rich and Carla, 190
Pitchard, Jamie, 194
Pitchard, Pam, 190
Pitman, Mark, 134, 138, 144, 146, 190
Pitman, Shirley, 144, 190
Place, Brooks, 174
Place, Diana, iv, 155
Place, Patricia, iv, 24, 73, 119, 144, 209
Plourde, Tom, 86, 87
Pollack, Jessie, 189
Powers, Lois, 173
Prest, Ashley, 29, 144
Prince, Donough (Don), 18, 26, 39, 151, 166, 208
Proctor, Hannah, 186
Pyle, Charlie, 64, 88, 151, 154, 163, 165, 166, 190, 201
Pyle, Sarah, 29, 67, 70, 97, 98, 117, 154, 163, 165, 169, 178, 190, 201

Quilty, Scott, 181
Quilty, Scott and Janet, 181
Radtke, Barbara, 29, 209
Radtke, Derald, 29, 144, 158, 165, 167, 168, 209-210
Rechkemmer, Marie, 154, 186
Rechkemmer, Lennie, 186
Regan, Maria, 179
Reimer, Ron, 144
Rice, Brooks, 165, 210
Rice, Nancy, 57, 208, 210
Roberts, Anthony, 81
Roche, Jim and Linda, 192
Rodier, Eileen, 65
Rogers, Chris, 123, 204
Rogers, Virginia, 171
Rokes, Eli, 154, 194
Rokes, Ralph, 160
Rokes, Robert (Bub), 28, 57, 101, 152, 154, 165, 172, 194, 210
Rokes, Tracy, 57
Rolph, Jill, 144
Ross, Donald, 39
Rowean, David, 29
Rupp, Jakob, iv, 194
Russell, Carol, 189
Russell, Gordon, 64, 112, 118, 119, 123
Samuelson, Tim, 56, 106, 194, 210
Sanchioni, Rino, 28
Sanderson family, 55, 173
Sanderson, George, 119, 172
Sanderson, Jamie, 193
Sanderson, Kathy, 173
Sanderson, Nate, 113, 173, 193
Sanderson, Nate and Natalie, 192
Savage family, 69
Savage, Larry and Diane, 68
Savage, Matt, 185, 189
Schaffer, Alex, 193
Schnakenberg, Gary, 160, 185
Schnare, Terry, 45, 55
Schott, John, 3, 4, 7, 8, 12, 13, 23, 27, 28, 30, 139, 149, 151, 214
Schroeppel, Robert, 29
Schultz family, 35
Scott, Cherie, 190

Scott, Dominick, 190
Scott, Meghan, 190
Severance, Kay, 127, 166, 172, 174, 185
Shattuck, Ron and Melissa, 99, 121, 122
Shea, Linda, 189
Sherman, Gordon, 28, 143, 144, 151, 165, 166
Sipe, Mary, 187
Sipe, Donald, 43, 187
Smith, Scott, 28
Smith, William, 165
Socia, Kelly, 29
Soper, Ann, 67, 169, 178, 190
St. Cyr, Amy, 137, 192
St. Cyr, Karen, 134, 192
St. Cyr, Paul, 28, 48, 76, 77, 80, 86, 89, 102
St. Jean, Chris, 192, 194
St. Jean, Cindy, 69, 124, 125, 178, 179, 213
St. Jean, Jack, iv
St. Jean, Jim, 124, 125, 196
Stanley, Mark, 151, 166
Stanley, Holly, 64, 151, 166, 174
Staub, Johanna, 32, 157, 162, 166, 186
Staub, Rob, 186
Stein, Anna, 190
Stein, Richard, 66
Stevens, Pam, 169
Stewart, Ann, 127, 162, 174, 191
Stewart, Betty, 134, 172, 210
Stewart, David, 29
Stewart, Deborah (Deborah Stewart Adams), 134, 156, 172, 190, 211
Stewart, Kris, 15, 21, 28, 51, 55, 57, 86, 91, 92, 93, 158, 162, 163, 171, 174, 178, 181, 182, 191, 194, 198, 208, 210-211
Stewart, Lisa, 66, 91, 93, 97, 98, 163, 174, 181, 194, 204
Stewart, Norman, 10, 23, 132, 138, 156, 199, 210
Stewart, Tom, 131
Stinson, Jordan, 195
Stone, Mike and Joan, 175
Sullivan, Chris, 194
Sullivan, Dillon, 194
Suprenant, John, 195
Susca, Paul, 190
Swan, Bill, 167
Sweet, Oscar (Ozzie), 151, 189

Swenson, Brian, 194
Taft, Elizabeth, iv, 155
Tamposi, Sam, 115
Tarr, Jeff, 28, 144, 157, 198
Tartalis, Mike, 97, 198
Taylor family, 97, 198
Taylor, Dijit, 117
Taylor, John, 151, 160, 165, 166
Taylor, Kate, 195
Tempone, Mary, 189, 190
Tennis, Michael and Marsha, 190, 191
Terry, Osiris, 194
Thiebault, Tom, 80
Thornblad, Heidi, 190
Thulander, O. Alan, 9, 12, 18, 20, 25, 27, 29, 36, 39, 41, 44, 46, 63-64, 66, 76, 77, 88, 102, 132, 134, 137, 149, 155-157, 158, 163, 167, 171, 179, 199, 200, 203, 208
Thulander, Barbara, 172
Thulander, Greg, 155
Tolman, Prescott (Guy), 95, 97
Tolton, Lynda, 140
Toppan, Bob, 25
Tremblay, Richard, 8, 18-19, 37, 39
Triplett, Bessann, 154, 189, 205
Tripp, David, iv, 191
Tripp, Wally, 189, 191
Truelson, Michael, 189
Turcott family, 69
Turcott, Shannon, 174, 192
Underhill, John (Jack), 26, 101, 161, 162, 187
Vadney family, 3, 29
Vadney, Evelyn, 171
Vadney, Gladys, 171
Vadney, Jennifer, 157, 191
Valentine, Joe, 69, 188
Van Cleave, Al and Joan, 189, 190
Van Cleave, Al, 132, 138, 173, 190
Varnum, Constance (Connie), iv, 18, 34, 35, 75, 119, 186, 200, 205, 207, 209
Varnum, Harold (Harry), 17, 20, 30, 35, 53, 132, 148, 199, 200
von Rosenvinge, James, 77, 166, 178
von Rosenvinge, Maureen, 127, 128, 129, 174
Wallace, Beth, 65, 144, 173, 178, 189, 208
Wallace, Ray, 144, 178, 180

Wasserloos, Charles, 28
Watson, Ben, 70, 174, 188, 189
Weisman, Hillary Graham, iv, 190
Welch, Richard, 183
Welch, Thomas, 93, 40
Westcott, Ben, 155
Wharton, Candace, 189
Wheeler family, 151, 178, 189, 190, 211
Wheeler, Kim, 173, 178, 189, 190, 211
Wheeler, Parker, 191
Wheeler, Randy, 34, 174, 189, 190, 191, 211
Wheeler, Theo Hardwick, 190, 211
Whipple, George, 28, 51, 56, 172, 181, 198
Whipple, Sandra, 190
Whipple-Simard, Heather, 185
Whittemore family, 155
Whittemore, Heather, 175
Wicklow, Dr. Barry, 123, 204
Wiederhold, Elizabeth (Betsy), 83, 103, 171, 182, 190
Wiederhold, Dr. Louis, 44, 48, 83, 132, 163, 170, 211
Williams, Quinn, 194
Wilson, Gail, 189
Wilson, Zachary, 183
Winslow family, 37
Wohle, Cole, 137, 165
Wohle, Rob and Christina, 164
Woodbury family, 179, 199
Woodbury, Carolyn, iv, 191
Woodbury, Harry, 198
Woodbury, Phil, 79, 80
Yoss, Anna, 29-30
Zahn, Peter, 57, 66
Zelko, Dale, 184

Made in United States
North Haven, CT
11 December 2022